CREATING A LEARNING ENVIRONMENT

A Learning Center Handbook

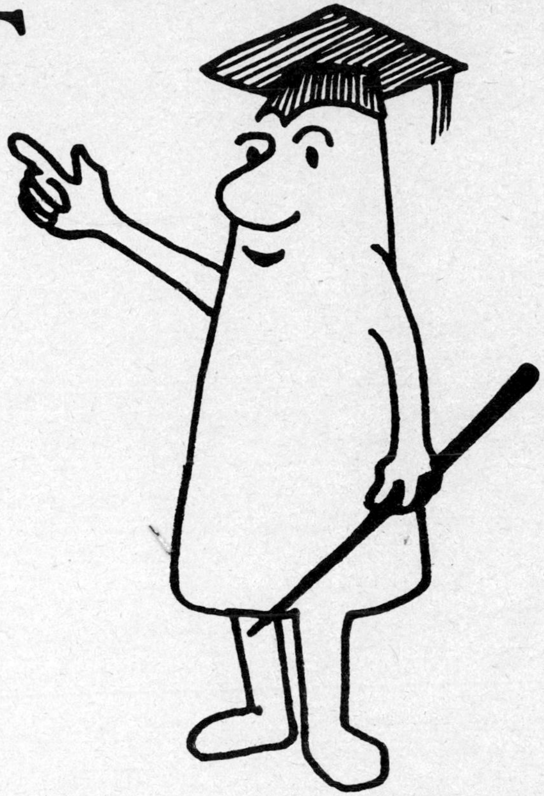

Ethel Breyfogle
Sue Nelson
Carol Pitts
Pamela Santich

Illustrated by Ronald Kremer

Goodyear Publishing Company, Inc.
Santa Monica, California

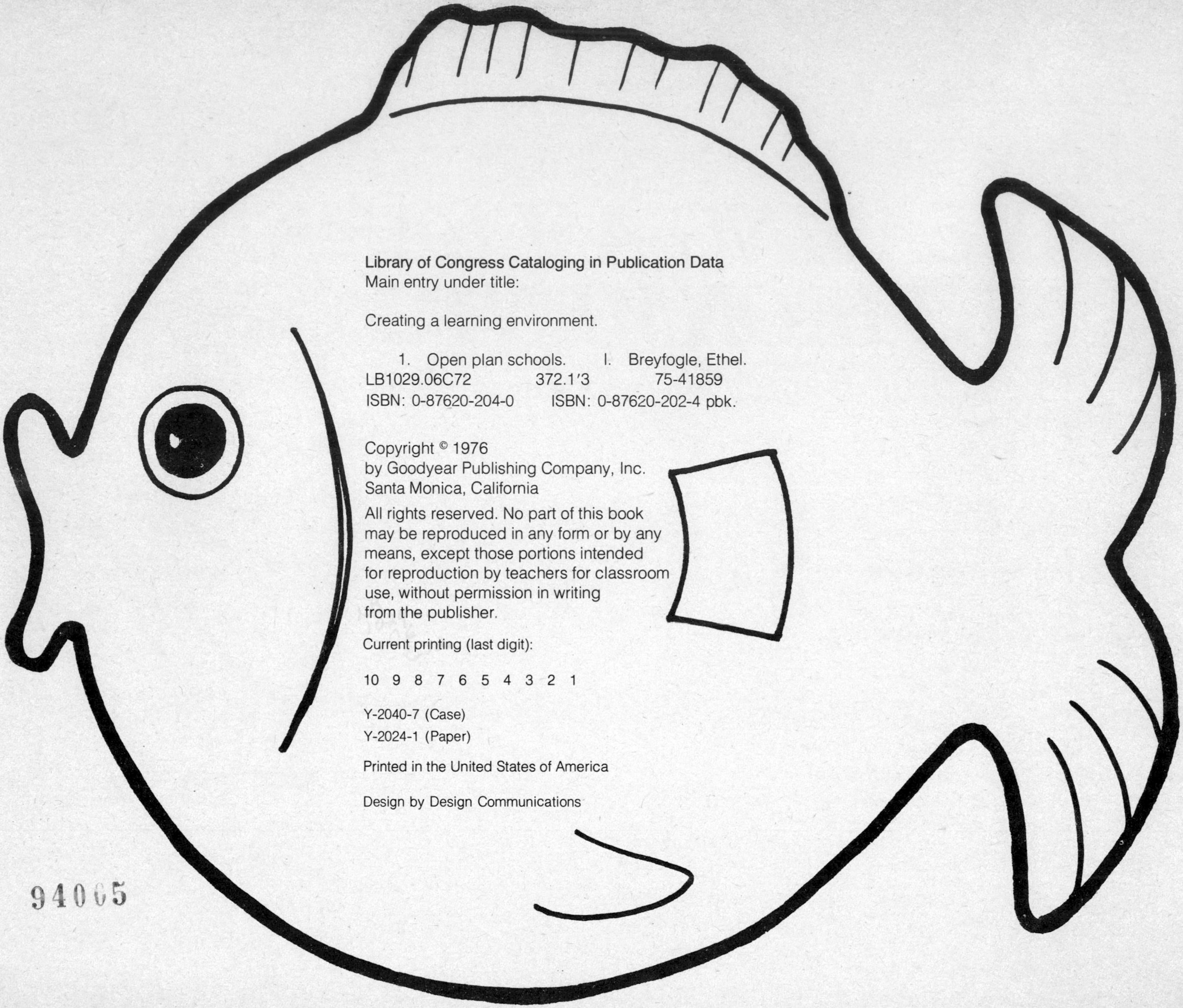

Library of Congress Cataloging in Publication Data
Main entry under title:

Creating a learning environment.

1. Open plan schools. I. Breyfogle, Ethel.
LB1029.06C72 372.1′3 75-41859
ISBN: 0-87620-204-0 ISBN: 0-87620-202-4 pbk.

Current printing (last digit):

10 9 8 7 6 5 4 3 2 1

Y-2040-7 (Case)
Y-2024-1 (Paper)

Printed in the United States of America

Design by Design Communications

Table of Contents

Preface

This handbook has been prepared to introduce teachers to the use of learning centers. We have provided full descriptions of sample learning centers, with instructions for their construction and use. We hope that teachers finding learning centers successful will be inspired to develop further centers on their own.

The objectives of this handbook are—

1. to suggest a philosophy of education that provides a background and purpose in the use of learning centers;
2. to guide the teacher in the organization of learning centers;
3. to suggest ways of implementing and managing learning centers;
4. to provide models of learning centers for kindergarten, primary, and intermediate grade levels.

Introduction

Philosophy for Development of Learning Centers

Nature and Use of Learning Centers
How to Begin Developing Learning Centers
Determining the Purpose of a Center
Selecting Activities for a Center
Constructing an Attractive Center

Management of Learning Centers

Room Arrangement
Scheduling
Record Keeping
Evaluation

Nature and Use of Learning Centers

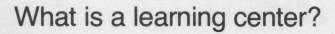

What is a learning center?

The learning center cannot replace the teacher; it cannot be the prime source of instruction in the classroom. However, it can be used to provide the necessary reinforcement for, expansion on, and enrichment of those concepts and skills previously introduced by the teacher.

For years teachers have experimented with new methods and techniques to accommodate the individual needs of the student. The learning center is one effective approach to individualized learning. A learning center is a collection of materials arranged around one or more "stations" where students can interact with the materials. At each station, the student will find instructions and materials for one particular activity. All of the activities available at a particular learning center are designed to reinforce a single educational objective (the "purpose" of the center).

The learning center is not a panacea for educational problems. Rather, it is a system for moving students away from teacher-centered learning experiences toward student-selected learning activities.

Why use learning centers?

Children are not alike. The classroom teacher must be aware of the differences in motivation, ability, and interest among her pupils. The student's individual needs are real and are more numerous than we often recognize. The learning center approach allows the teacher to develop certain activities and materials that cater to individual differences. Because of the greater array of learning activities, each student can become more involved in the educational process. The student will assume more responsibility about what he learns and will begin to evaluate the effectiveness of his efforts. The student will advance at his own rate—a rate that is governed by his ability, his interest, and his motivation.

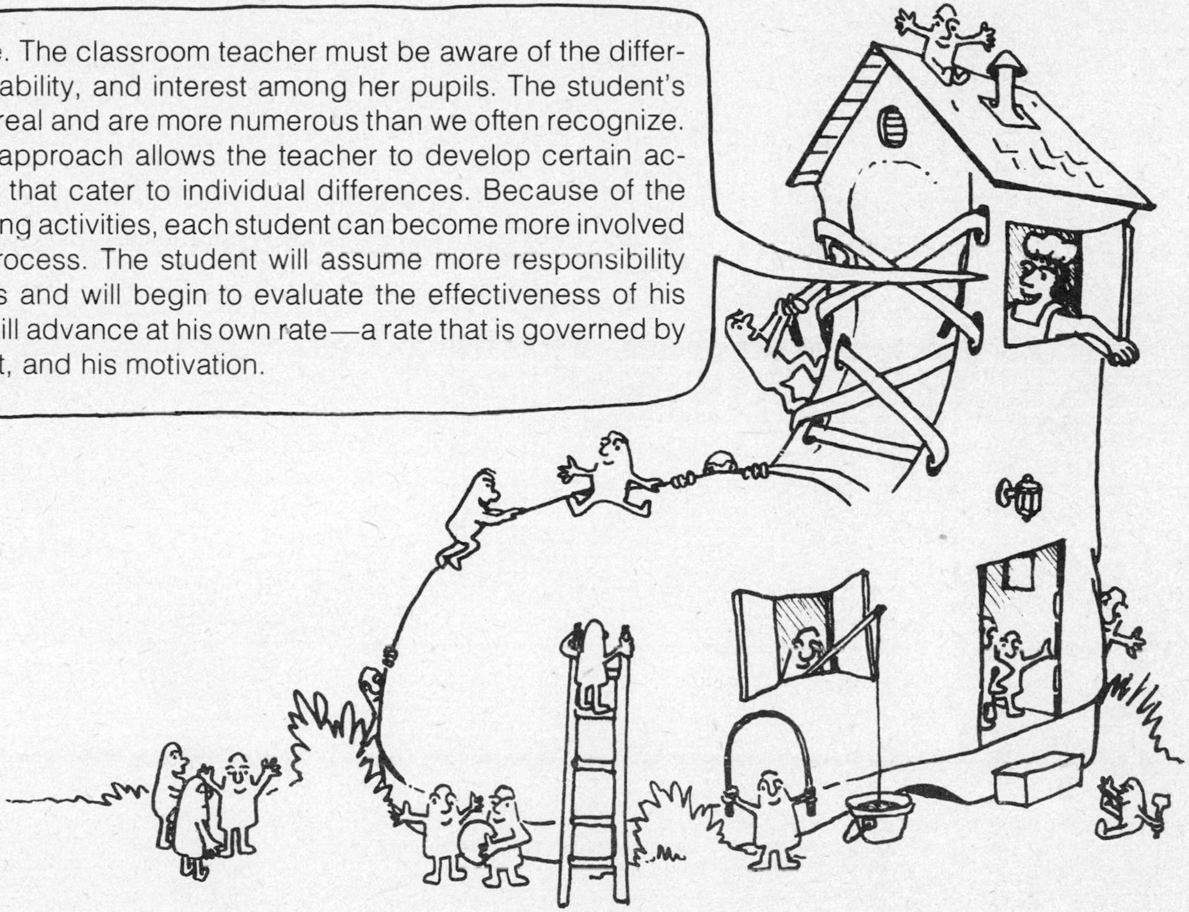

Learning centers make small-group activities a part of the learning process. The student can choose to work in group situations or to work independently. The centers can be structured to give each student experience in both situations during a period of time. Learning to function as a group member is vital to the development of each child. Working together, students exchange ideas and learn to share responsibility for the learning process.

There is no "correct" way of establishing groups. The teacher must consider the skill or task to be accomplished by the group; then she can divide the class into groups according to ability, interest, subject matter, friendships, or any other dimensions that seem appropriate. The most productive small group is one that creates an interaction through which students assume a dominant role in their own educational program.

How do students feel about learning centers?

Students will react positively to learning centers if the teacher is attentive to individual interests, learning styles, ability differences, and achievement ranges in developing the centers. When the student is involved in setting the goals, selecting the learning activities, choosing the pace at which he will work, and evaluating his own work, then the student will experience success in learning. Experiences with such success will in turn enhance the self-image of the student.

How to Begin Developing Learning Centers

Where do I begin?

In developing educationally sound, stimulating learning centers that will meet the needs of your students, the key is preplanning. Plan each center around definite behavioral objectives that will be achieved through work in the center. Pretesting or a survey of student needs may be a source of ideas for objectives and types of activities to be included in the centers you plan. Variety and attractive packaging will enhance appeal and motivation. Whether the intent of a center is development of skills, enrichment, or sheer fun, the center should be activity oriented.

First, determine the **purpose** of the center. Second, choose **activities** that will help students to meet the goal you have chosen. Third, be creative in the **construction** of an attractive center.

Determining the Purpose of a Center

You can develop a learning center oriented toward some specific purpose within almost any area of the curriculum. The list of possible subject areas is almost endless.

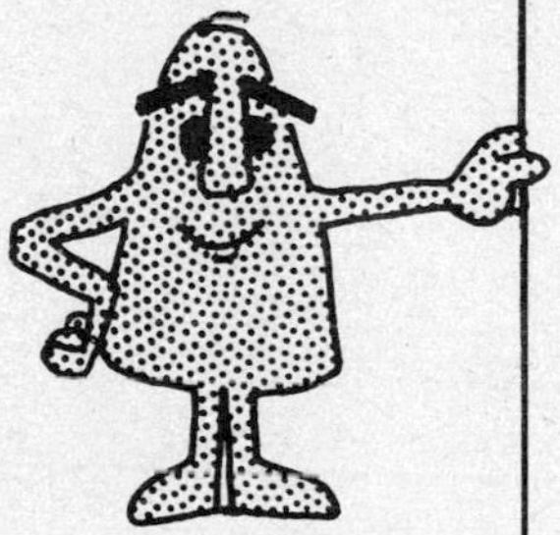

Reading

- Phonetic skills
- Structural analysis skills
- Comprehension
  - Sequence
  - Main idea
  - Vocabulary
  - Cause and effect
  - Inference
- Study skills
- Library skills and resources
- Oral interpretation

Language development

- Puppet theater
- Literature-listening experiences
- Story-telling experiences
- Flannel-board experiences
- Listening skills
- Oral reporting
- Creative writing
- Research and report writing
- Handwriting skills
- Spelling skills

Mathematics

- Computational skills
- Problem-solving skills
- Measurement skills
- Geometry concepts and skills

Science

- Experimentation skills
- Geology concepts
- Weather concepts

Social Sciences

- Map-reading skills
- Ecology concepts
- Multicultural experiences

Suppose that you decide to develop a learning center oriented toward development of computational skills (within the subject area of mathematics). The next step is to choose a specific behavioral objective or purpose—a very precise statement of the skill or experience that you hope students will achieve through the center. For example, you might choose as the goal of your center the reinforcement of the skill of three-place addition with regrouping.

At this point, it would be a good idea to pause and conjure up a catchy title and theme for the center. The objective is to find a title and theme that will appeal to the students and make them want to try the activities provided.

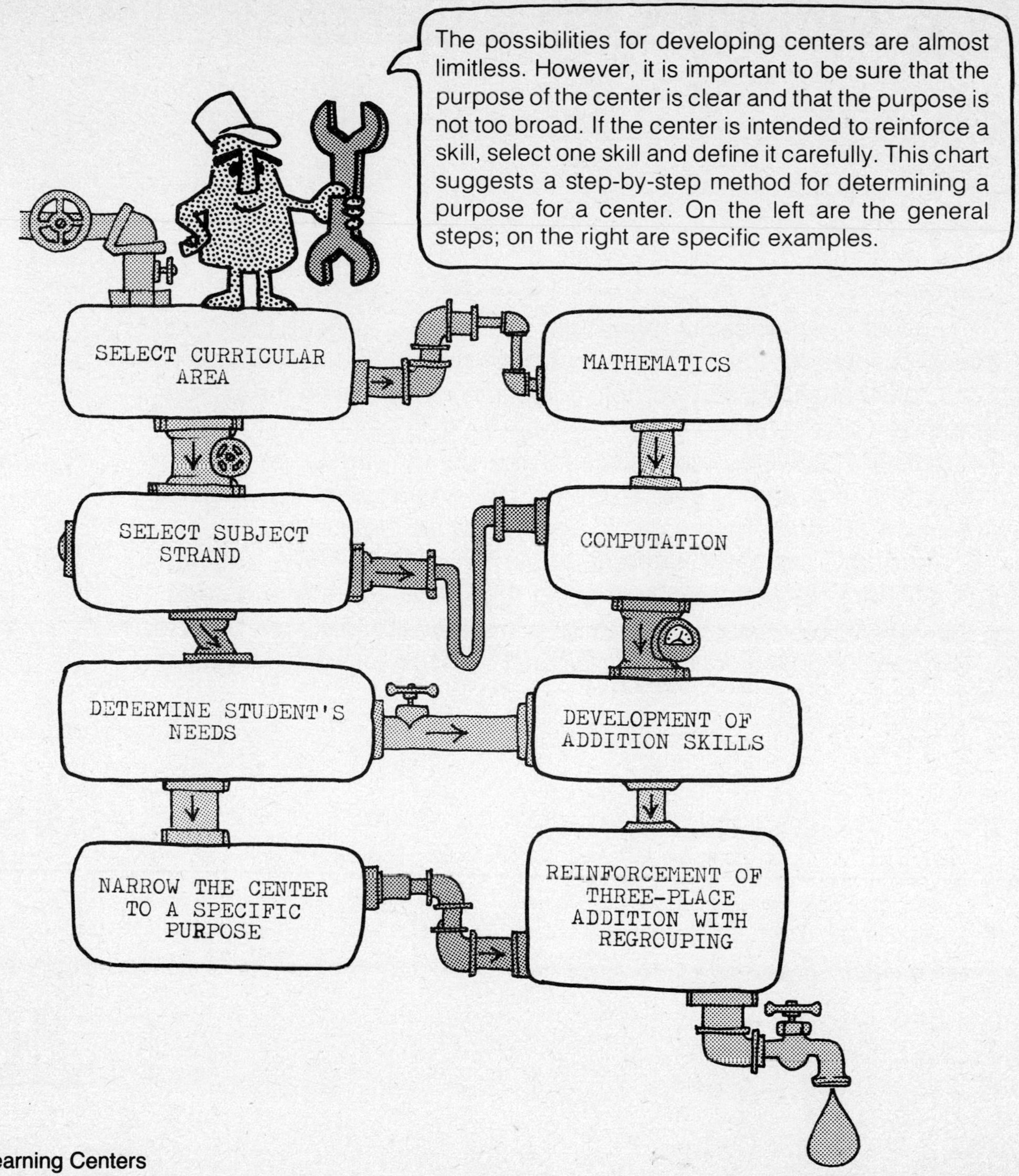
The possibilities for developing centers are almost limitless. However, it is important to be sure that the purpose of the center is clear and that the purpose is not too broad. If the center is intended to reinforce a skill, select one skill and define it carefully. This chart suggests a step-by-step method for determining a purpose for a center. On the left are the general steps; on the right are specific examples.
SELECT CURRICULAR AREA
MATHEMATICS
SELECT SUBJECT STRAND
COMPUTATION
DETERMINE STUDENT'S NEEDS
DEVELOPMENT OF ADDITION SKILLS
NARROW THE CENTER TO A SPECIFIC PURPOSE
REINFORCEMENT OF THREE-PLACE ADDITION WITH REGROUPING

Selecting Activities for a Center

"Appropriate" activities are those that meet the pupils' needs and lead to the accomplishment of the purpose chosen for the center. In other words, you should select activities that will help **your** students to master the instructional objective chosen for the center.

The different activities you select for the center should provide for individual differences among **your** students. Consider the individual learning styles of the children in your class. Each pupil prefers certain learning styles. Some pupils are sight learners, some kinesthetic, some auditory; some are abstract thinkers, some need to manipulate concrete objects. Ideally, the activities available at a particular center will allow each pupil to select a mode of input and output that will best help him to reach the goal of the center.

For example, if the purpose of the center is to reinforce three-place addition with regrouping, the center might include the following alternative activities:

1. worksheets for those pupils operating at an abstract level;
2. number lines for those pupils operating at a representational level; and
3. manipulative counting chips for those pupils operating at a concrete level.

The activities you select should be chosen, not only to meet individual differences in background and learning style, but also to offer variety that will stimulate interest.

The only limit on the variety of activities you could present is the limit of your own imagination in devising possible activities. Among the many activities we have used in different centers are the following:

Board games	Manipulative materials
Worksheets	Electric boards
Task cards	Records and tapes
Card games	Art activities
Concentration boards	Crossword puzzles

Constructing an Attractive Center

Learning centers with intriguing titles and stimulating pictures will invite and motivate students. Use your imagination and artistic talents to create a pleasing and exciting center for learning.

Be practical when constructing a learning center; make the center durable. A durable learning center is one constructed so as to survive repeated use in the classroom. Use protective coverings to prolong the utility of center components. Products such as clear contact paper, plastic sleeves, or plastic lamination will prolong the life of materials and ensure their reusability.

If a crossword puzzle or worksheet is covered with a protective material, many students may use the same puzzle or sheet. Washable felt-pen markings can then be erased with a damp cloth; markings made with wax pencils can be erased with a tissue or with a square of indoor/outdoor carpeting. The cleaned puzzle or sheet can then be returned to the center for further use.

When constructing a learning center, pay attention to the directions for students. Write directions that are "teacher independent." That is, write instructions that **your** students will understand and follow without additional verbal directions from you. Check your instructions against the following ideal properties:

1. the directions are written in words and sentences that your students can read and understand;
2. the instructions are in sequential order, with no steps left out; and
3. the directions are given in clear and succinct terms.

Room Arrangement

Use your imagination and meet the needs of your students.

The basic technique is to create a cluster of "work stations" at various spots within the room for each center.

The most convenient learning-center module is a large table (designed for four to eight students) or a cluster of flat-top individual desks.

Desks with slanting tops cannot support gameboards nor be fitted together readily to form larger tables. However, such desks can be used in study centers or to provide work space for individual activities. Materials for a study center might be located on shelves or walls, with slant-top desks used to provide writing or study surfaces. Games can be played on a rug or even on a bare floor.

With a little imagination, you can include in your learning centers any furniture that is available to you: bookcases, dividers, racks, portable chart supports, easels, overstuffed chairs, couches, straight chairs, and so on.

WEATHER REPORT
FRIDAY
MAY 5, 1975

MATCH THE SETS

Use bulletin boards as part of a center.

An old overstuffed chair, a rocking chair, or a sofa can add the comfort of home to a reading or library corner.

Old pieces of furniture can be renewed with bright contact paper or paint.

The area near the sink is a good place for art centers or terrariums.

Include single-student areas where individuals can work privately.

At each station in each center, place the materials that will be needed for the activities to be performed there. In addition, have a Basic Materials Supply Center in an easily accessible location, with a supply of such extra items as paper, paste, scissors, and rulers.

When arranging the room, be aware of traffic patterns to doors, restrooms, and drinking fountains.

Children should be able to move freely from desk to floor without bothering others.

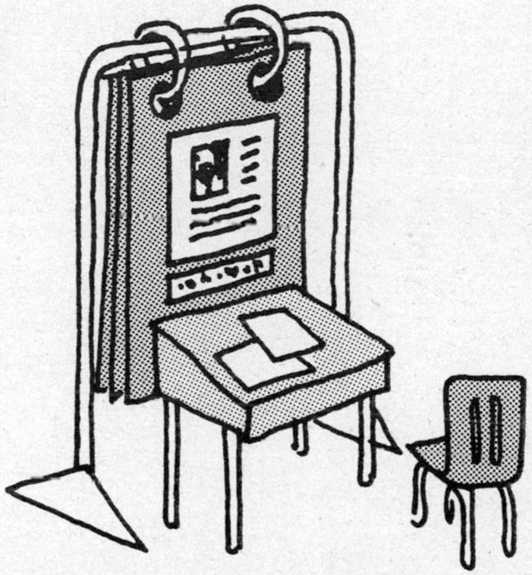

Make arrangements with the principal and the custodian about changes you are planning in your room arrangement.

FIND A BOOK AND READ ABOUT ME
SIZE ? FOOD ? AGE ?
WHAT WILL HAPPEN NEXT ?
Aa Bb Cc Dd Ee Ff Gg Hh Ii Jj Kk Ll
TASKS
CASSET TAPES

SOUTH VIEW

WHERE IN THE WORLD ARE YOU ?
WHERE ON EARTH HAVE YOU BEEN ?
SIZE THINGS UP!
TRY A TASK... AND RECORD YOUR RESULTS
HOW MANY ?
TASKS
TASKS
TASKS
SAND
KREMER

ART...
INSTRUCTIONAL
CENTER

A WORLD IN A WATER DROP
TRY A TINY TASK
WHICH ONE HAS WATER FLEAS ?
TINY TASKS
OLD MAGAZINES

NORTH VIEW

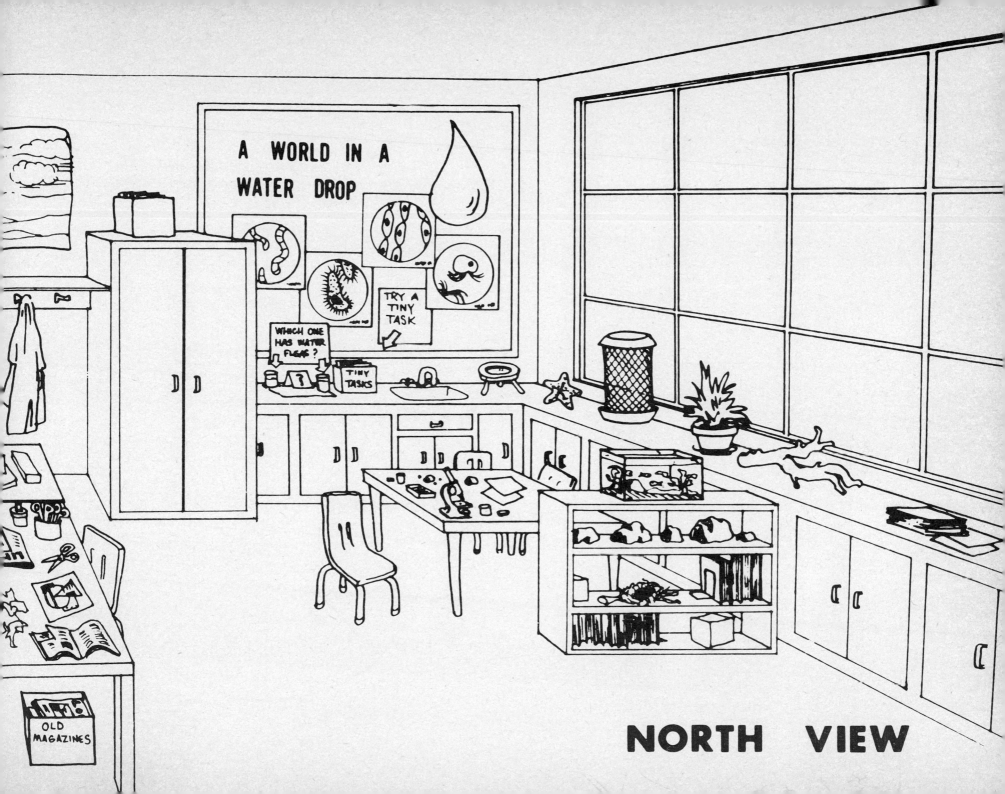

Scheduling

The amount of time to be scheduled for each learning center depends upon the subject areas included in the centers, the individual needs of the students, and the requirements of the curriculum. There is no "correct" schedule. The teacher must design a schedule with which she is comfortable and one that meets the needs of her students.

A schedule provides the student with an outline for effective use of his or her time. If the student knows what he will be doing each day, he gains a sense of security. Two basic systems are available for scheduling students to centers: the rotational system and the contract system.

Individual assignment sheets or an assignment wheel (rotated each day or each period) can be used to provide instructions for a rotational system.

Rotational Scheduling System

1. Centers are set up around the room.
2. Each student is assigned to a specific center at a specific time.
3. This system is most readily used when small groups of students rotate around the different centers in some fixed pattern.

The rotational system is a good one to use when first introducing learning centers to the classroom. It allows teacher and students a chance to become familiar with the centers approach, while providing some structure for the classroom day and routine.

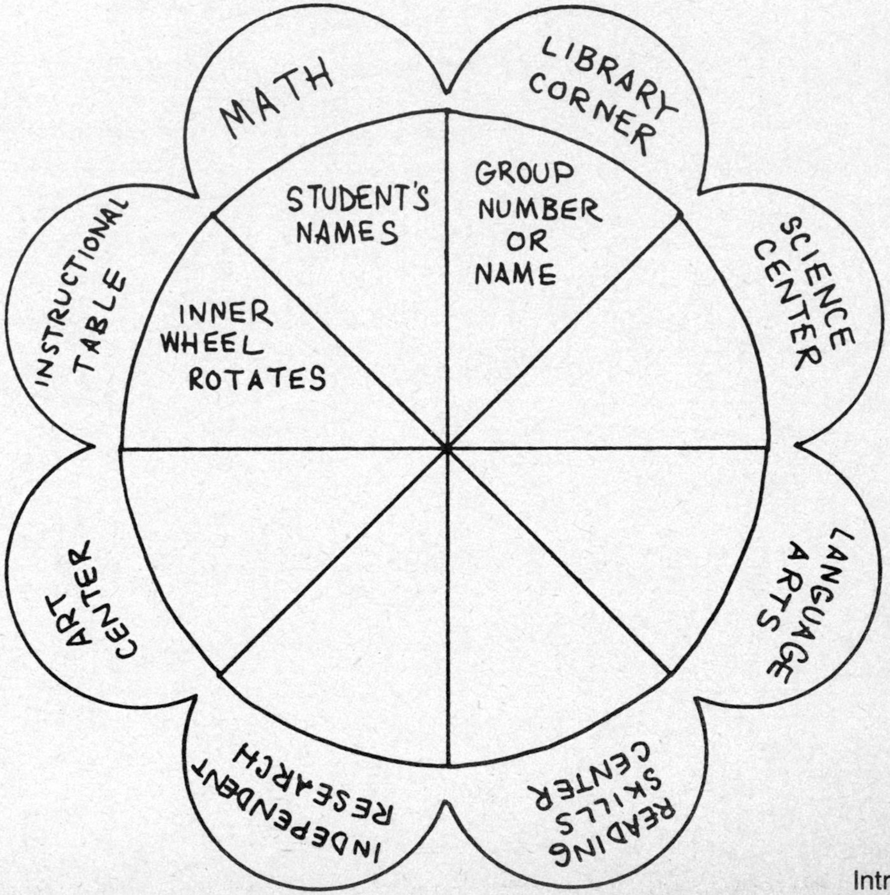

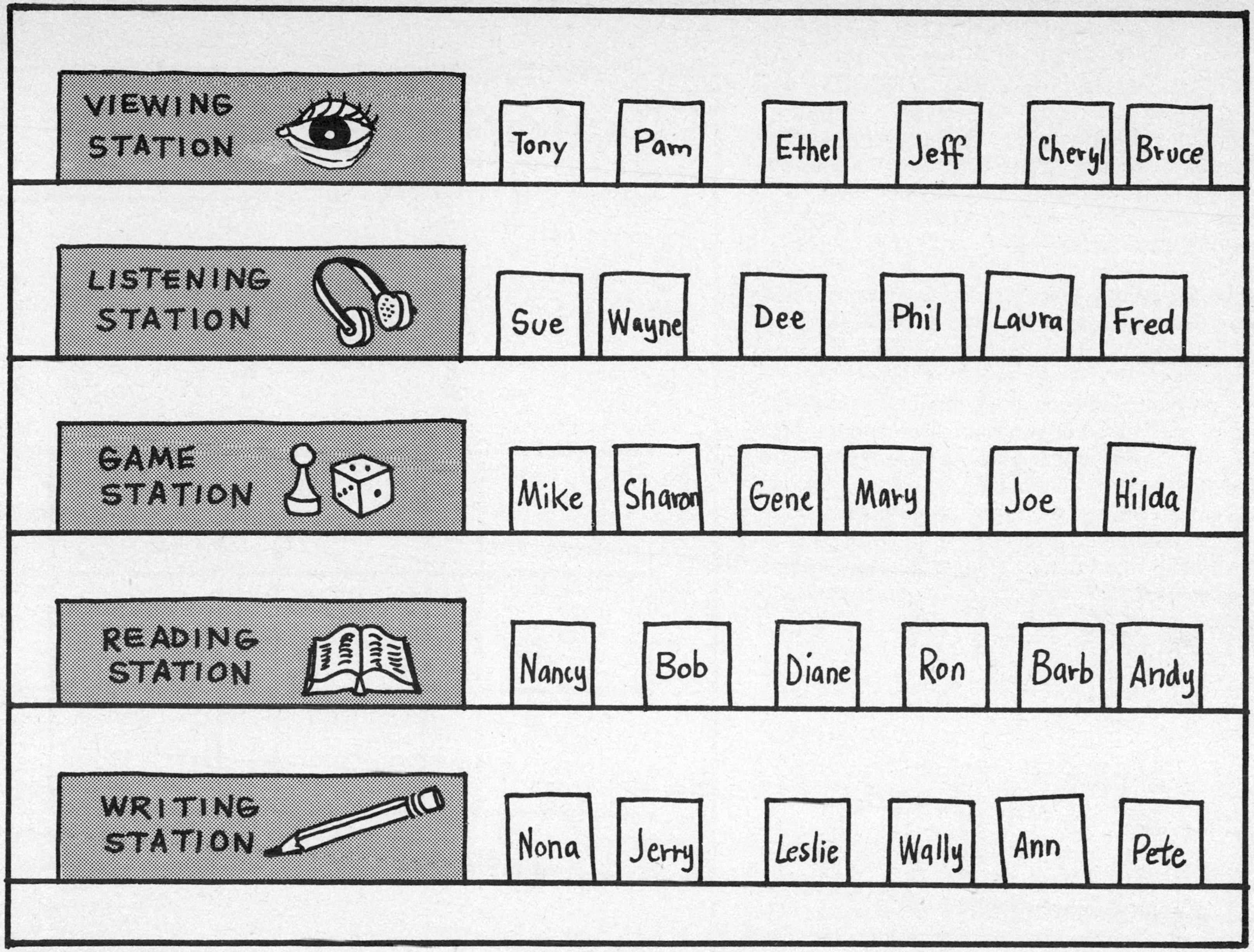

A pocket chart is useful for rotational scheduling. The station cards can be rotated easily for normal rotation, but group makeup can also be altered when desired.

Contracting Scheduling System

A contract is a written agreement between teacher and student, describing the work to be done by the student and the schedule for that work. Class discussion of goals and responsibilities can serve as preparation for contracting.

Verbal contracts are the first step. Written and signed contracts between teacher and pupil can lead to independent research and study.

Conferences between teacher and student are basic to the contracting system. The student must evaluate his own work and his own use of time. Students often tend to contract for more than they can actually handle, and then they are unable to complete the contracted work by the agreed date. In such a case, the teacher should help the student renegotiate the contract to require a reasonable load of work.

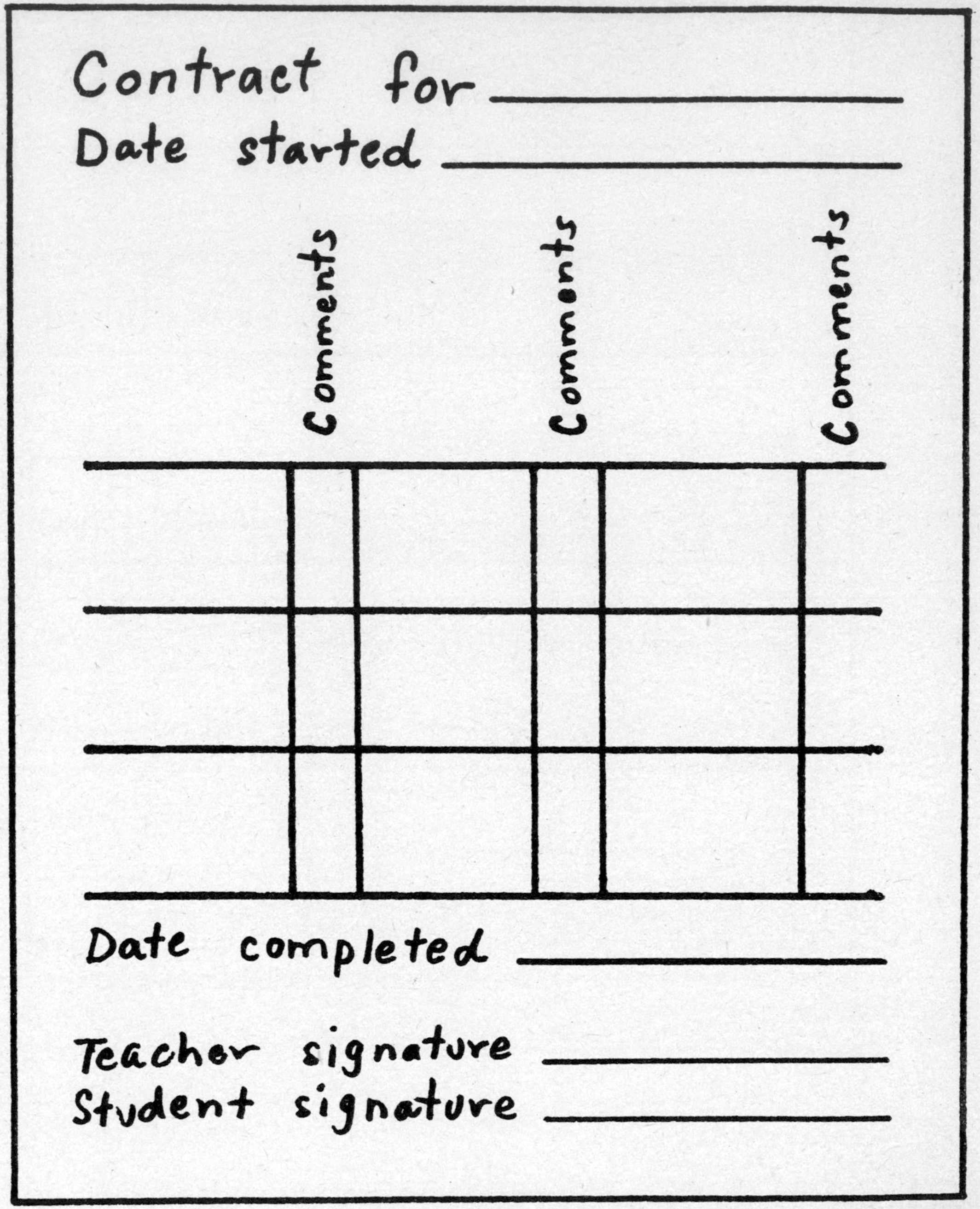

An example of an individual assignment sheet for rotational scheduling. The comments space might be used for the teacher's comments to the student on suggested activities or objectives, or this space might be used for the student's comments about the work he has done each day.

Name: ____________ My Weekly Reading Centers	
Viewing Center 	Monday Comments:
Reading Center 	Tuesday Comments:
Skill Center 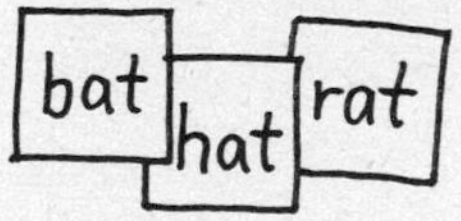	Wednesday Comments:
Writing Center 	Thursday Comments:
Game Center 	Friday Comments:

Record Keeping

In order to evaluate each student's progress, the teacher must keep adequate records for each student.

Record keeping is a continuous process, involving both the student and the teacher. Records show the amount of work the student has accomplished; an evaluation tests and reports the quality of the work.

The types of records needed for a center will vary, depending on the subject area covered by the center. The following examples can be adapted to various types of centers.

1. Student file of completed work

a. Set priorities for work to be filed; there is no need to file self-corrected work.
b. Establish a take-home work system for daily, weekly, and monthly papers.
c. Attach to each file a teacher-comment sheet.
d. Write comments in each file every week, so that work can be returned. The comment sheet is a resource for the teacher in preparing for conferences with students.

2. Reading and math skill records

a. Use district forms or available diagnostic materials that state objectives.
b. List objectives on a student record sheet.

3. Center task-completion charts

a. A master chart can be used for a center, listing all task (activity) numbers and all students' names. Each child can check off the tasks as he completes them. For younger children, the teacher might check off completed tasks, or the child might color in a square on the chart. An example of a master chart is shown on page 28.
b. For younger children, it is often useful to give each child a record sheet for work at a particular center. The child colors in a space on the chart as he completes each task. Four examples of such individual record sheets are shown on pages 212–215. The sheets can be kept in a folder in the center; if desired, the teacher could periodically transfer the information to a master chart.

4. Classroom center-completion chart

a. It is often useful to display a large chart in the classroom listing all students' names and the names of the various centers in the classroom. As the child completes all the tasks at a center, he indicates this fact on the chart by coloring in or placing a sticker in the appropriate space.
b. This chart is helpful to both teacher and student in suggesting where the student should concentrate his efforts to complete his work at unfinished centers.

Name ____________________

Age ____________________

DATE	PAGES COVERED	BASIC VOCABULARY	WORD ATTACK	STRUCTURAL ELEMENTS	BLENDING	WORD MEANING	COMPREHENSION	STUDY SKILLS	COMMENTS

Example of a reading record

TASK ____________

WORKERS	1	2	3	4	5	6	7	8	9
Judy		✓	✓	✓					✓
Billy									
Janet		✓							
Mike			✓		✓				
Pam	✓	✓							
Ethel								✓	
Ronald	✓				✓			✓	✓
Susan	✓	✓	✓	✓	✓	✓	✓	✓	✓
Carol		✓	✓		✓	✓			✓
Wayne									
Kerry									
Joseph									
Fred									
Sharon									
Marlo						✓		✓	
Gene									

Evaluation

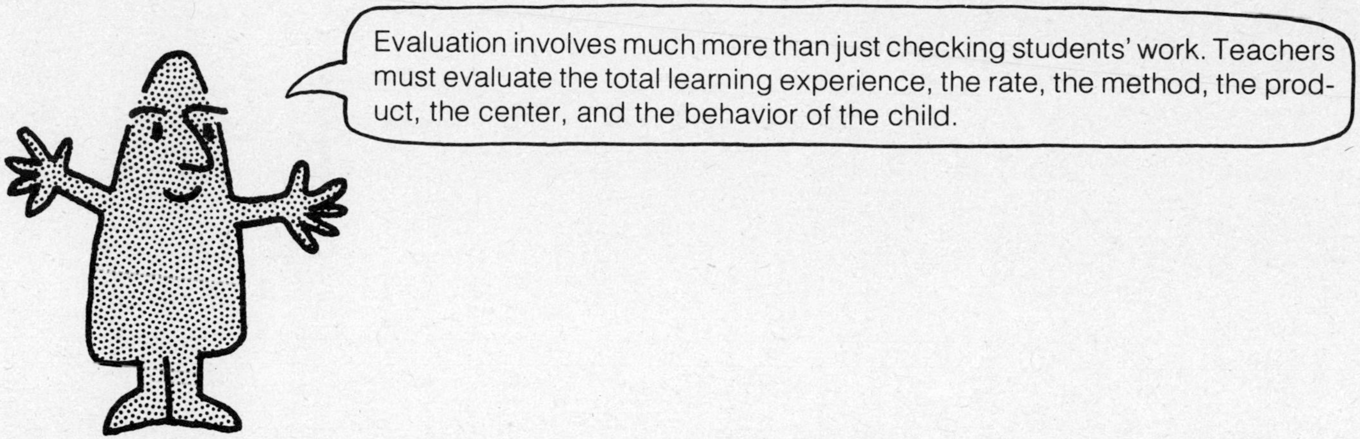

Evaluation involves much more than just checking students' work. Teachers must evaluate the total learning experience, the rate, the method, the product, the center, and the behavior of the child.

1. There are several general behavioral goals that should evolve from a learning-center experience and that should influence evaluation.
   a. Children will know how to work cooperatively in groups.
   b. Children will develop independent work habits.
   c. Children will develop more effective ways of planning their time.
   d. Children will discover creative ways of working.
   e. Children will know how to explore areas of interest.
   f. Children will recognize the sequential steps in a lesson.
   g. Children will understand techniques of evaluation.
   h. Children will know how to use methods of evaluation.
2. Evaluation is included on any record sheet in the form of comments.
3. Students may share projects or tell about discoveries and/or experiences.
4. During pupil-teacher conferences, students offer and receive suggestions for improvement.
5. Spot checking during activity periods is an important evaluation tool. The teacher should immediately enter comments on student folders.
6. Self-correcting materials give students immediate feedback for self-evaluation.
7. Suggested evaluation forms are shown on the following two pages.

MONTHLY EVALUATION OF STUDENT BEHAVIOR AT CENTERS

PUPIL ______________________________ AGE ____________

DATE ____________

RATING SCALE

1	2	3	4	5
Low				High

A. How well does the student . . .

1. Follow oral directions? 1 2 3 4 5
2. Follow written directions? 1 2 3 4 5
3. Complete center tasks? 1 2 3 4 5
4. Select appropriate tasks? 1 2 3 4 5
5. Interact with other pupils in a sharing or helping situation? 1 2 3 4 5
6. Work in a manner which does not interrupt or distract others? 1 2 3 4 5
7. Use his time? 1 2 3 4 5
8. Move from center to center? 1 2 3 4 5
9. Complete contracted plans made in teacher-pupil conferences? 1 2 3 4 5

B. Number of contracts completed this month. ____________

C. What suggestions should be included in the next teacher-pupil conference?

MARKING SYSTEM:

\+ knows concept, assign to more difficult task

✓ meeting objective, continue through task

\- needs assistance

TITLE OF ACTIVITY (CROSSWORD PUZZLES)

OBJECTIVE: (The student will be able to use the Dolch words in sentences for correct meaning.)

DATE	NAME	1	2	3	4*	5	6	7	8	9	10

1

KINDERGARTEN CENTERS

Language Arts and Reading

Alphabet Center

Activity 1: Alphabet Puzzles
Activity 2: Alphabet Matching Boards
Activity 3: Alphabet Tracing Boards

Initial Consonant Center

Activity 1: Sound Wheels
Activity 2: Spin a Sound
Activity 3: Magnetic Sound Board

Alphabet Center

Purpose: To provide practice in writing and matching letters of the alphabet, both capital and small letter forms.

Activity 1: Alphabet Puzzles

Construction

On each of twenty-six **3" x 5" cards,** print a capital letter and its corresponding small letter. Draw a zig-zag line between the two letters. **Contact** the cards for durability. Cut through each card along the zig-zag line. Place the card pieces in a large **envelope** or in a **box.**

Procedure

The child fits the puzzle parts together, matching each capital letter with its corresponding small letter.

Evaluation

This is a self-evaluating activity because only correct matches will "fit."

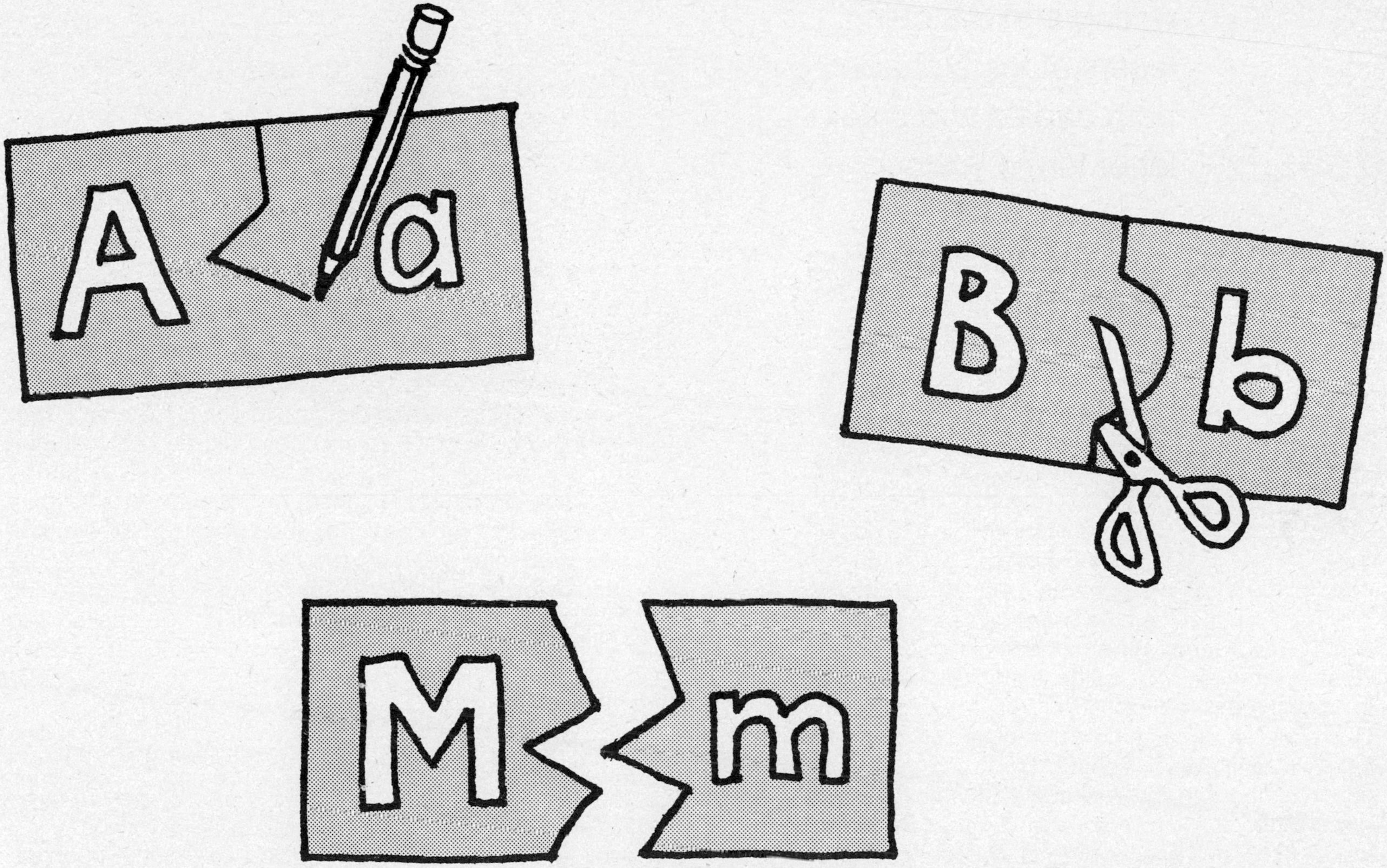
A a
B b
M m

Alphabet Center

Purpose: To provide practice in writing and matching letters of the alphabet, both capital and small letter forms.

Activity 2: Alphabet Matching Boards

Construction

Up to six children will be able to work in this center, using all six of the **playing boards.** Cut three red boards and three blue boards. Line the boards into 2" squares. Letter the blue boards with capital letters and the red boards with small letters. Cut 78 red and 78 blue **squares,** 2" on a side. Letter the red squares to make three complete sets of small letters; letter the blue squares to make three complete sets of capital letters. **Laminate** or **contact** the boards and the squares for durability. Package each alphabet set in an **envelope;** mark the envelope with a red or blue dot made with a felt-tip pen to show which kind of alphabet set is included.

Procedure

The child draws one letter square from the envelope, says its name, and places it under its matching letter on the board. He continues until he has matched each letter on the board. The child may begin by matching capital letters to capital letters (blue squares on blue board), then match small letters to small letters (red squares on red board), and finally match small letters to capital letters (red squares on blue board) or vice versa (blue squares on red board).

Evaluation

This activity can be evaluated by teacher observation.

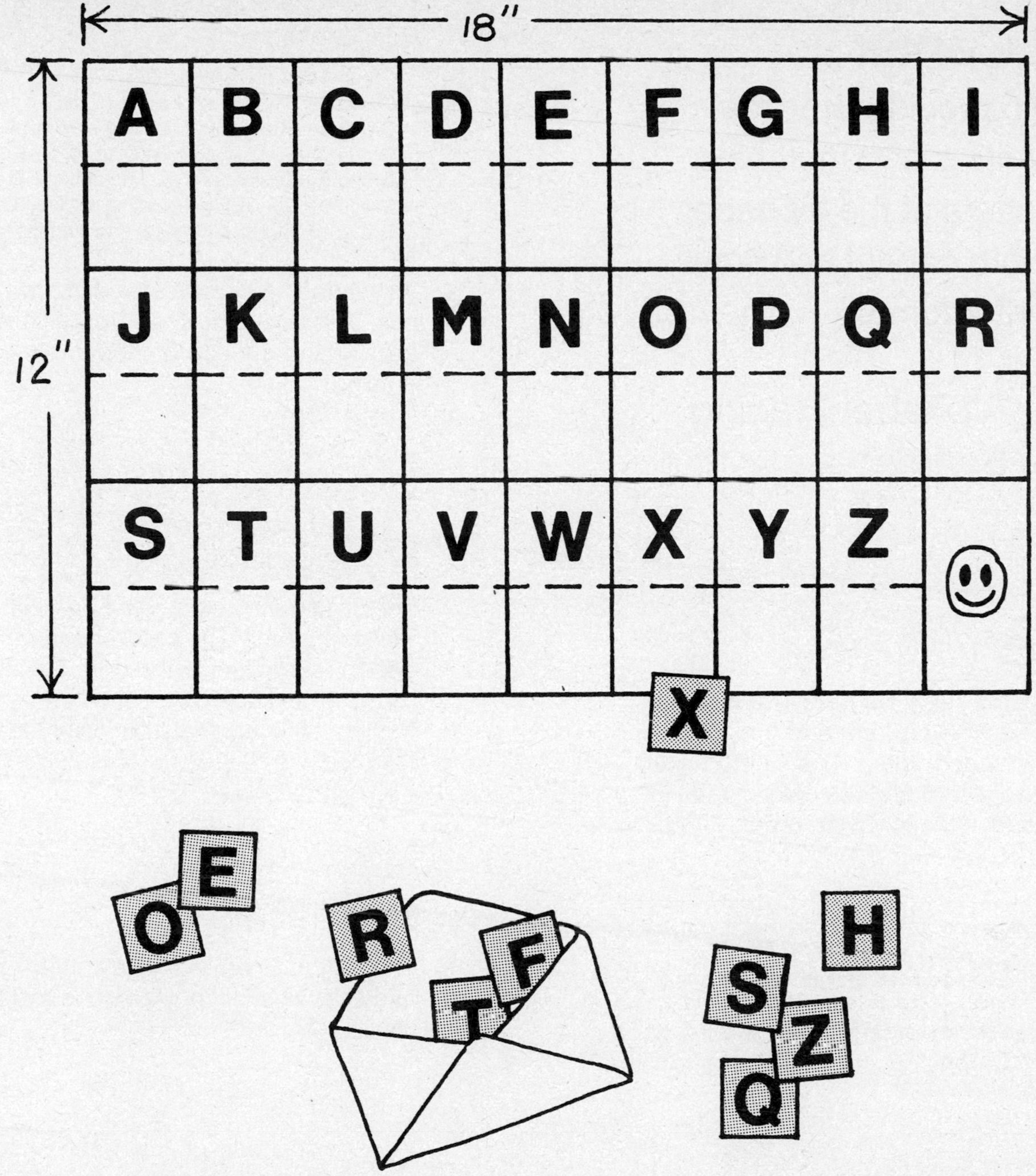
18"
12"
A B C D E F G H I
J K L M N O P Q R
S T U V W X Y Z
X
O E
R T F
S H Z Q

Alphabet Center

Purpose: To provide practice in writing and matching letters of the alphabet, both capital and small letter forms.

Activity 3: Alphabet Tracing Boards

Construction

Fifty-two **tracing boards** (9" x 12") are used in the center: one for the small-letter form and one for the capital-letter form of each letter. The boards are ruled as shown on page 216 and are color-coded in ten groups to be used in the following order.

Small letters:

Group 1 Circular strokes and straight strokes: o, a, d, g, q, b, p, c, e.
Group 2 Straight strokes and curved strokes: l, t, i, f, j, n, m, r, h, u, s.
Group 3 Straight strokes and slanting strokes: v, w, y, x, z, k.

Capital letters:

Group 4 Straight strokes: E, F, H, I, L, T.
Group 5 Slanting strokes: V, W, X.
Group 6 Straight and slanting strokes: A, M, N, Y, Z, K.
Group 7 Curving strokes: C, O, S, U, J.
Group 8 Straight and curving strokes: B, D, G, P.
Group 9 Curving and slanting strokes: Q.
Group 10 Straight, curving, and slanting strokes: R.

All the tracing boards are contacted and placed in a **box.** The box should also contain **wax markers** for tracing and a piece of indoor/outdoor **carpeting** for erasing.

Procedure

The child traces each letter on the board with a wax marking pencil. The child should erase each board before returning it to the box. The child then moves on to the next board in order. The teacher should limit tracing time so that the child does not become fatigued.

Evaluation

The student can evaluate much of his own work; further evaluation may be done by teacher observation.

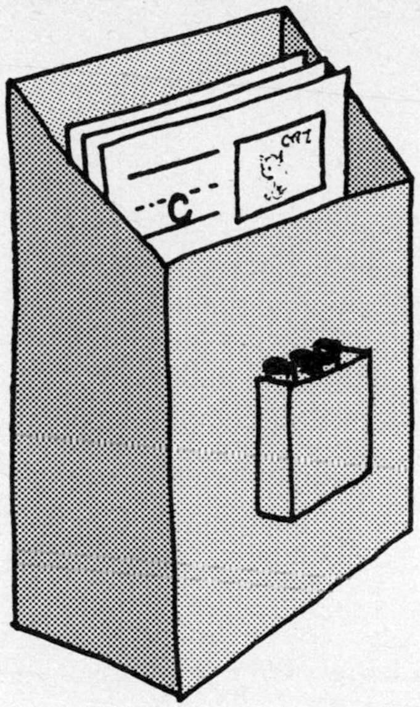

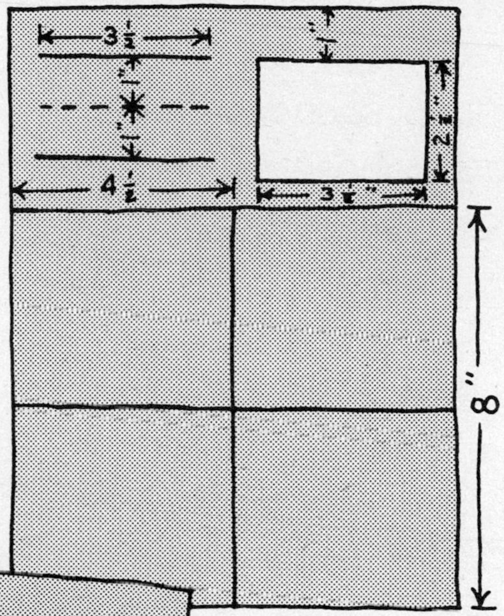
3 ½
4 ½
3 ½"
8"

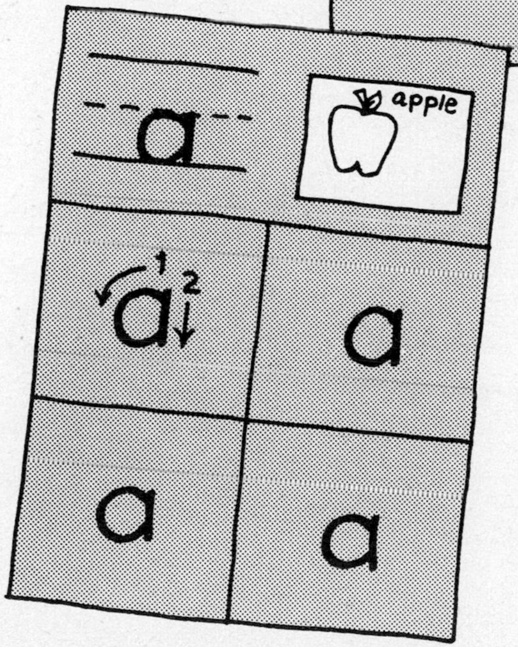
a
apple
1
2
a
a
a
a

Initial Consonant Center

Purpose: To provide practice in matching initial consonant sounds with pictures whose names begin with those sounds.

Activity 1: Sound Wheels

Construction

Cut four sets of four 12" diameter circles of colored tag for sound wheels. Draw seven 3" circle outlines on each wheel. Upper and lower case letters are written on a center 4" circle. Cut four sets of twenty-eight 3" diameter circles of tag matching the sound wheels. Pictures of objects with the initial sounds are pasted on 3" circles. The sound wheels and sorting circles may be laminated or covered with contact. Use the following sets for sound wheels.

Group 1: F, D, M, G.
Group 2: B, S, T, W.
Group 3: N, P, K/C, J.
Group 4: H, L, R, V.

Procedure

One or two children are given a set of wheels and the corresponding set of picture circles. The children place the matching pictures on the appropriate wheels.

Evaluation

This activity may be evaluated by teacher observation. If the backs of the picture circles are coded, the activity may be self-evaluated.

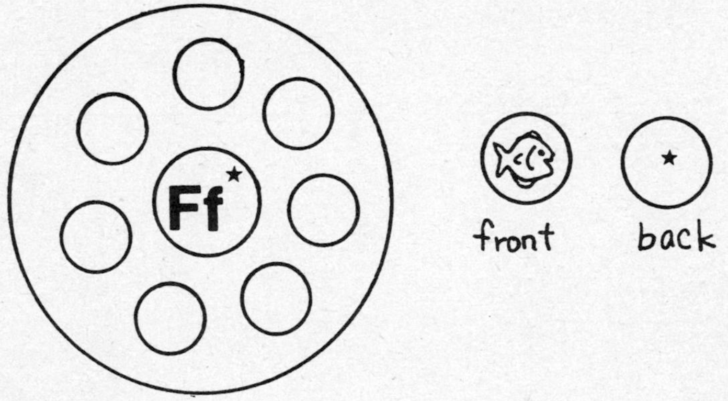

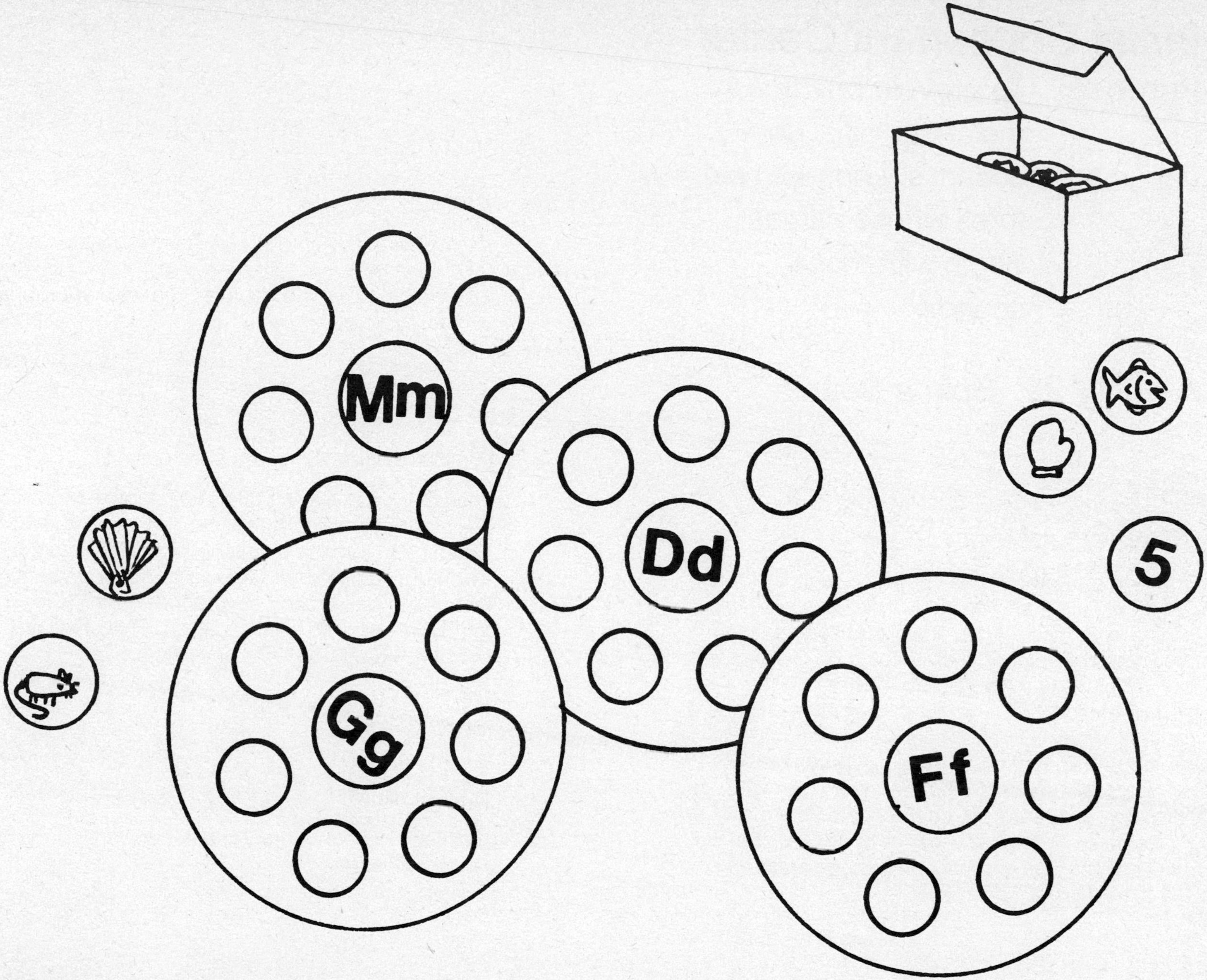
Mm
Dd
Gg
Ff
5

Initial Consonant Center

Purpose: To provide practice in matching initial consonant sounds with pictures whose names begin with those sounds.

Activity 2: Spin a Sound

Construction

Draw the game board as shown on **tagboard.** Each square is 2" x 2" and contains a **picture** whose name begins with one of the initial consonant sounds shown on the spinner; there should be five pictures for each of the four consonants. The spinner area is a 5"-diameter circle. Glue the tagboard on a **chipboard** backing, cover with clear **contact,** and attach a **spinner** made from tagboard or metal. Obtain two sets of ten **chips** (each set a different color), or make the chips from tagboard; the chips should be about 1" to 2" diameter. A separate game board can be prepared for each set of consonants shown in Activity 1.

Procedure

Each of the two players takes ten chips of one color. The first player spins the spinner; he then uses one of his chips to cover a picture with the initial sound of the letter indicated. (If all the pictures representing that sound are already covered, the child loses the turn.) The first child to place all ten of his chips on the board is the winner.

Evaluation

Evaluation is done through teacher participation or teacher observation.

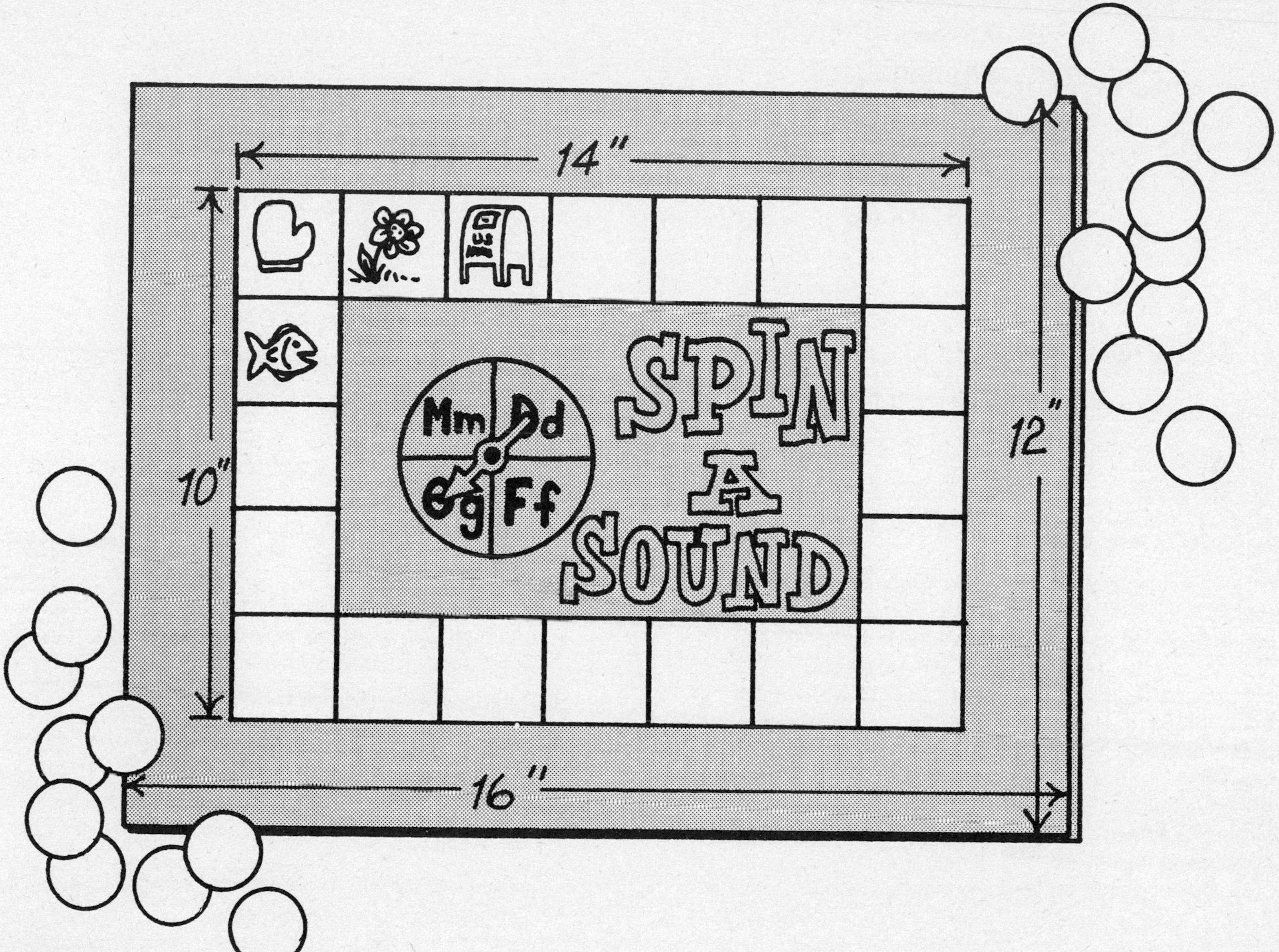
14"
10"
12"
16"
Mm
Dd
Gg
Ff
SPIN
A
SOUND

Initial Consonant Center

Purpose: To provide practice in matching initial consonant sounds with pictures whose names begin with those sounds.

Activity 3: Magnetic Sound Board

Construction

Obtain a large sheet of white **tagboard** (approximately 22" x 28"). Across the top of this chart, print a set of four initial consonant sounds. In a random manner around the rest of the chart, paste six to eight **pictures** corresponding to each initial sound. Under each of the four letters and each of the pictures, paste a piece of **magnetic paper** about ½" x 1". Cover the chart with clear **contact.** Cut fifteen pieces of heavy colored **tagboard,** each ½" x 1", and place a small piece of **magnetic tape** on the back of each strip. One magnetic sound board can be constructed for each set of consonants given in Activity 1.

Procedure

The teacher or the child places a colored strip underlining one letter at the top of the board. The child then places a colored strip under each picture whose name begins with that initial sound.

Evaluation

This activity may be evaluated through teacher observation or teacher participation.

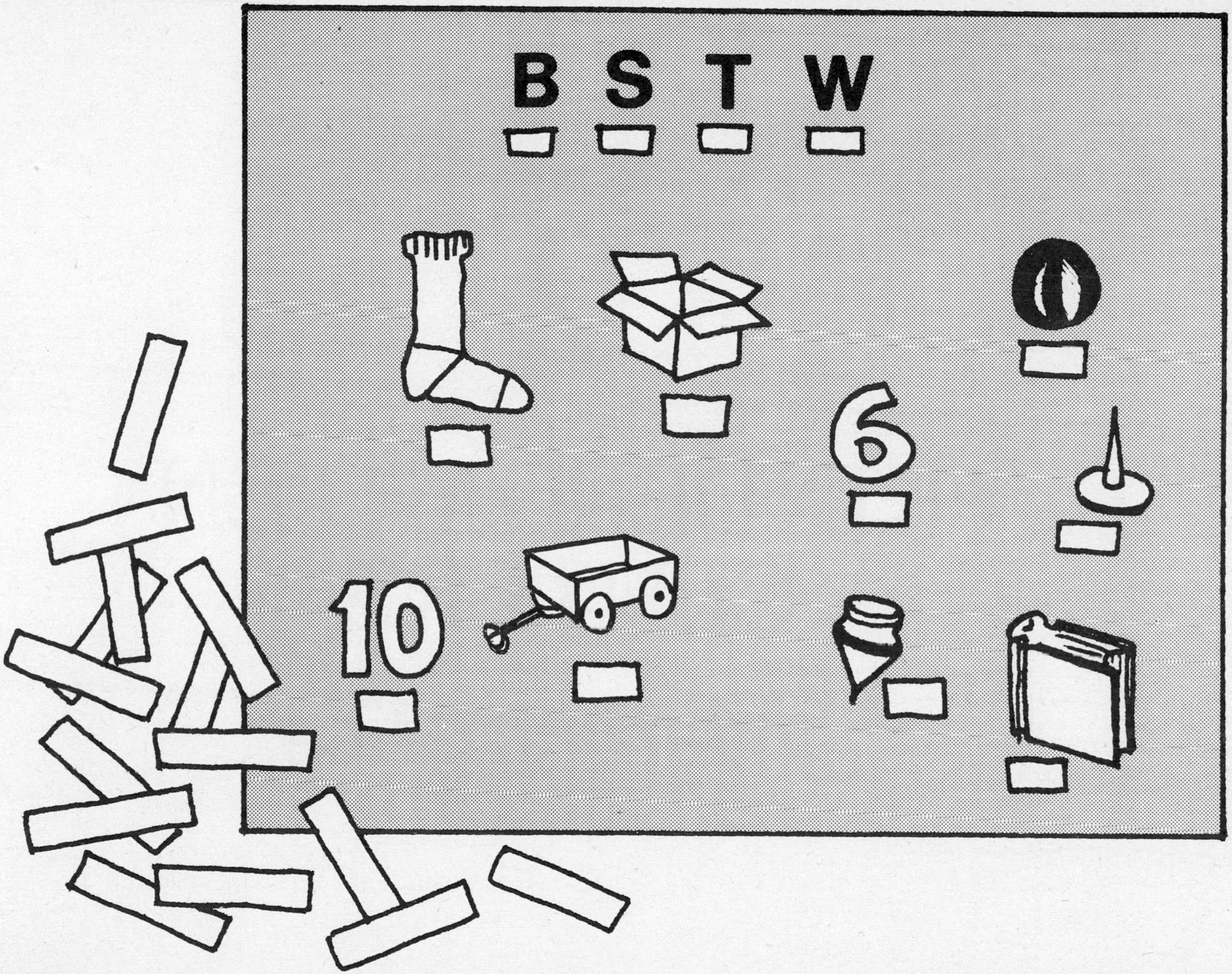
B S T W
6
10

2

KINDERGARTEN CENTERS

Mathematics

Geometric Shapes Center

Activity 1: Magnetic Matching Board
Activity 2: Bead Pattern Cards
Activity 3: Match the Pattern

Numerals Center

Activity 1: Number Match
Activity 2: Spin and Cover
Activity 3: Number Kites

Geometric Shapes Center

Purpose: To provide practice in matching and reproducing patterns of geometric shapes.

Activity 1: Magnetic Matching Board

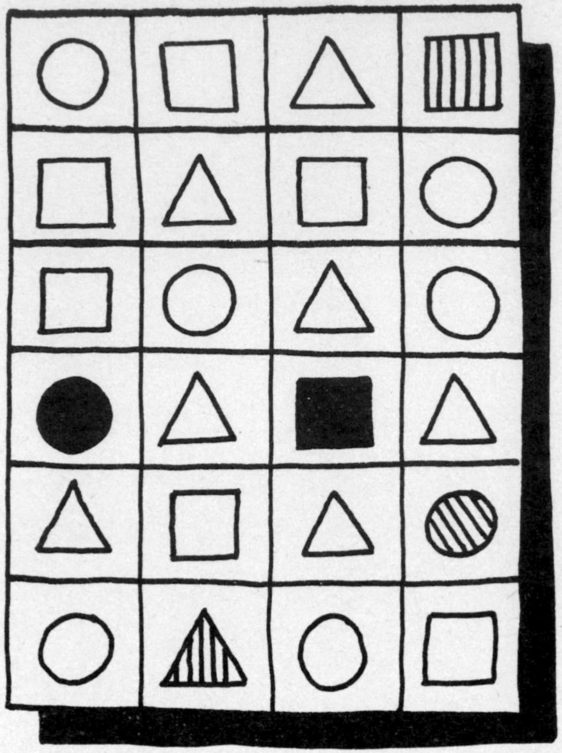

Construction

The board is constructed of **chipboard.** The left side is covered with colored **tagboard,** appropriately lettered. The right side is covered with **magnetic paper,** divided into 24 squares, each containing a colored geometric shape. Both sides of the board are covered with clear **contact** for protection. Matching cards are made of **chipboard** and **tagboard;** 24 cards should be prepared, each containing a colored shape matching one of the squares on the board. The cards are covered with clear **contact** or laminated, and a small piece of **magnetic tape** is placed on the back of each card.

Procedure

The child is given a box of 24 cards; he is to place each over the matching shape on the board.

Evaluation

This activity can be evaluated through teacher observation.

11"
16"
Can you match the shapes and colors ?
SHAPES

Geometric Shapes Center

Purpose: To provide practice in matching and reproducing patterns of geometric shapes.

Activity 2: Bead Pattern Cards

Construction

Cut twelve 2½" x 6" cards of white **tagboard.** Draw a bead pattern on each card as shown on pages 217–219. Back the cards with **chipboard,** and **laminate** or **contact** them for durability. Punch a hole about ½" from the bottom of each card, and tie a **shoestring** through this hole.

Procedure

Give the child a tub of **beads.** The child is to string beads on each shoestring, producing a pattern that matches the pattern shown on the attached card.

Evaluation

Evaluation is done by teacher observation.

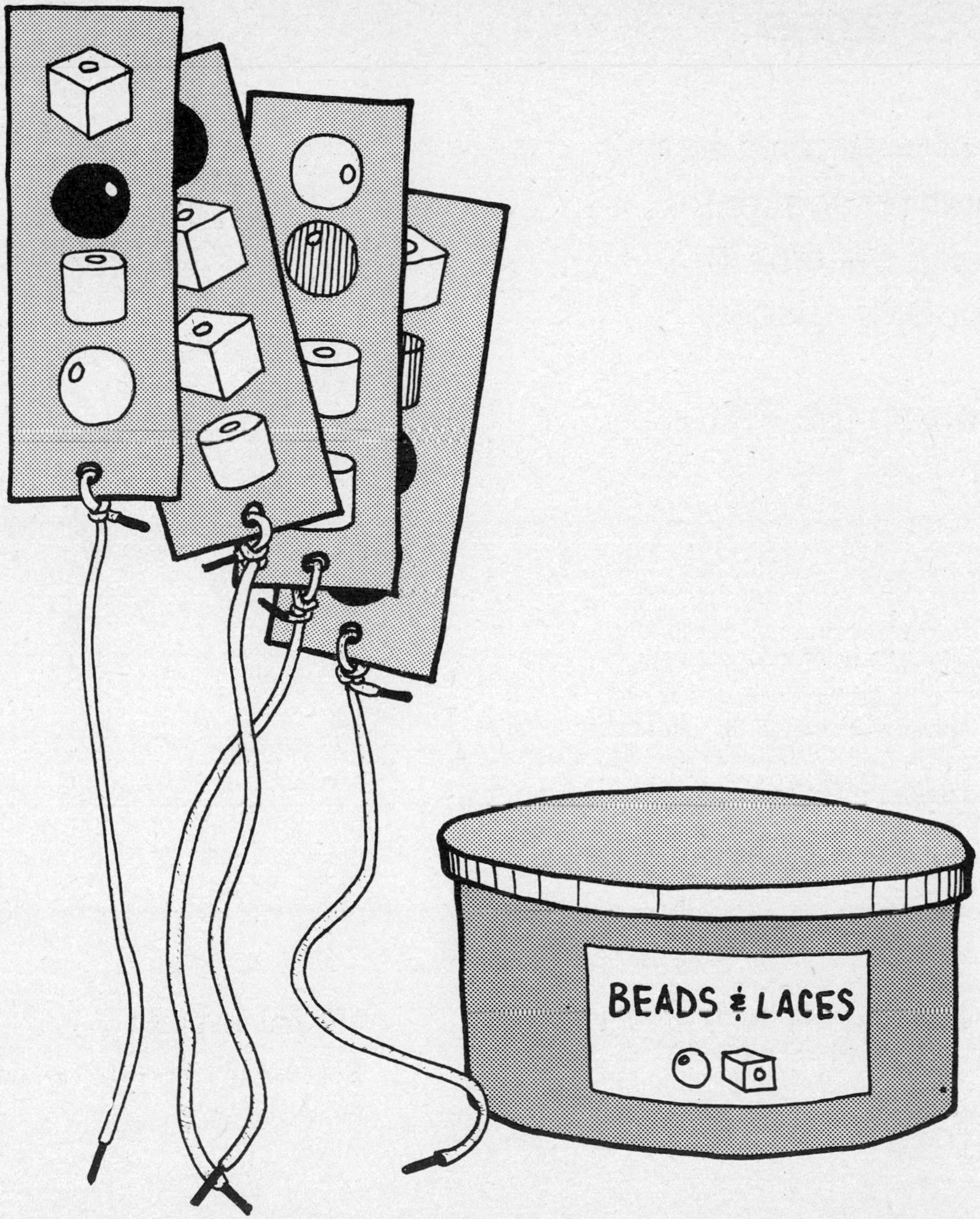
BEADS & LACES

Geometric Shapes Center

Purpose: To provide practice in matching and reproducing patterns of geometric shapes.

Activity 3: Match the Pattern

Construction

Make the board of three pieces of heavy **cardboard** or **chipboard** (dimensions shown in drawing), hinged together. The middle section is divided into two equal parts. The left side contains six **acetate pockets,** open at the inside edge. The right side is covered with **magnetic paper,** ruled with black pen, and covered with clear **contact** for protection. Cover the outside sections with colored **tagboard** and clear **contact.** The right section has a pocket (6" deep) to hold the pattern cards. Prepare at least 24 pattern **cards** (12½" x 2¼"); each should show the beginning of a series of combinations of shapes and colors. Prepare 2" squares of **tagboard,** each containing one of the various colored shapes used in the pattern cards; prepare several squares for each of the shapes and colors. Back each square with a small piece of **magnetic tape.**

Procedure

Place from one to six pattern cards on the board. The child is asked to continue each series of shapes by placing the small squares on the right half of the center board.

Evaluation

Evaluation of this activity is through teacher observation.

13"
26"
13"
18"
What
comes
next?

Numerals Center

Purpose: To provide practice in matching number pictures from zero to ten with corresponding numerals.

Activity 1: Number Match

Construction

Cut a piece of **chipboard** 17" x 17". Cover the chipboard with a piece of **tagboard.** Divide the tagboard into sixteen 4" squares. Make a 2" square in the top lefthand corner of each of these squares. In the remaining portion of each square, place a set of dots that represents an integer from one to ten. (Six integers must be repeated to fill all sixteen squares.) Cut sixteen 2" squares of **tagboard.** On each of these squares, place the numeral that corresponds to a set of dots on the large board. Cover the master board and the small squares with clear **contact.**

Procedure

The child will match the numerals with the corresponding set of dots.

Evaluation

This activity is evaluated through teacher observation.

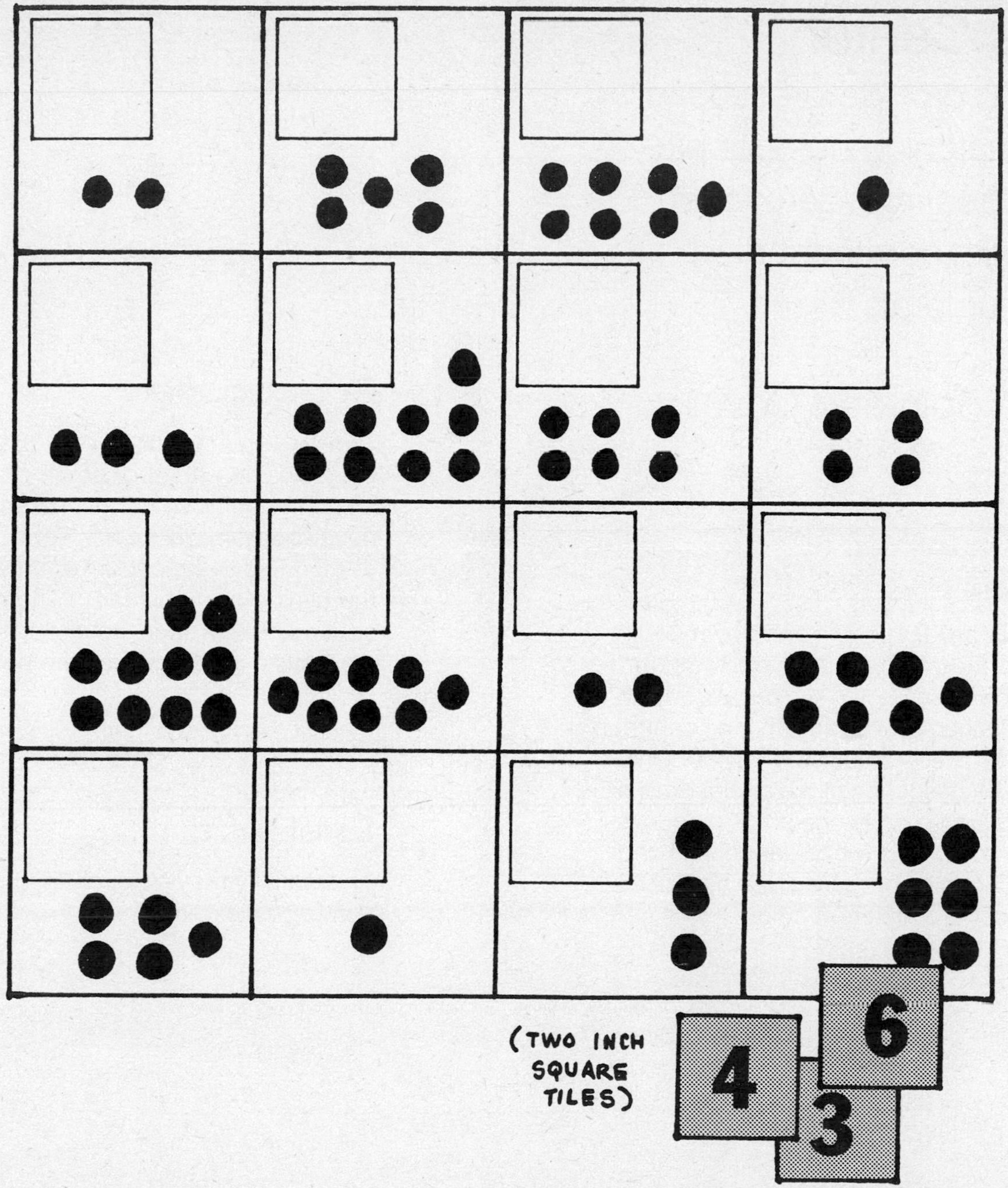
(TWO INCH
SQUARE
TILES)
4
3
6

Numerals Center

Purpose: To provide practice in matching number pictures from zero to ten with corresponding numerals.

Activity 2: Spin and Cover

Construction

Cut a piece of **chipboard** 19" x 19", and cover it with a piece of **tagboard.** Draw a pattern on the tagboard as shown (each square will be 1½" on a side). In each square, place a numeral as shown. The central circle is drawn with a 3" radius and divided into eleven sections. In each section of the circle, draw a pattern of dots corresponding to one of the numerals from 0 to 10. Cover the board with clear **contact** and attach a **spinner.** Obtain or prepare three sets of 25 cover **chips** (each set of a different color).

Procedure

Two or three children may play the game, each player having a set of cover chips. The first player spins the spinner; he then uses one of his chips to cover the numeral he has spun. (If all numerals corresponding to the pattern spun are already covered, the player loses that turn.) The game ends when all squares have been covered; the player who has placed the most chips on the board wins the game.

Evaluation

This activity may be evaluated by teacher observation or participation.

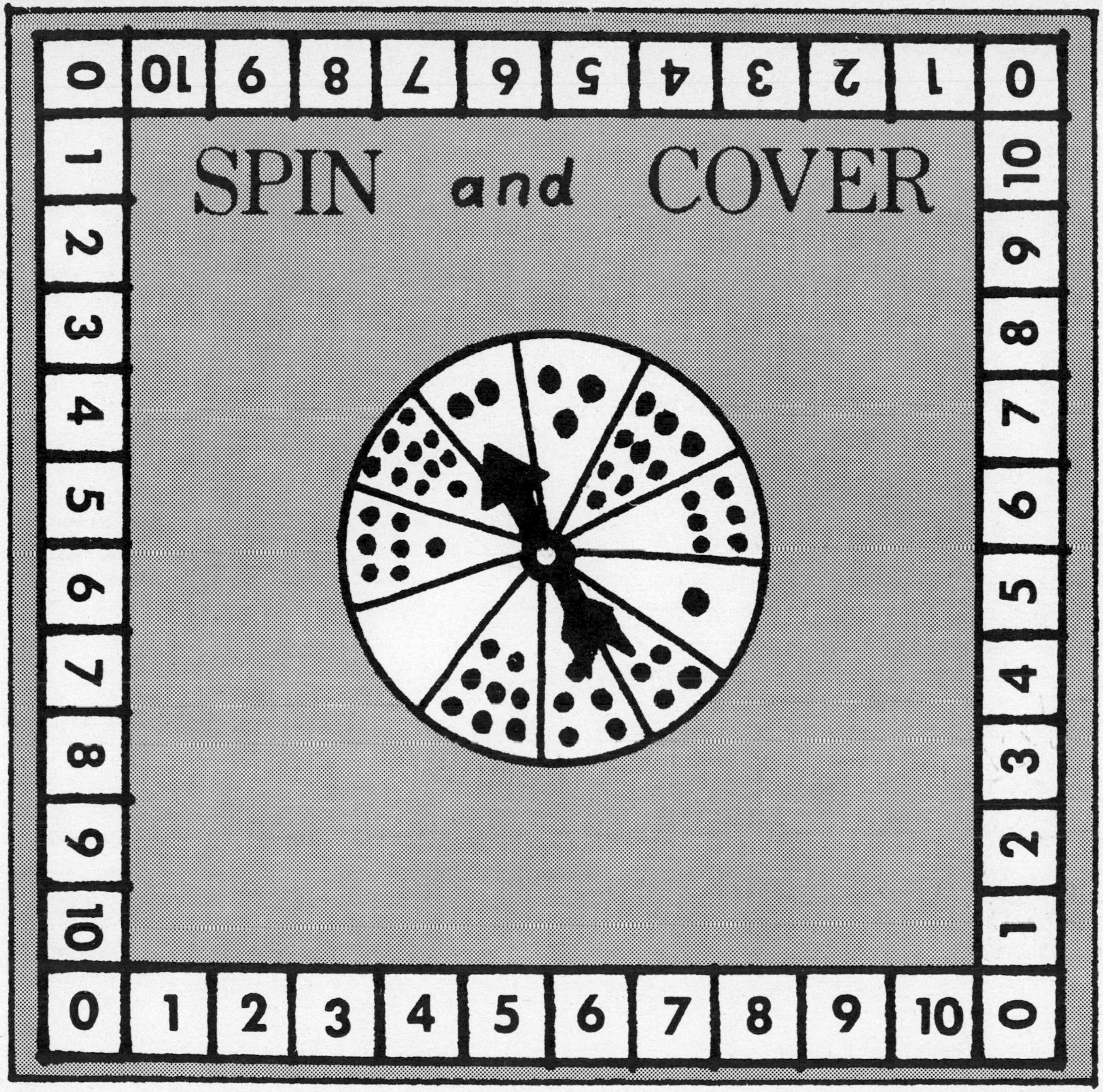
SPIN and COVER
0 1 2 3 4 5 6 7 8 9 10 0

Numerals Center

Purpose: To provide practice in matching number pictures from zero to ten with corresponding numerals.

Activity 3: Number Kites

Construction

Cut eleven "kites" out of **tagboard.** Draw one of the numerals from 0 to 10 on each kite. (Suggested designs are shown on pages 220–230.) Laminate or contact each kite for durability. Attach a "tail" of **yarn** to each kite. Obtain a box of **clothespins.**

Procedure

The child must clip the correct number of clothespins to the tail of each kite, matching the numeral shown on the kite.

Evaluation

This activity is evaluated by teacher observation.

1
4
3

3

PRIMARY CENTERS

Language Arts and Reading

Alphabet Center

Activity 1: Sound Pointers
Activity 2: Fish Wheels
Activity 3: Shake and Spell
Activity 4: Alphabet Doughnuts
Activity 5: Letter Order Boards
Activity 6: Alphabet Dot to Dot
Activity 7: Open Ended Games

Reading Center

Activity 1: Leo
Activity 2: Sound Boards
Activity 3: Concentration
Activity 4: Book Banners
Activity 5: Where Do I Belong?

Fairy Tale Center

Activity 1: Listening Station
Activity 2: Vocabulary Station
Activity 3: Syllable Chips
Activity 4: Creative Writing
Activity 5: Save the Princess
Activity 6: Research Station
Activity 7: Puppet Theater

Alphabet Center

Purpose: To provide reinforcement activities for vowel sounds, consonant sounds, and letter order.

Activity 1: Sound Pointers

Construction

Prepare twenty-one 7" squares of **cardboard** and 21 matching squares of colored **tagboard** or **construction paper.** Glue a paper square on the front of each cardboard square. On each square, write the capital and small letter forms of a consonant at the top. At the bottom of the square, paste three **pictures,** one of which has a name beginning with the letter shown at the top. Cover each square with clear **contact.** To each square, attach (with a **paper fastener**) a 4" arrow cut from **plastic, cardboard,** or other durable material.

Procedure

The child says the name of the letter on each card, says the name of the three pictures, and then moves the arrow to point to the picture whose name begins with the designated letter.

Evaluation

This activity may be evaluated through teacher observation. If press-apply dots are used to key the correct picture on the reverse side of the cards, the activity can be self-evaluating.

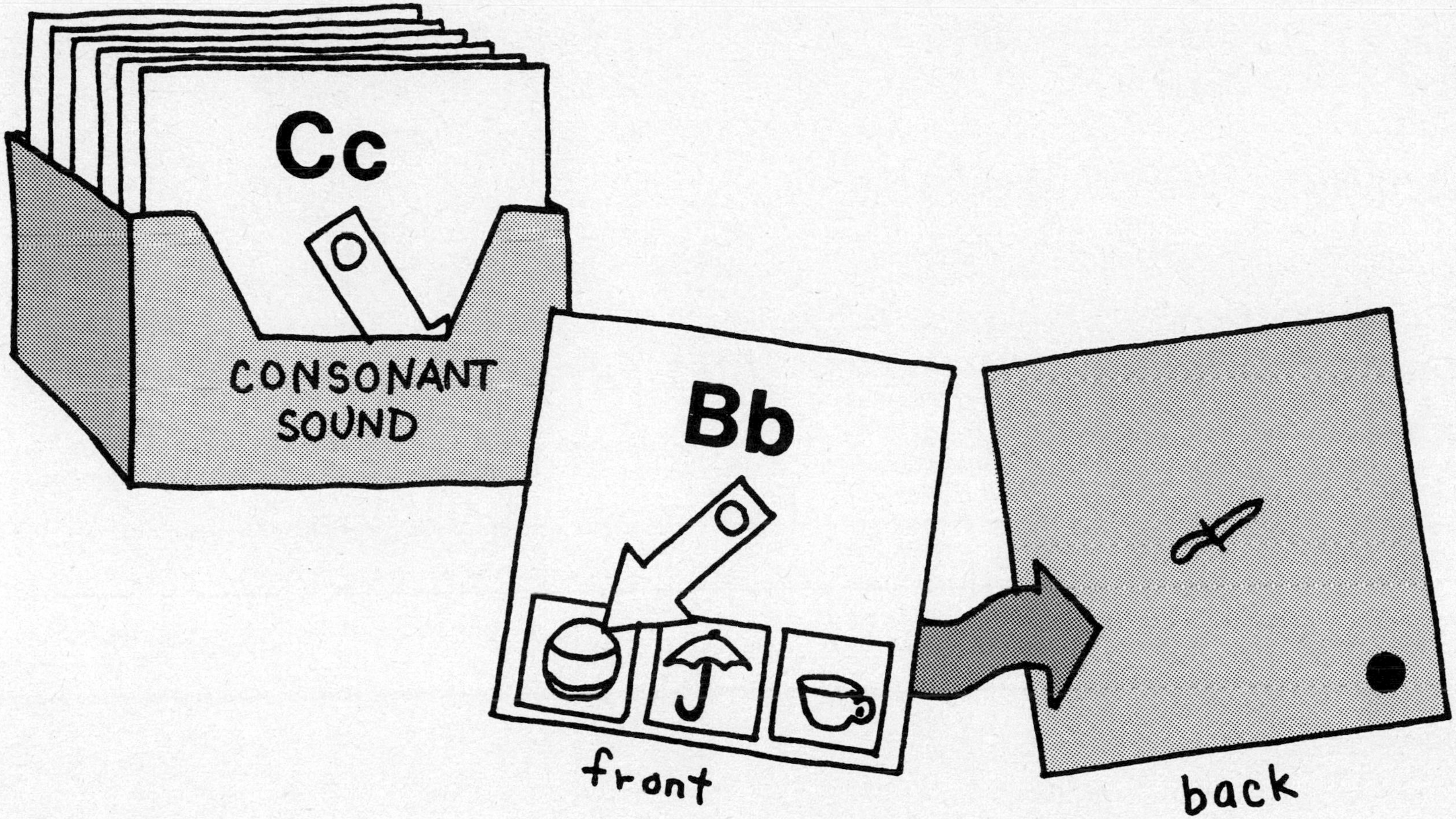
Cc
CONSONANT
SOUND
Bb
front
back

Alphabet Center

Purpose: To provide reinforcement activities for vowel sounds, consonant sounds, and letter order.

Activity 2: Fish Wheels

Construction

Trace the fish pattern on page 231 onto each of twelve 8" x 10" pieces of colored **tagboard.** Prepare 12 **tagboard** circles (6" diameter). On the front of each fish, place a group of letters that forms the body of several words. On each wheel, place a series of initial consonants (or consonant groups) that will complete the words. Attach each wheel to the back of the corresponding fish with a **paper fastener.** Ditto a series of **worksheets** from the example provided on page 232.

Procedure

The child chooses a fish. As he turns the wheel, he writes on his worksheet each of the words that is formed. He then writes on the worksheet a sentence using each of the words.

Evaluation

The teacher corrects the worksheets.

My Words
Name
1.
2.
3.
4.
5.
6.
7.
8.
tall

Alphabet Center

Purpose: To provide reinforcement activities for vowel sounds, consonant sounds, and letter order.

Activity 3: Shake and Spell

Construction

Obtain or make three **wooden cubes,** 1" on a side. Use **press-apply dots** to put letters on the faces of the cubes. Use a **paper cup** or **plastic lid** as a shaker for the cubes. Ditto a set of **score sheets** from the sample provided on page 233.

Procedure

The game is intended for three players. The first player shakes the cubes in the cup and drops them on the table. If he can make a word with the three letters rolled (and is able to say the word), he writes the word on the score sheet and scores one point. If he can use the word in a sentence, he scores another point. The second player then rolls the cubes. The game can be varied by changing the letters on the cubes. (You will probably want to use one cube with vowels, the other two cubes with consonants—this will maximize the chances of success in making a word on each turn.)

Evaluation

Children can evaluate their own play with the score sheet; further evaluation can be made by teacher observation.

PLAYER 1
PLAYER 2
PLAYER 3
1. dog 1
2. pat 2
1. 0
2. log 2
1. hat 2
2. not 1
TOTAL
TOTAL
SHAKE AND SPELL

Alphabet Center

Purpose: To provide reinforcement activities for vowel sounds, consonant sounds, and letter order.

Activity 4: Alphabet Doughnuts

Construction

Cut several 9"-diameter circles from **tagboard** or **cardboard.** Cut a 3"-diameter hole in the center of each circle; save the center circles that you have cut out. Cut small **pictures** from old workbooks, spelling books, magazines, and so on. Paste pictures on the doughnuts so that all the pictures shown on a single ring have names that begin or end with the same letter; add one more matching picture to the separate center circle.

Procedure

The child says the name of each of the five pictures on a doughnut. He listens carefully to the beginning (or ending) sounds. He must then choose a center for the doughnut with a picture whose name has the same beginning (or ending) sound.

Evaluation

This activity can be evaluated by teacher observation. If the reverse side of the circle or the doughnut is coded, the activity can be made self-evaluating.

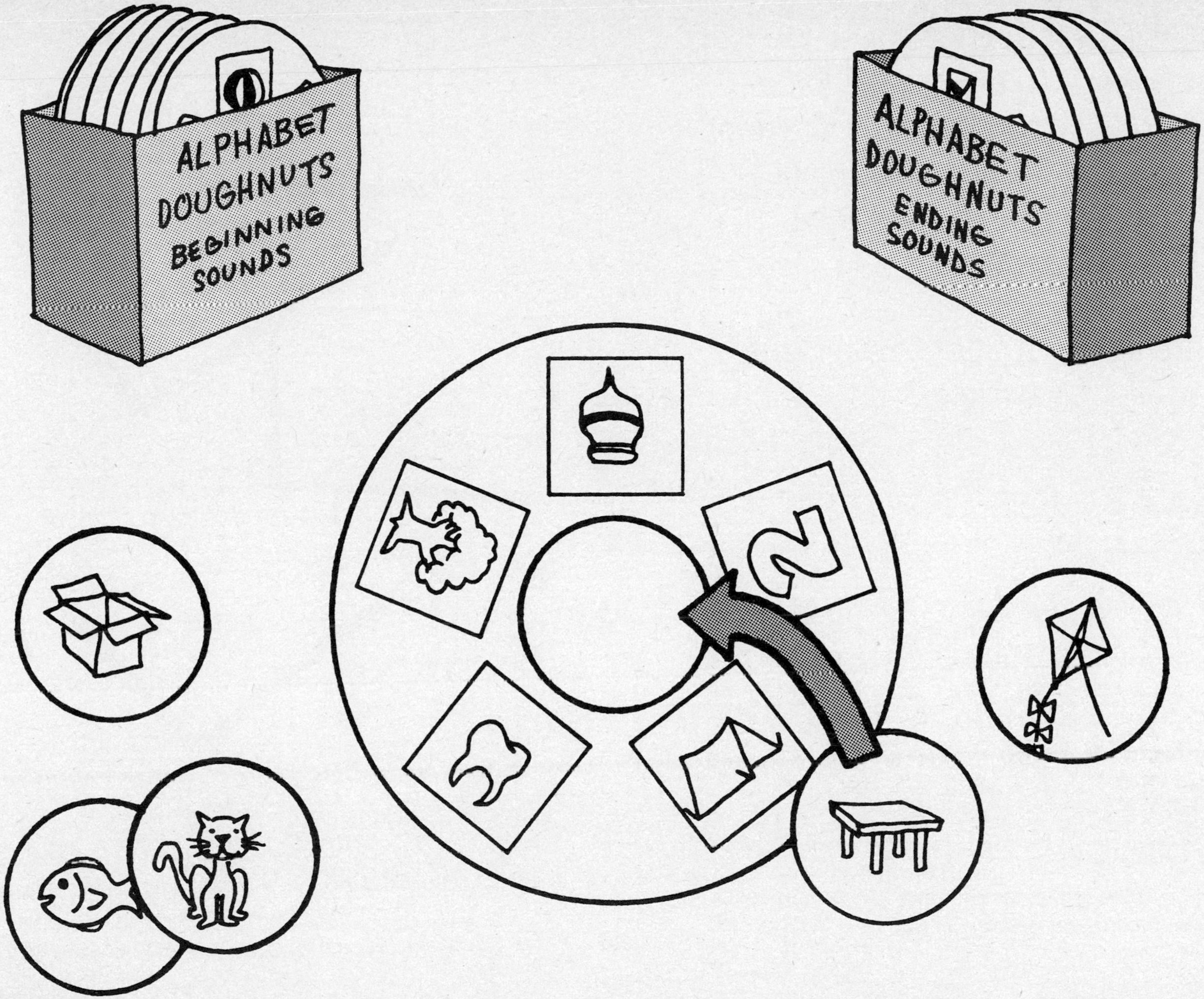
ALPHABET
DOUGHNUTS
BEGINNING
SOUNDS
ALPHABET
DOUGHNUTS
ENDING
SOUNDS

Alphabet Center

Purpose: To provide reinforcement activities for vowel sounds, consonant sounds, and letter order.

Activity 5: Letter Order Boards

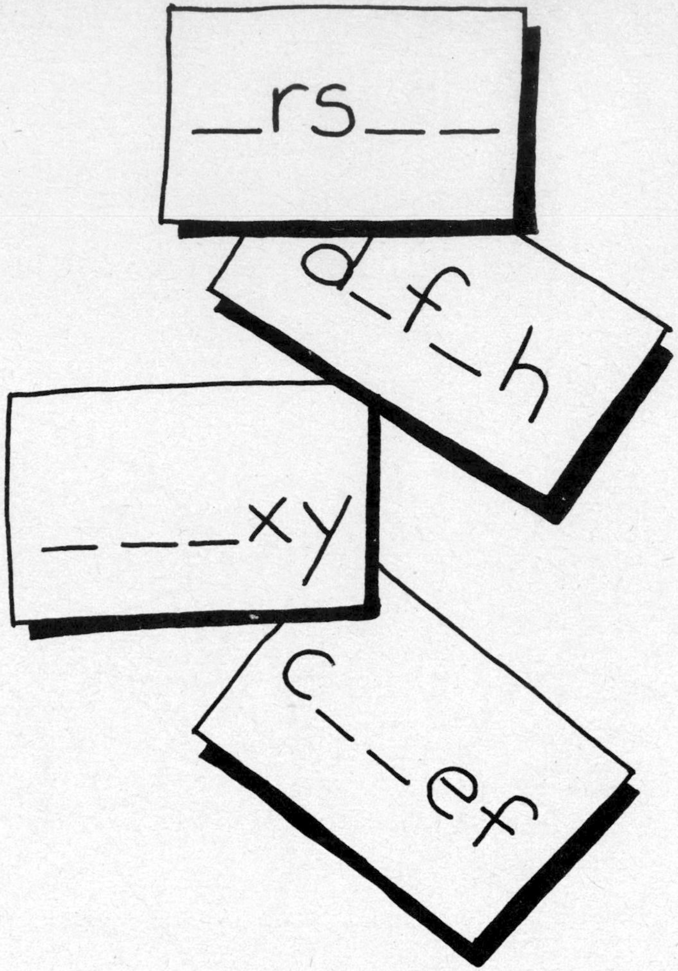

Construction

Obtain twenty-four 5" x 8" **index cards** or pieces of **tagboard.** On each card, write a short sequence of the alphabet with some letters replaced by blanks. Cover each card with clear **contact, laminate** each, or place each in a **plastic sleeve.** Use **press-apply dots** to number the cards. Obtain **wax marking pencils** and use squares of acrylan **carpeting** for erasing.

Procedure

The child fills in the missing letters in the sequence on each card, using the wax pencil to mark on the coated surface.

Evaluation

This activity can be evaluated by teacher observation, or can be self-evaluated with an answer key.

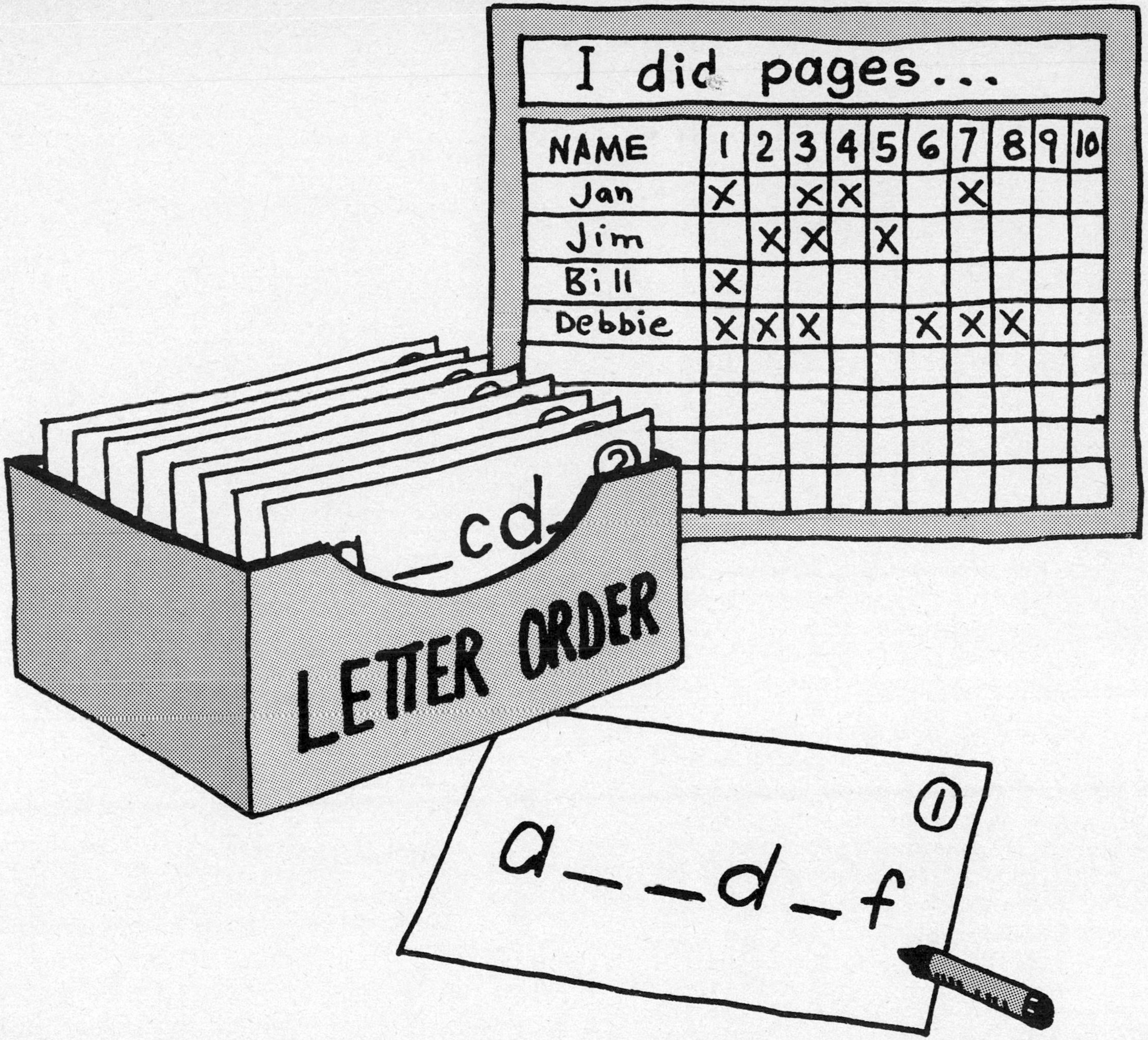
I did pages...
NAME
1
2
3
4
5
6
7
8
9
10
Jan
Jim
Bill
Debbie
_cd_
LETTER ORDER
a__d_f
1

Alphabet Center

Purpose: To provide reinforcement activities for vowel sounds, consonant sounds, and letter order.

Activity 6: Alphabet Dot to Dot

Construction

Prepare dot-to-dot **pictures** using alphabet sequences rather than numbers as keys to line sequence. (Suggested pictures are shown on pages 234–235.) Commercially printed pictures can be obtained inexpensively in book or tablet form at a supermarket or variety store. (If necessary, use typewriter correcting tape or fluid to blank out numerals and replace them with inked letters.) Cover the unused sheets with **plastic sleeves** or clear **contact** paper; add **tagboard** or **cardboard** backing if needed for durability. Use **press-apply dots** to put identifying numbers on the various puzzles. Obtain **wax marking pencils** and scraps of acrylan **carpet** for erasing. Prepare a **record sheet** for the activity.

Procedure

Using the wax pencil, the child joins the dots in alphabetical sequence to complete the picture on each sheet.

Evaluation

Evaluation can be done by teacher observation. Self-evaluation can be done with a master key.

NAME
1 2 3 4 5 6 7 8 9 10 11 12
John
Amy
Sam
l. m. n.
DOT TO DOTS
B. C E F. D G. A

Alphabet Center

Purpose: To provide reinforcement activities for vowel sounds, consonant sounds, and letter order.

Activity 7: Open Ended Games

Construction

Prepare two game boards as shown on **cardboard** or **tagboard,** covered for durability. Prepare several decks of **cards** (2½" x 4"), with each deck containing two dozen or more cards. Write a word on each card; each deck can be used to reinforce some particular sound element such as blends, digraphs, long vowel with silent "e," or paired vowels. Obtain a pair of **dice** and at least eight **markers.**

Procedure

Three or four children can play at each game board. The deck is placed face down on the table. The first player takes a card. If he can say the word, he rolls the die and moves according to the number of dots shown. If he cannot read the word, he does not move his marker. The card is returned to the bottom of the deck. The next player then takes a turn. The first player to move completely around the board to the finish line is the winner.

Evaluation

Both self-evaluation and teacher observation can be used with this activity.

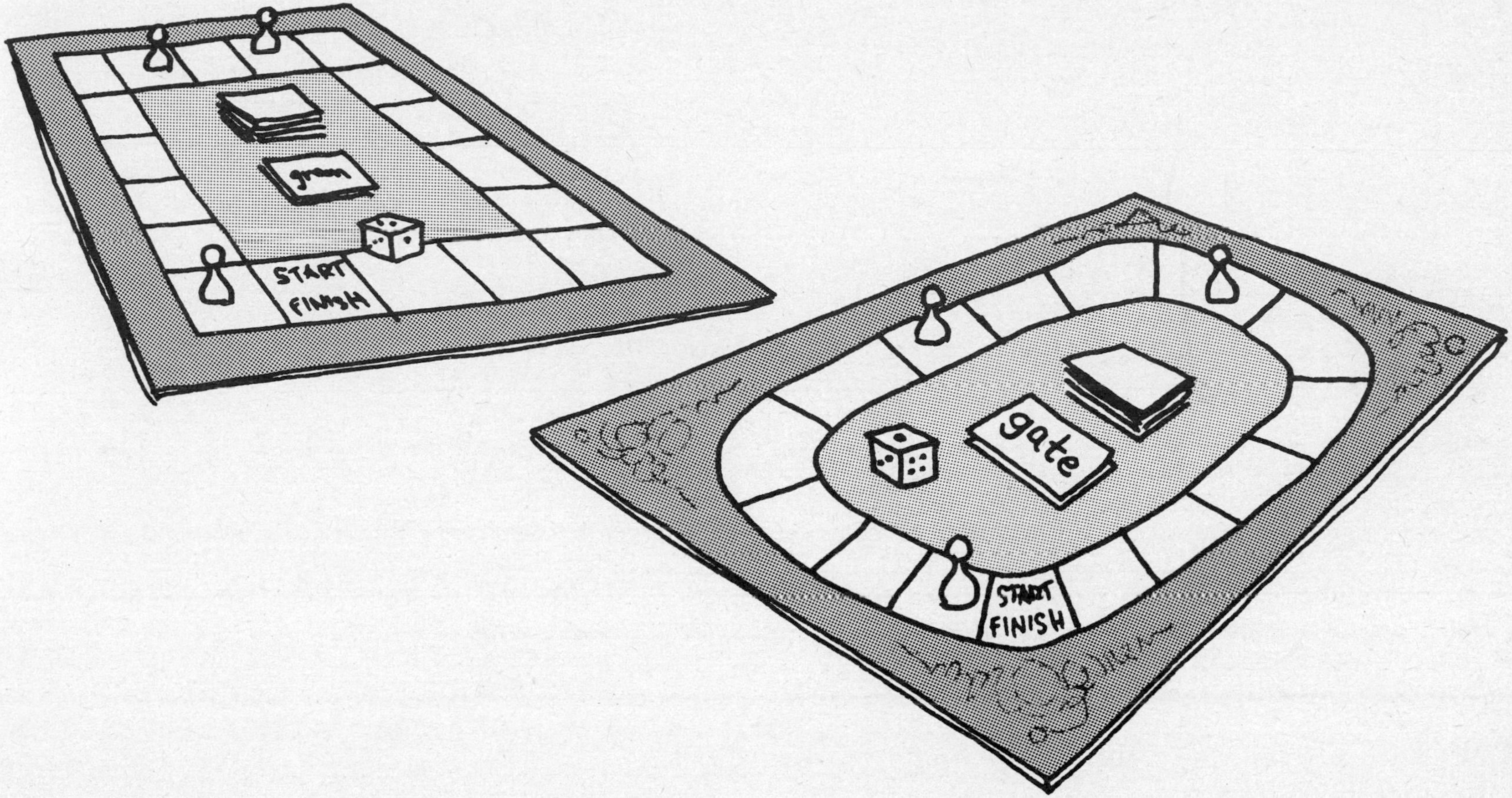
gram
START
FINISH
gate
START
FINISH

Reading Center

Purpose: To provide reinforcement activities for vocabulary, word-attack skills, and comprehension.

Activity 1: Leo

Construction

Build Leo (the "function machine") from a **cardboard box** or **ice-cream carton,** using **tagboard** to make the chute that will turn a card over and send it back out the mouth. Use **yarn** to make a mane for Leo. Prepare a set of 3" x 5" **cards** with a sentence on the front in which one word is replaced by a blank; the missing word is written on the back of the card. Prepare a vocabulary **chart** listing all of the missing words used in the deck of cards.

Procedure

A group of children can work together. Each child selects a card, reads the front aloud to the group, and selects a word from the vocabulary chart that will complete the sentence. He then drops the card in the top of the "function machine" and checks his answer against the word on the card that comes out Leo's mouth.

Evaluation

This activity is self-checking, for the correct word is on the back of each card. Choose words and sentences carefully to avoid ambiguities. In the example shown here, "detective" could be used as a title to complete the sentence shown, but the need for a capital letter to start the sentence makes that an incorrect choice.

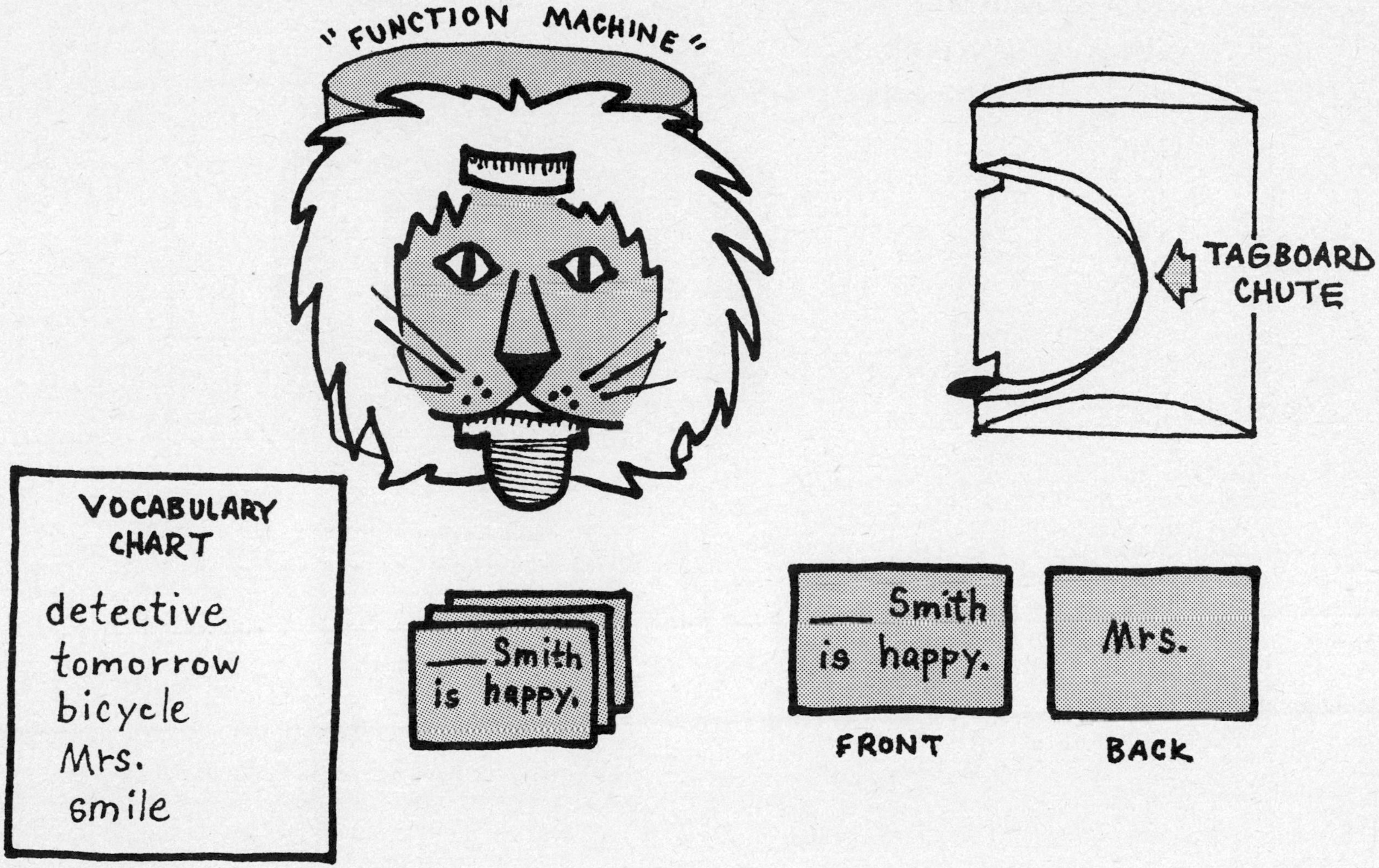
"FUNCTION MACHINE"
TAGBOARD CHUTE
VOCABULARY CHART
detective
tomorrow
bicycle
Mrs.
smile
___ Smith is happy.
___ Smith is happy.
Mrs.
FRONT
BACK

Reading Center

Purpose: To provide reinforcement activities for vocabulary, word-attack skills, and comprehension.

Activity 2: Sound Boards

Construction

Prepare the game boards (model shown on page 236) on six 11" x 14" **tagboard** sheets. For each game board, prepare nine small sound **cards.** On the front of each sound card is a phonetic symbol representing a sound; on the back are the numbers of the words on the game board that contain that sound. Put the sound cards in an **envelope** coded to match the game board. Prepare a **record card** for each student in the class.

Procedure

The child takes a game board and the corresponding envelope of sound cards. He places a sound card over each word on the game board, matching the sounds to the words.

Evaluation

The child can check his own work by turning each sound card over; the small number in the upper corner of the word square should match one of the numbers on the back of the sound card. When the child correctly completes a game board, he punches out the corresponding number on his record card. Teacher observation can be used to supplement the self-evaluation.

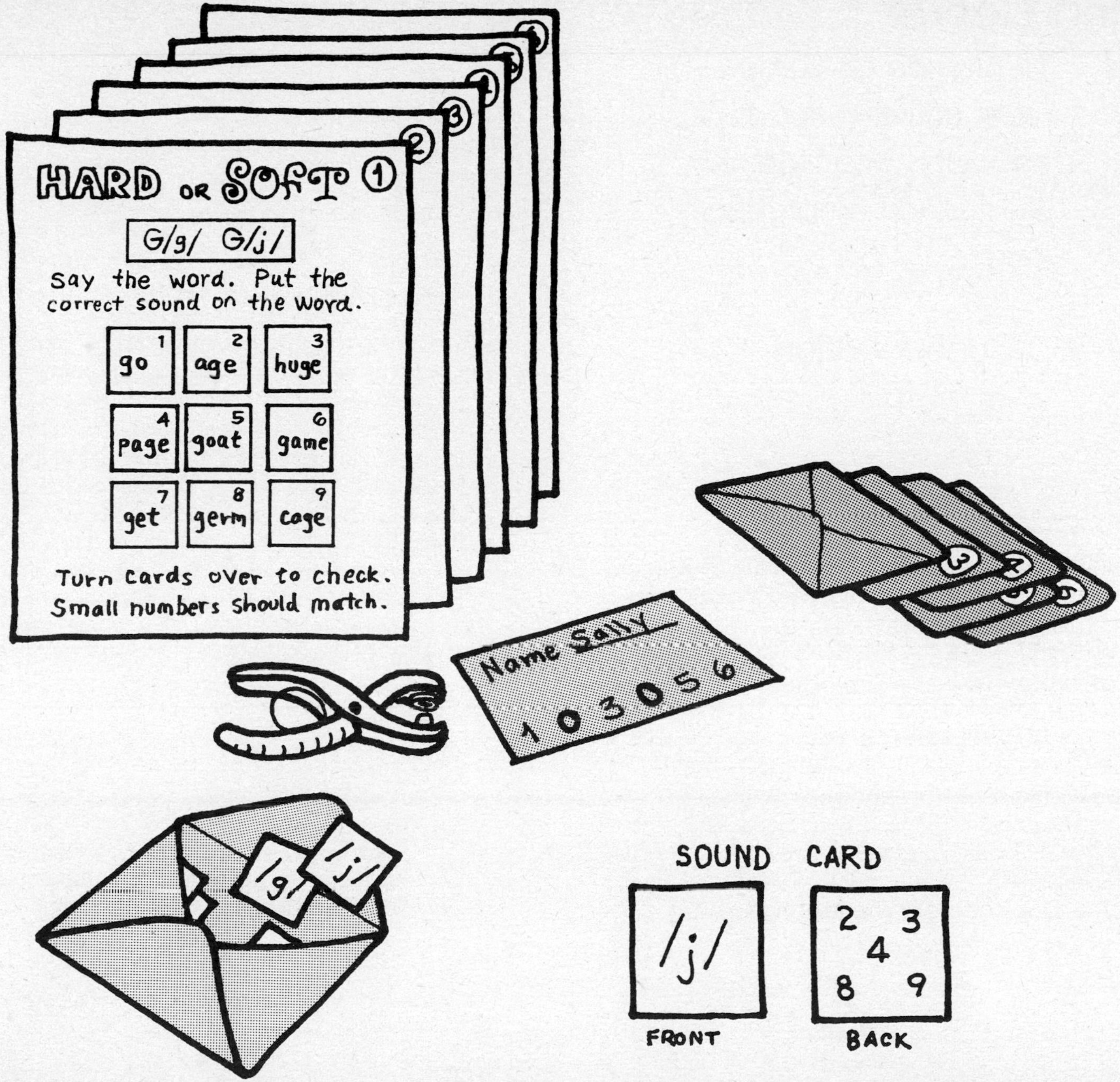
HARD or SOFT 1
G/g/ G/j/
Say the word. Put the correct sound on the word.
1 go
2 age
3 huge
4 page
5 goat
6 game
7 get
8 germ
9 cage
Turn cards over to check. Small numbers should match.
Name Sally
1 0 3 0 5 6
/g/
/j/
SOUND CARD
/j/
FRONT
2 3 4 8 9
BACK

Reading Center

Purpose: To provide reinforcement activities for vocabulary, word-attack skills, and comprehension.

Activity 3: Concentration

Construction

Build the game board from two sheets of **cardboard** 26" x 19", and matching sheets of **tagboard** for facing. Attach 15 **library book pockets** to each sheet. Label pockets on one side with letters from A through O, and those on the other side with numerals 1 through 15. Cover with clear contact. Hinge the two sheets together with **Mystik tape** (1½" wide). Prepare 30 **index cards** (3" x 5") to form 15 word pairs. The board may be programmed for matching compound word parts (as shown), antonyms, or synonyms. Split the pairs so that one card of each pair will be in a pocket on the left side of the board, the other card of the pair in some pocket on the right side of the board.

Procedure

The children playing are divided into two teams. A child on one team chooses a letter (from A through O) and a numeral (from 1 through 15). The teacher or the child removes the chosen cards and shows them to the class. If the cards form a pair, a point is awarded to the team of the child who chose the cards, and the pair of cards is removed from the board. If the cards do not form a pair, they are returned to their pockets. A child from the other team then has a chance to choose two cards. The game continues until all cards have been removed; the team with the greatest number of points wins.

Evaluation

Self-evaluation is possible if the matching word is penciled in small print in a corner of each card.

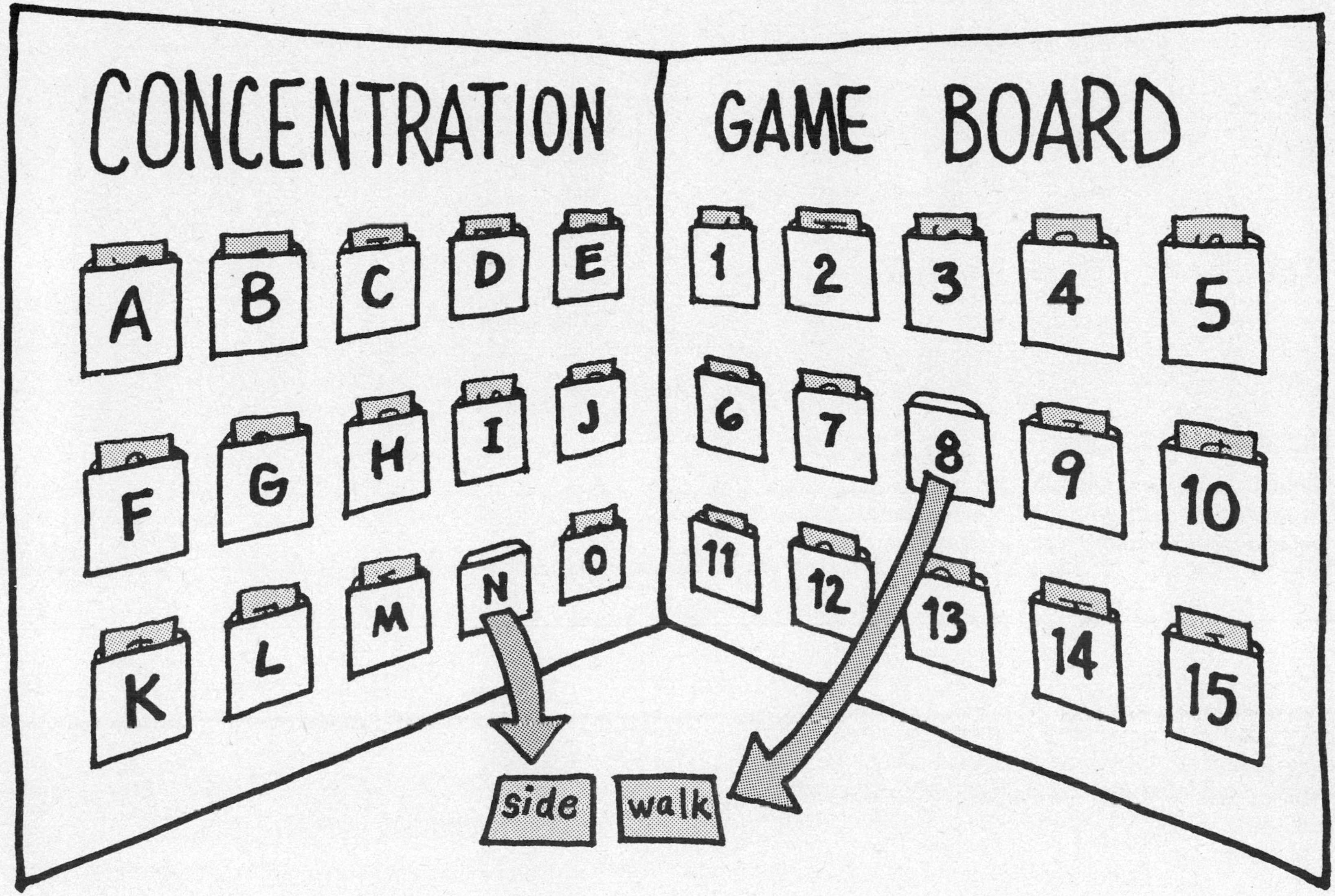
CONCENTRATION GAME BOARD
A
B
C
D
E
F
G
H
I
J
K
L
M
N
O
1
2
3
4
5
6
7
8
9
10
11
12
13
14
15
side
walk

Reading Center

Purpose: To provide reinforcement activities for vocabulary, word-attack skills, and comprehension.

Activity 4: Book Banners

Construction

Obtain a supply of the following art materials: **coat hangers, cloth, felt, yarn, needles and thread, felt-tip pens, dowels, scissors.** Prepare a few sample banners for display.

Procedure

The child uses any of the art materials available at this station to make a banner about a book he has read. The banner should include the title of the book, the name of its author, an illustration or object representing the book, and the child's name. The banners may be hung on wire or string stretched across the classroom.

Evaluation

Completion of a banner represents successful completion of the activity.

Sally
UMBRELLA
BY TARO YASHIMA
DRUMMER HOFF
BY EMBERLEY
David
JUST ME
BY ETS
Terri
Make a banner for your book.

Reading Center

Purpose: To provide reinforcement activities for vocabulary, word-attack skills, and comprehension.

Activity 5: Where Do I Belong?

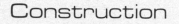

Construction

Make six pocket charts as shown; each is constructed from a 20" x 30" piece of **tagboard.** (Before folding, the long axis of the sheet is vertical.) For each chart, prepare sixteen 3" x 5" **cards.** Four of the cards bear the names of general categories; the other cards bear **pictures** cut from magazines (three pictures to fit into each category). Put all of the cards for each chart into an **envelope.**

Procedure

The child takes an envelope and a pocket chart. He puts the category cards across the top of the chart, and then sorts the other cards so that each picture is placed under the appropriate category.

Evaluation

This activity can be evaluated by teacher observation, or by self-evaluation (if the backs of the cards are coded with category names or colored dots).

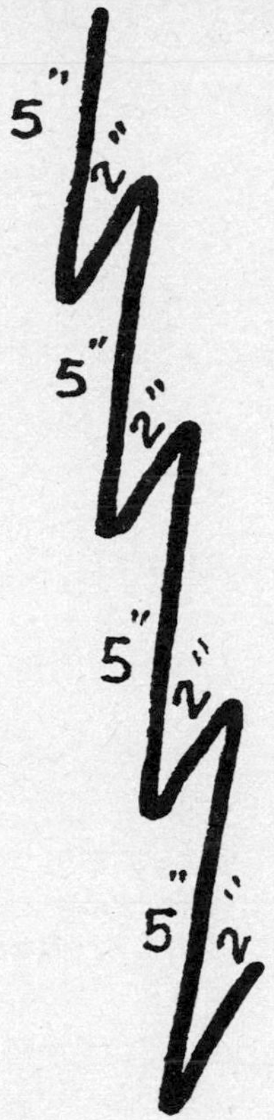

SIDE VIEW OF FOLDING FOR POCKET CHART

Fairy Tale Center

Purpose: To reinforce language skills through opportunities to read, listen to, and dramatize fairy tales.

Activity 1: Listening Station

Construction

Obtain a **cassette tape recorder** with one or more pairs of **earphones.** Record a fairy tale on each cassette. For each fairy tale, prepare a question wheel from two 12"-diameter circles of **tagboard** and a brass **paper fastener.** Ditto **answer sheets** (the answer sheet shown here can be printed on one quarter of an 8½" x 11" sheet). Provide **pencils** and a **folder** for completed answer sheets. Place the following instructions on a **poster** or task card at the station.

1. Listen to tape.
2. Choose the question wheel that goes with the tape.
3. Answer the questions on an answer sheet.
4. Put your paper in the folder.

Procedure

The child follows the instructions step by step.

TASK CARD

* Listen to tape.

* Choose the wheel that goes with the tape.

* Answer the questions on an answer sheet.

* Put your paper in the folder.

Evaluation

The teacher evaluates the activity by checking the student's answer sheet.

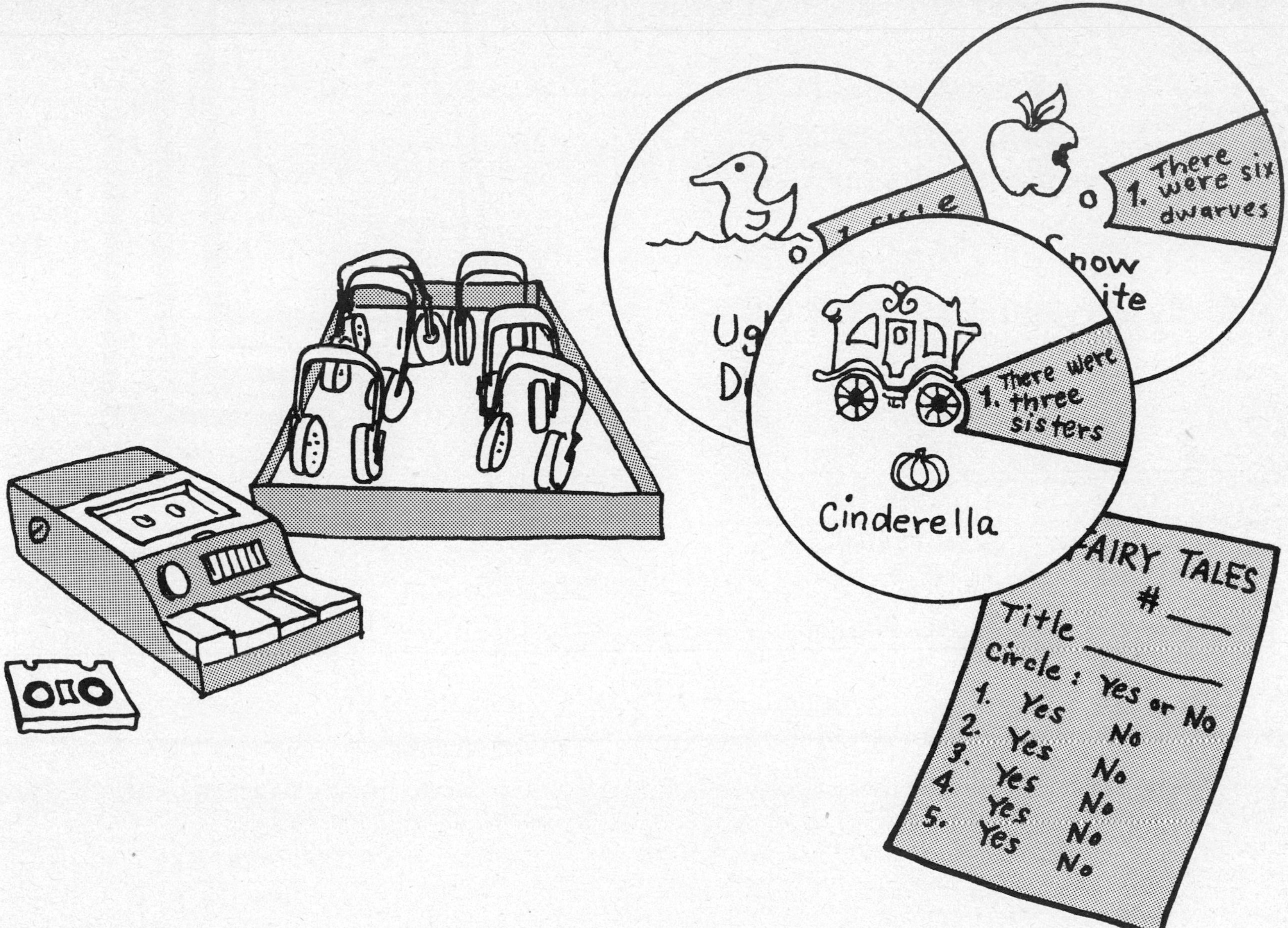
1. There were six dwarves
Snow
ite
Ug
D
1. There were three sisters
Cinderella
FAIRY TALES
#
Title
Circle : Yes or No
1. Yes No
2. Yes No
3. Yes No
4. Yes No
5. Yes No

Fairy Tale Center

Purpose: To reinforce language skills through opportunities to read, listen to, and dramatize fairy tales.

Activity 2: Vocabulary Station

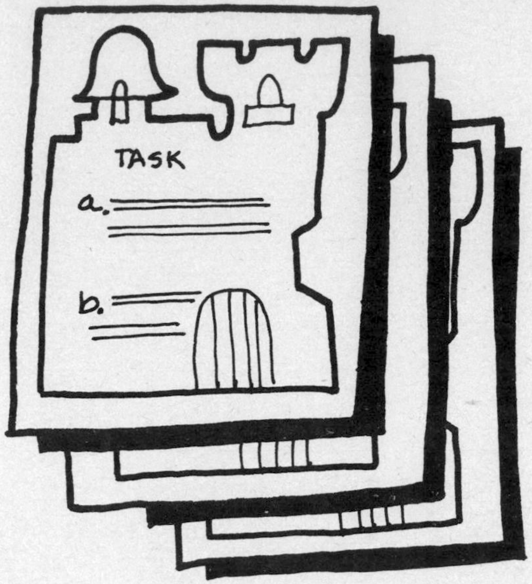

Construction

Build the carrel from a 19" x 26" piece of **cardboard** and two 13" x 19" pieces. Cover the cardboard with colored **tagboard** and use felt-tip pens to letter and decorate the carrel. Make the pocket for task sheets from a folded 12" x 12" piece of **tagboard.** Cover the finished carrel with clear **contact** for durability. Hinge the carrel together with 1½" Mystik tape.

Duplicate a set of castle-shaped **task cards** from the sample provided on page 239. Letter each task sheet with appropriate instructions (samples are given on pages 237–238). Provide **pencils, writing paper,** and a **folder** for completed work.

Procedure

The child selects a task card and follows the instructions on it.

Evaluation

The teacher evaluates the activity by correcting the paper written by the student.

THE WORLD OF FAIRY TALES
TASK 1
TASKS
VOCABULARY
1. giant
2. elf
3. princess
4. crown
5. king
6. queen
7. fairy
8. witch
9. dragon
10. castle
11. kingdom
12. throne
13. magic
14. enchanted
15. treasure
16. prince
17. fortune
18. creatures
19. golden
20. tower
21. beast
22. village
23. tales
24. knight

Fairy Tale Center

Purpose: To reinforce language skills through opportunities to read, listen to, and dramatize fairy tales.

Activity 3: Syllable Chips

Construction

Prepare five 10" x 10" **tagboard** cards, dividing each card into 2" squares. In each square, write a word taken from one of the fairy tales. (Use one-syllable and two-syllable words only.) Obtain 100 **poker chips;** use **press-apply dots** to label the chips with a numeral "1" on one side and a numeral "2" on the reverse side. Put the chips in a **box.** Prepare an **answer key** for each card, color coded to match the appropriate card.

Procedure

The child takes a word card. He says each word quietly. He counts the number of syllables he hears in the word. He places a numbered chip on the word to show how many syllables it has.

Evaluation

The answer key is used for self-evaluation.

FAIRY TALES

village	princess	throne	golden	fairy
tale	handsome	elf	castle	tower
enchant	prince	creature	king	fortune
kingdom	witch	magic	peddler	knight
beast	dragon	queen	treasure	robber

ANSWER KEY

2	2	1	2	2
1	2	1	2	2
2	1	2	1	2
2	1	2	2	1
1	2	1	2	2

Fairy Tale Center

Purpose: To reinforce language skills through opportunities to read, listen to, and dramatize fairy tales.

Activity 4: Creative Writing

Construction

Build the carrel from two 13" x 19" pieces of **cardboard.** Cover the cardboard sheets with colored **tagboard,** build the pockets from folded sheets of **tagboard,** letter and decorate the carrel, and cover with clear **contact.** Hinge the carrel together with **Mystik tape.** Prepare six 5" x 8" **cards,** each bearing the first paragraph of a fairy tale. Provide **pencils** and **writing paper.**

Procedure

The child chooses a "story starter" card. He copies the paragraph from the card, and then finishes writing the story. He places the finished story in the pocket provided.

Evaluation

The teacher reads the story and provides written or spoken feedback to the student.

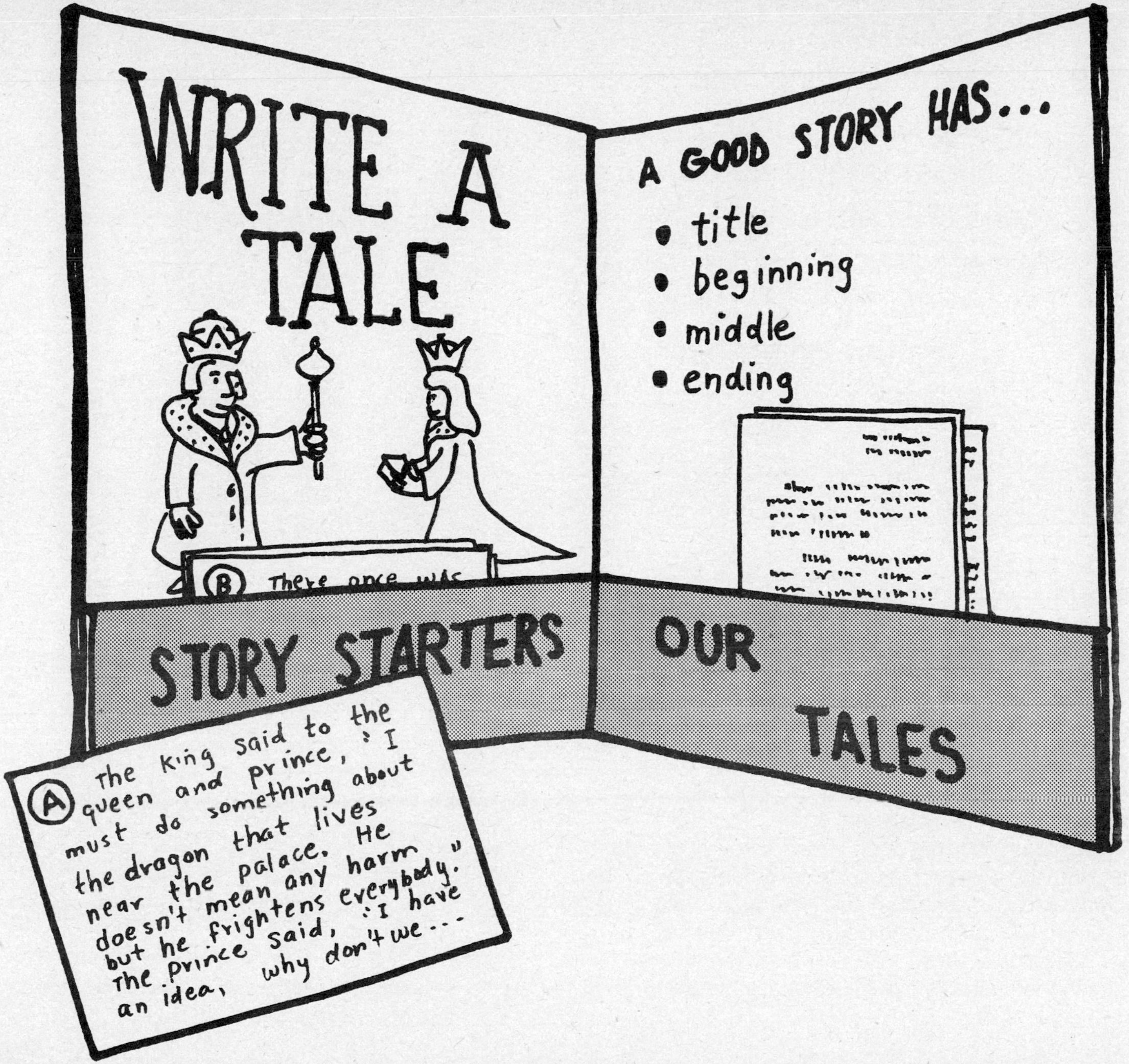
WRITE A TALE
A GOOD STORY HAS...
• title
• beginning
• middle
• ending
B There once was
STORY STARTERS
OUR TALES
A The king said to the queen and prince, "I must do something about the dragon that lives near the palace. He doesn't mean any harm but he frightens everybody."
The prince said, "I have an idea, why don't we...

Fairy Tale Center

Purpose: To reinforce language skills through opportunities to read, listen to, and dramatize fairy tales.

Activity 5: Save the Princess

Construction

Draw the game board on a 13" x 19" piece of colored **tagboard.** Attach a **cardboard** backing to the board and cover the playing surface with clear **contact.** Provide a **die,** four **markers,** and a deck of **vocabulary words.**

Procedure

Up to four children may play the game. The first player draws a card from the deck. If he can read the word, he rolls the die and moves the number of spaces indicated. If he cannot read the word, he does not move. The card is returned to the bottom of the deck and the next player takes his turn. The first child to reach the castle ("save the princess") is the winner.

Evaluation

This activity may be evaluated through teacher observation or participation.

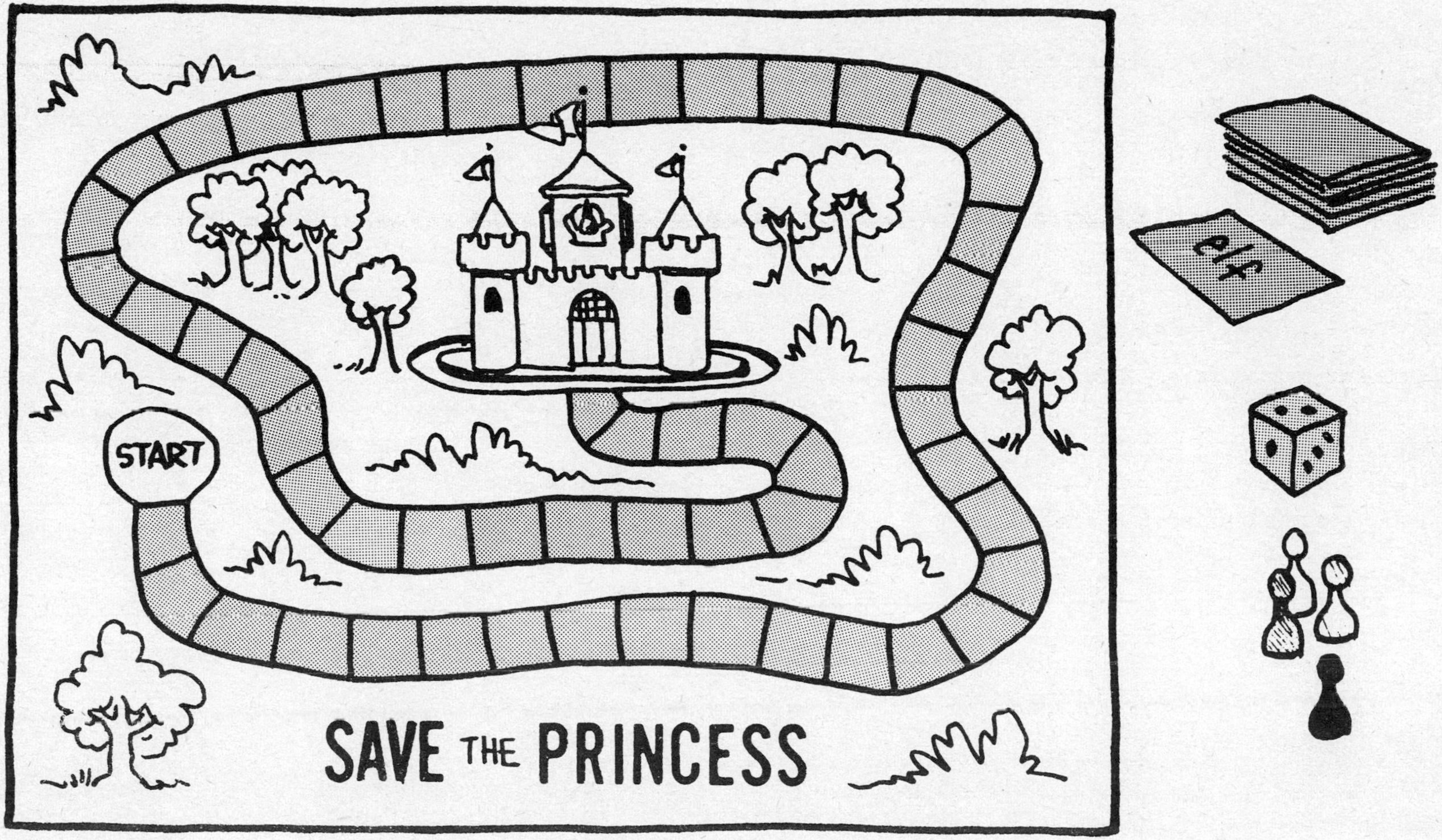
START
SAVE THE PRINCESS
e/f

Fairy Tale Center

Purpose: To reinforce language skills through opportunities to read, listen to, and dramatize fairy tales.

Activity 6: Research Station

PROJECTS
1. Compare two fairy tales
List: Characters Vocabulary Events
How are they alike
How are they different
2. Make a world map of fairy tales.

Construction

Prepare a **poster** or other decoration for the station. Prepare a series of project **instruction sheets**. Provide the following materials: **writing paper, large-sized drawing paper, pencils, crayons, colored pencils, printed outline world maps.** Samples of project instructions are given on the opposite page.

Procedure

The child selects a project instruction sheet and follows the directions on it. Research may be done both in class and at home.

Evaluation

The child presents the results of his research orally to the class or to the teacher alone. The teacher evaluates the work and provides feedback.

Sample Project Instructions

Project 1

Read two fairy tales. For each fairy tale, make a list of the characters in the story. In what ways are the two lists alike? In what ways are they different?

Project 2

Read a fairy tale. Make a vocabulary list of the unusual words that you find in the story. For each word in the list, write a new sentence of your own using that word.

Project 3

Read a fairy tale. Make a list of the main events in the story. Draw a picture of each event.

Project 4

Read two fairy tales. Write a short fairy tale of your own, using at least one character from each of the two stories you read.

Project 5

Make a world map of fairy tales. On the map, write the name of each fairy tale in the place where that tale comes from.

Project 6

Read a fairy tale. Draw a map of the places described in the story. Add any pictures or words that will help make your map interesting.

Fairy Tale Center

Purpose: To reinforce language skills through opportunities to read, listen to, and dramatize fairy tales.

Activity 7: Puppet Theater

Construction

The puppet theater can be constructed from a large **refrigerator carton.** Be as creative as you like in adding decorations, curtains, scenic backdrops, and so on. Provide **sign-up sheets** and **art supplies** for making hand puppets.

Procedure

Each child signs up to join a particular group. The group then chooses a fairy tale, makes the puppets needed to dramatize the story, and prepares the puppet show. Scripts can be written in advance or developed through improvisation.

Evaluation

Each group can present its show for the rest of the class. Evaluation can be made through teacher observation and through class discussion.

SIGN UP FOR A PUPPET SHOW GROUP
1
2
3
4
5
SCRAPS

4

PRIMARY CENTERS

Mathematics

Basic Facts Drill and Practice Center

Activity 1: Bean Addition Station
Activity 2: Roll Your Own Problems
Activity 3: Pick a Page
Activity 4: Hear the Facts
Activity 5: Play a Game

Place Value Center

Activity 1: Bean Sticks and Boards
Activity 2: Graph Paper Numbers
Activity 3: Expanded Notation
Activity 4: Listening
Activity 5: Fido's Football Game

Time Center

Activity 1: Time Match
Activity 2: Clock Cards
Activity 3: Pinwheels
Activity 4: Give Me a Hand
Activity 5: Race of Time
Activity 6: The Clockshop
Activity 7: Time Sheets

Basic Facts Drill and Practice Center

Purpose: To provide various activities reinforcing basic addition and subtraction facts (0 through 18).

Activity 1: Bean Addition Station

Construction

Cut a large number of 4" x 12" strips of **construction paper.** On the front of each strip, print an addition problem and mark spaces for pasting beans. On the back of the strip, mark a space for the answer. Put the problem strips in a **box.** Provide **dry beans** and **paste** or **glue.** Prepare a 10" x 12" **clasp envelope** for each student, and put these envelopes in another **box.**

Procedure

The child selects a strip and reads the addition problem on it. He pastes the appropriate numbers of beans in the spaces provided, to show the two sets that are being joined. He then counts the beans and writes the answer to the problem on the back of the strip. Completed strips are placed in the child's envelope for use as flash cards in review work with a partner.

Evaluation

Evaluation can be made through teacher observation and through use of the flash cards with the child.

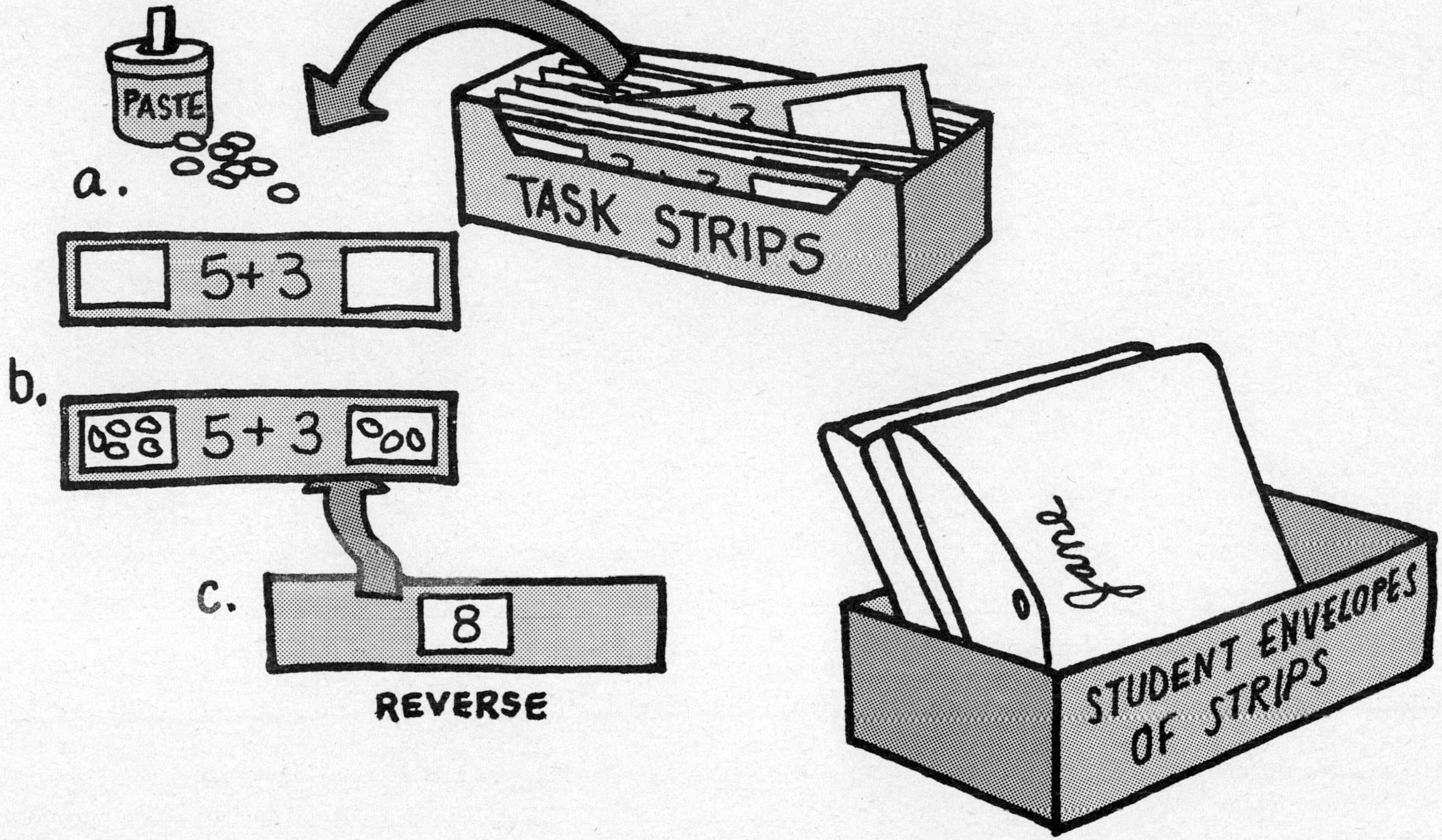
PASTE
a.
5+3
TASK STRIPS
b.
5+3
c.
8
REVERSE
Jane
STUDENT ENVELOPES
OF STRIPS

Basic Facts Drill and Practice Center

Purpose: To provide various activities reinforcing basic addition and subtraction facts (0 through 18).

Activity 2: Roll Your Own Problems

Construction

Duplicate a number of blank **problem sheets** (sample given on page 240); cut the sheets in half to produce separate addition and subtraction forms. Paste sample forms on the outside of 10" x 12" **clasp envelopes** and write instructions on the envelopes. Put the blank forms in the envelopes. Use small **wooden cubes** and **press-apply dots** to prepare two dice with written numerals on the faces for each packet. Obtain four regular **dice** (two for each packet). Make two small **boxes;** put one pair of each kind of dice in each box. Provide a **box** for completed worksheets.

Evaluation

Evaluation can be made by teacher correction of the worksheets.

Patterns for wooden dice:

Use dice A and B with addition set; use dice A and C with subtraction set.

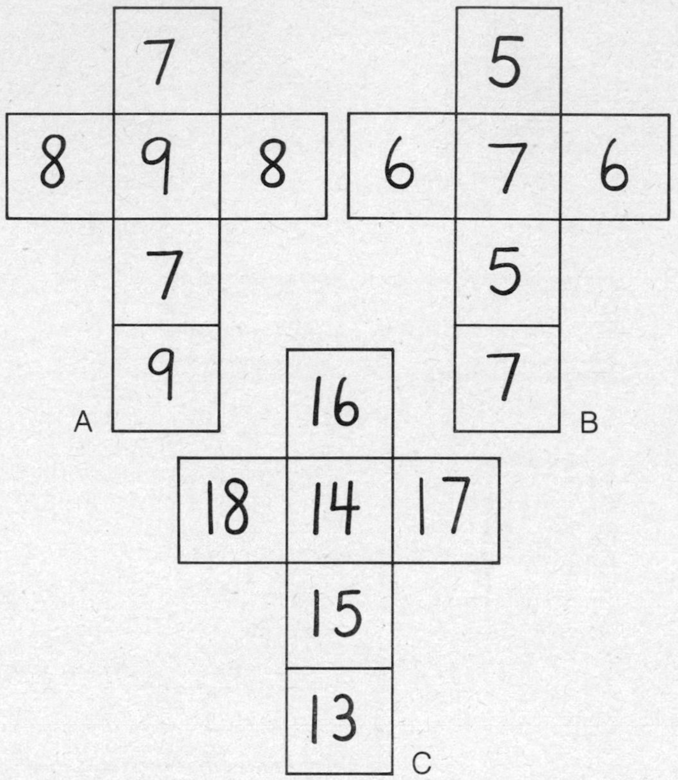

Procedure

The child selects a pair of matching dice and rolls them to obtain a pair of numbers. He writes these numbers in the spaces of a problem on the worksheet and then finds the answer to the problem he has created. Children may make problem sheets for one another also.

Addition
Addition
Make your own problems.
You will need:
pencil
paper
2 dice.
Make up problems for a friend!
4 1/4"
Add
DICE

Subtraction
Subtraction
Make your own problems.
You will need:
pencil
paper
2 dice
Make up problems for a friend!
4 1/4
Subtract
DICE

Basic Facts Drill and Practice Center

Purpose: To provide various activities reinforcing basic addition and subtraction facts (0 through 18).

Activity 3: Pick a Page

Construction

Obtain 24 **workbook pages** in mathematics (six sheets for each level of facts, 0–12, 0–18). Mount each page on a 9" x 12" piece of colored **tagboard,** mount an answer key on the back of the sheet, and cover the page with clear **contact.** Use a **press-apply dot** to put a number on each page. Provide **wax marking pencils** and small squares of indoor/outdoor **carpet** for erasing. Use 3" x 5" **index cards** to prepare one record card for each student; place these cards in a **box,** and put the worksheets in **boxes.**

Procedure

The child selects a worksheet and writes answers on it with the wax pencil. He then corrects his own work by using the answer key on the back of the sheet. He then writes the number of the completed worksheet in one of the circles on his record card.

Evaluation

This activity is self-evaluating.

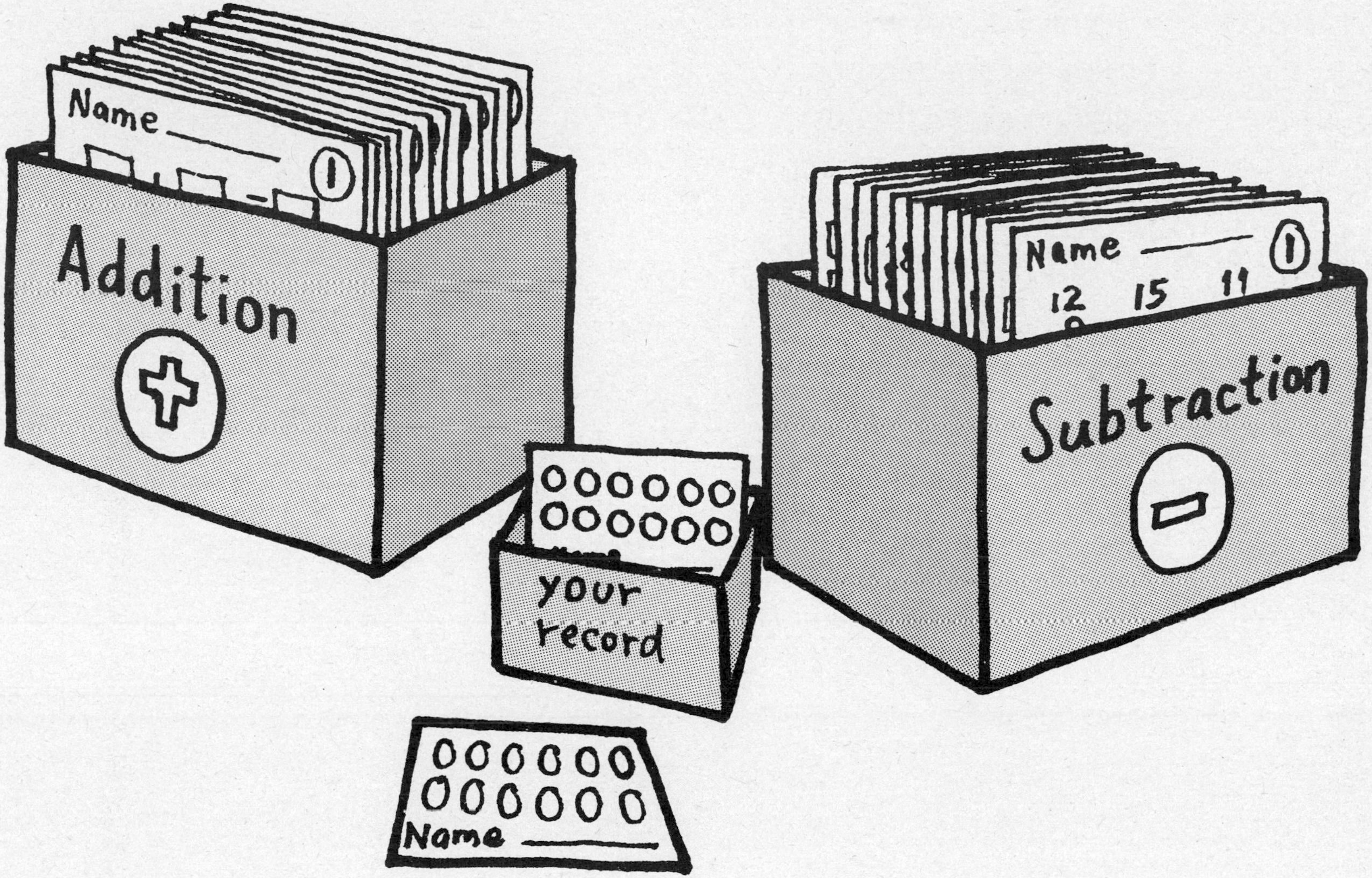
Name
Addition
your
record
Name
Name
12 15 11
Subtraction

Basic Facts Drill and Practice Center

Purpose: To provide various activities reinforcing basic addition and subtraction facts (0 through 18).

Activity 4: Hear the Facts

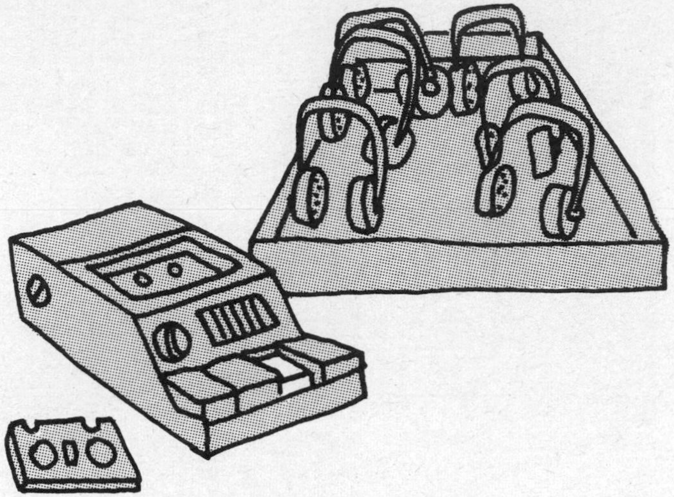

Construction

Obtain or prepare **cassette tapes or records** with instructions for drill and practice activities on the basic facts. Provide a **tape or record player** with **earphones, pencils** and **paper,** and a **poster** giving general instructions.

Procedure

The child selects a tape or record and follows the directions given on it.

Evaluation

This activity can be self-evaluating if answers are given at the end of the recording, or it can be evaluated through teacher correction of the papers.

★ Select a tape.

★ You will need: pencil
paper

★ Follow the directions on the tape.

★ Write the tape number on your paper.

Basic Facts Drill and Practice Center

Purpose: To provide various activities reinforcing basic addition and subtraction facts (0 through 18).

Activity 5: Play a Game

Construction

Draw a "Move It" game board on an 11" x 22" sheet of colored **tagboard** (sample shown on page 241). Back the board with **cardboard** and cover it with clear **contact.** Prepare a deck of **cards** giving addition combinations with answers of 6, 7, 8, 9, or 10. Cut twenty 1" squares from a sheet of colored **construction paper.** Write a numeral on each square, making four squares for each of the numbers from 6 through 10. Put these squares in a 5" x 7" **clasp envelope.** Prepare two similar sets of squares, each of a different color. Now make another game board, another deck of problem cards, and three more sets of squares—this time for addition problems with answers of 11, 12, 13, 14, or 15.

Procedure

Three children play at a game board; each player takes an envelope of colored squares. The deck of problem cards is shuffled and put face-down on the table. The first player takes a card, reads the problem aloud, and gives the answer. He then takes one of his colored squares with that number and uses it to cover a corresponding numeral on the game board. If the player gives the wrong answer to the problem, he loses his turn. The problem card is returned to the bottom of the deck and the next player takes a turn. Any player can choose to remove another player's square and replace it with his own instead of covering an empty circle. The first player to get four of his own squares in a diagonal row or in the horizontal row across the center of the board is the winner.

Evaluation

This activity can be evaluated through teacher observation or participation.

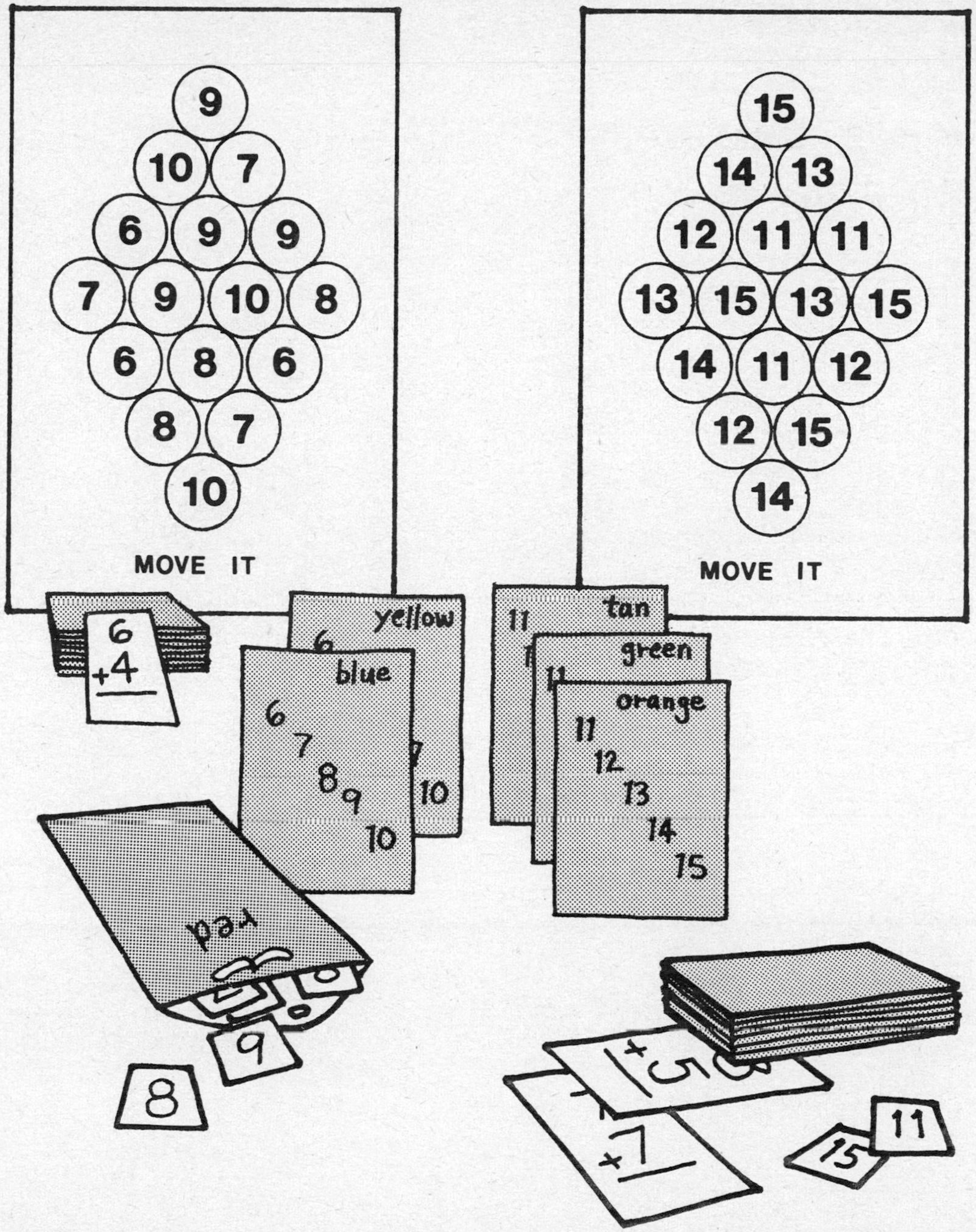

9
10 7
6 9 9
7 9 10 8
6 8 6
8 7
10
MOVE IT
15
14 13
12 11 11
13 15 13 15
14 11 12
12 15
14
MOVE IT
6
+4
yellow
blue
6 7 8 9 10
tan
green
orange
11 12 13 14 15
red
9
8
+5
+7
11
15

Place Value Center

Purpose: To provide various activities to reinforce the concept of place value.

Activity 1: Bean Sticks and Boards

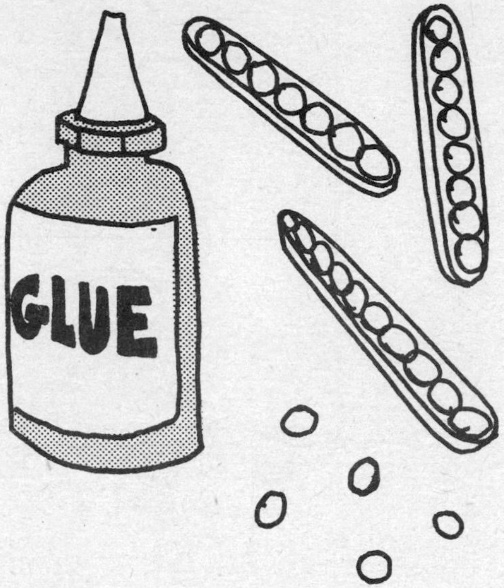

Construction

Take six sheets of colored **tagboard;** divide each sheet into four parts and write a number between 1 and 100 in each part. Cover the boards with clear **contact.** Obtain at least 500 **dry beans** (such as pinto beans) and 20 **popsicle sticks.** Place the beans and sticks in a **box.**

Procedure

Students may make bean sticks by gluing ten beans onto each stick; the finished bean sticks can then be stored in the box with the remaining loose beans. Each child selects a board. Using beansticks as tens and loose beans as ones, he places the correct number of beans in each square on the board.

Evaluation

This activity may be evaluated through teacher observation.

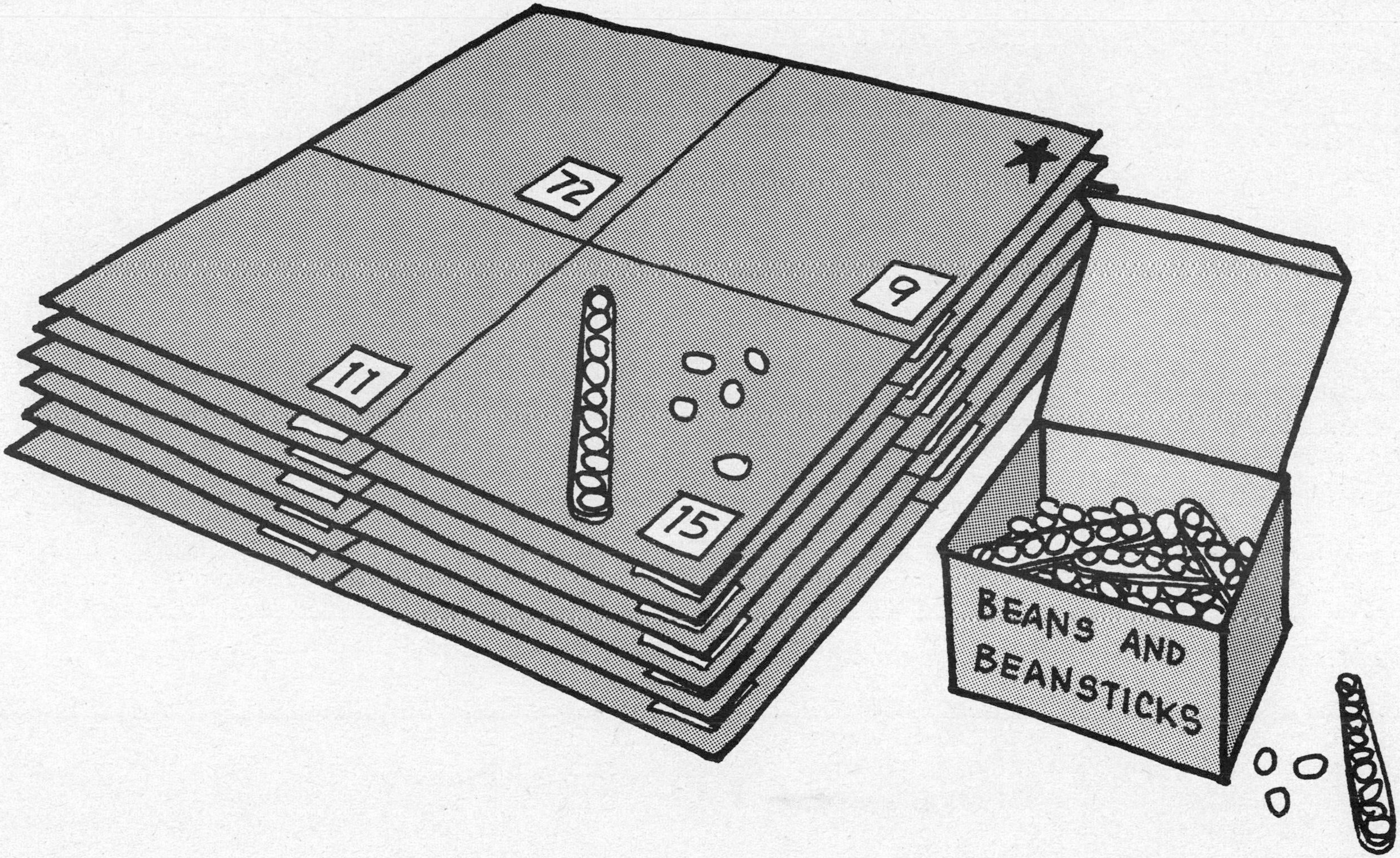
72
9
11
15
BEANS AND
BEANSTICKS

Place Value Center

Purpose: To provide various activities to reinforce the concept of place value.

Activity 2: Graph Paper Numbers

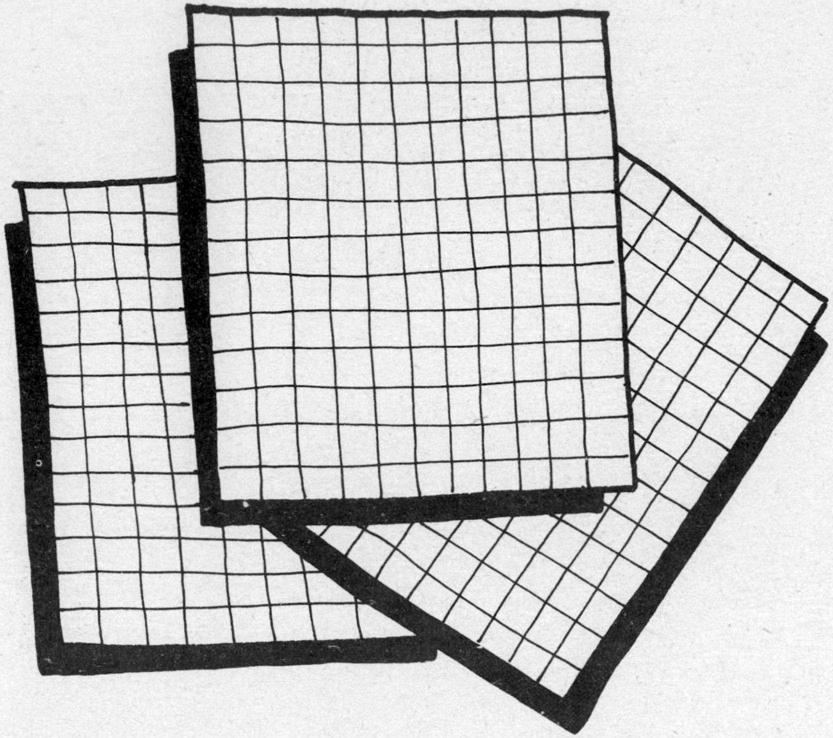

Construction

Obtain at least 30 sheets of **grid paper** (with about 1 cm squares), or duplicate the sheets from the example on page 242. Prepare a dozen task cards on 3" x 5" **index cards** and place them in a box. Provide **scissors, glue,** and sheets of 12" x 18" **construction paper.**

Procedure

The child selects a task card. He prepares a sheet of construction paper as shown, recording his own name and the identifying code of the task sheet. Using the grid paper, the child cuts tens and ones to paste on the construction paper as representations of the numbers indicated on the task card.

Evaluation

This activity can be evaluated by teacher correction of the work sheets.

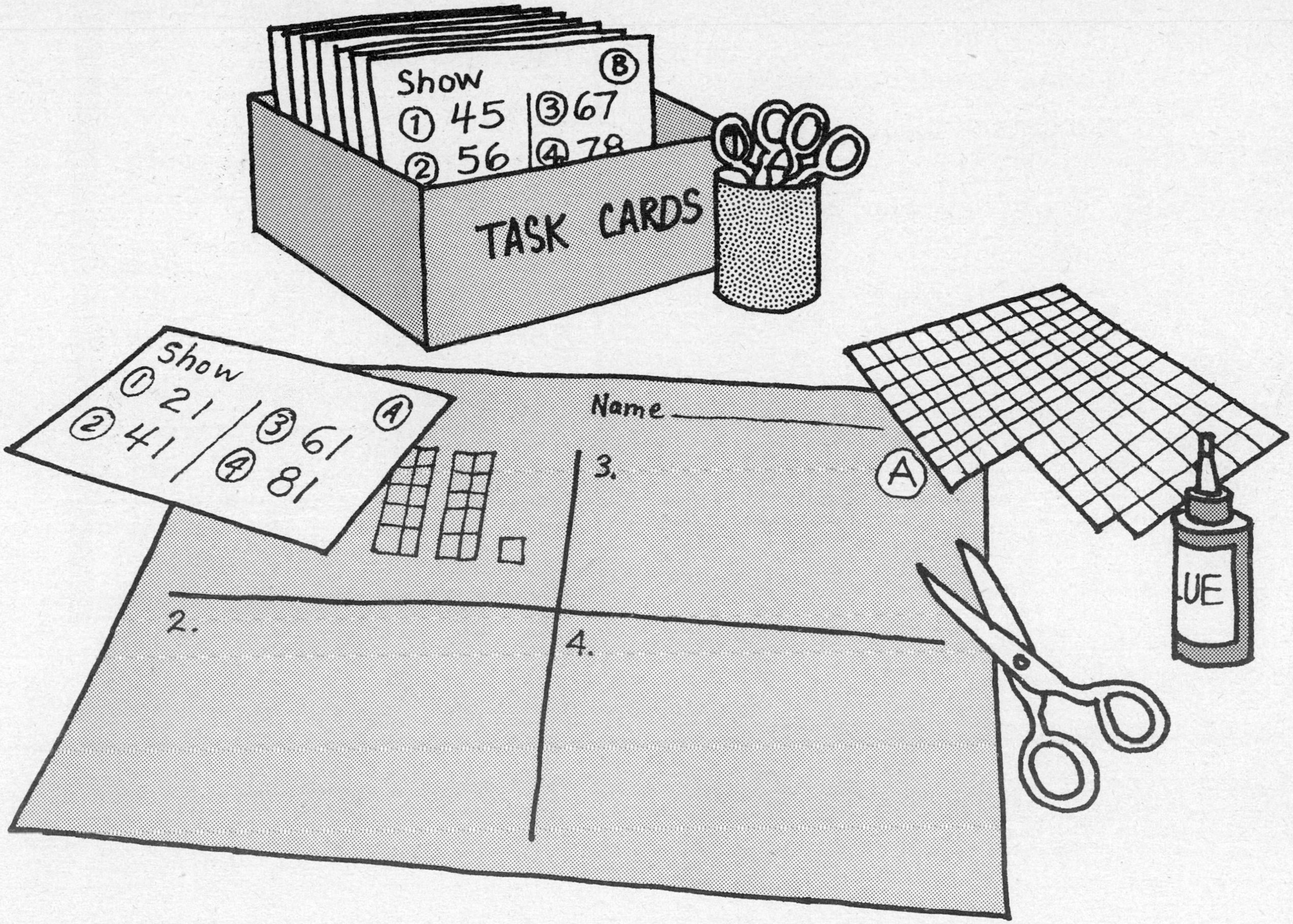
Show
B
① 45
② 56
③ 67
TASK CARDS
Show
① 21
② 41
③ 61
④ 81
A
Name
3.
A
2.
4.
UE

Place Value Center

Purpose: To provide various activities to reinforce the concept of place value.

Activity 3: Expanded Notation

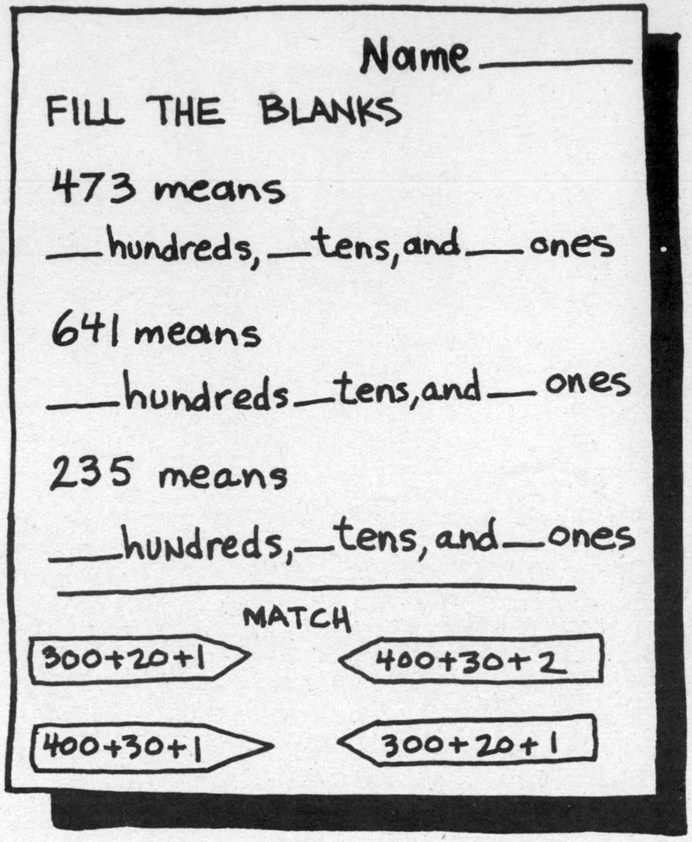

Construction

Prepare six different **worksheets** on ditto masters and duplicate enough copies to supply your class. Put the copies of each worksheet in a **manila folder** and staple an answer key inside the folder. Place the folders in a **box.**

Procedure

The child selects a worksheet and answers the questions. He then uses the answer key inside the folder to correct his work.

Evaluation

This activity is self-evaluating.

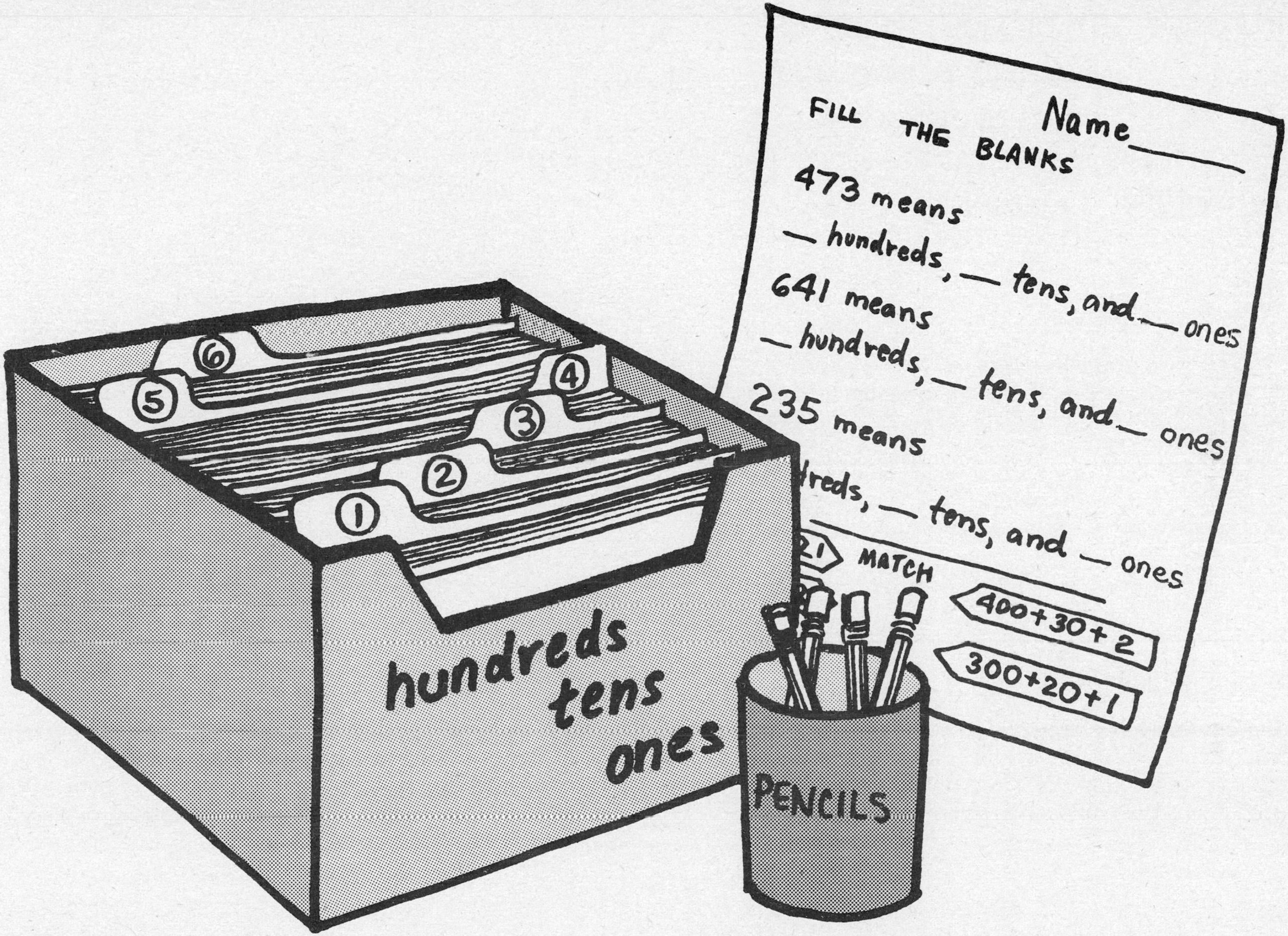

Name
FILL THE BLANKS
473 means
— hundreds, — tens, and — ones
641 means
— hundreds, — tens, and — ones
235 means
— tens, and — ones
MATCH
400+30+2
300+20+1
hundreds
tens
ones
PENCILS

Place Value Center

Purpose: To provide various activities to reinforce the concept of place value.

Activity 4: Listening

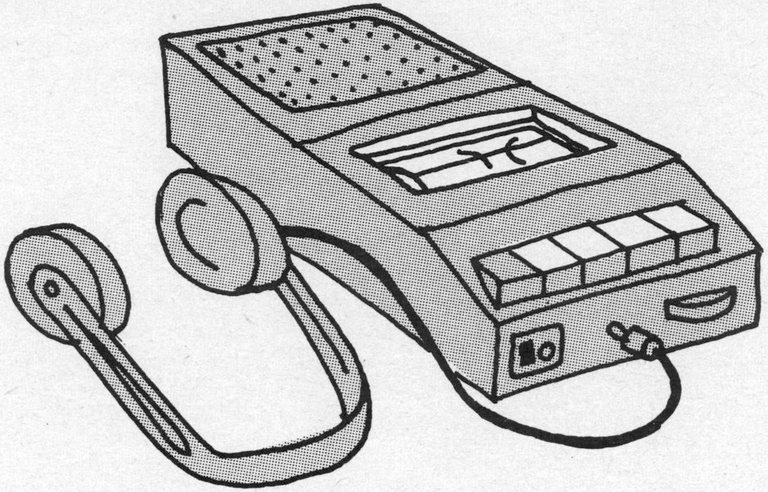

Construction

Prepare six **worksheets** as shown for each cassette tape to be used. On a 15-minute **cassette,** read the identification of each problem and one of the three numbers listed on the worksheet. Mount the worksheets on 9" x 12" sheets of colored **tagboard,** and cover them with clear **contact.** Provide **wax marking pencils** and the **cassette playback unit** with **earphones.**

Procedure

The child selects a tape cassette and the matching worksheets. As he listens to the tape, he circles the numeral on the worksheet that matches the number read on the tape for each problem.

Evaluation

This activity may be evaluated through teacher correction of the worksheets, through self-correction with answer keys, or through provision of a self-correcting oral key at the end of the tape recording.

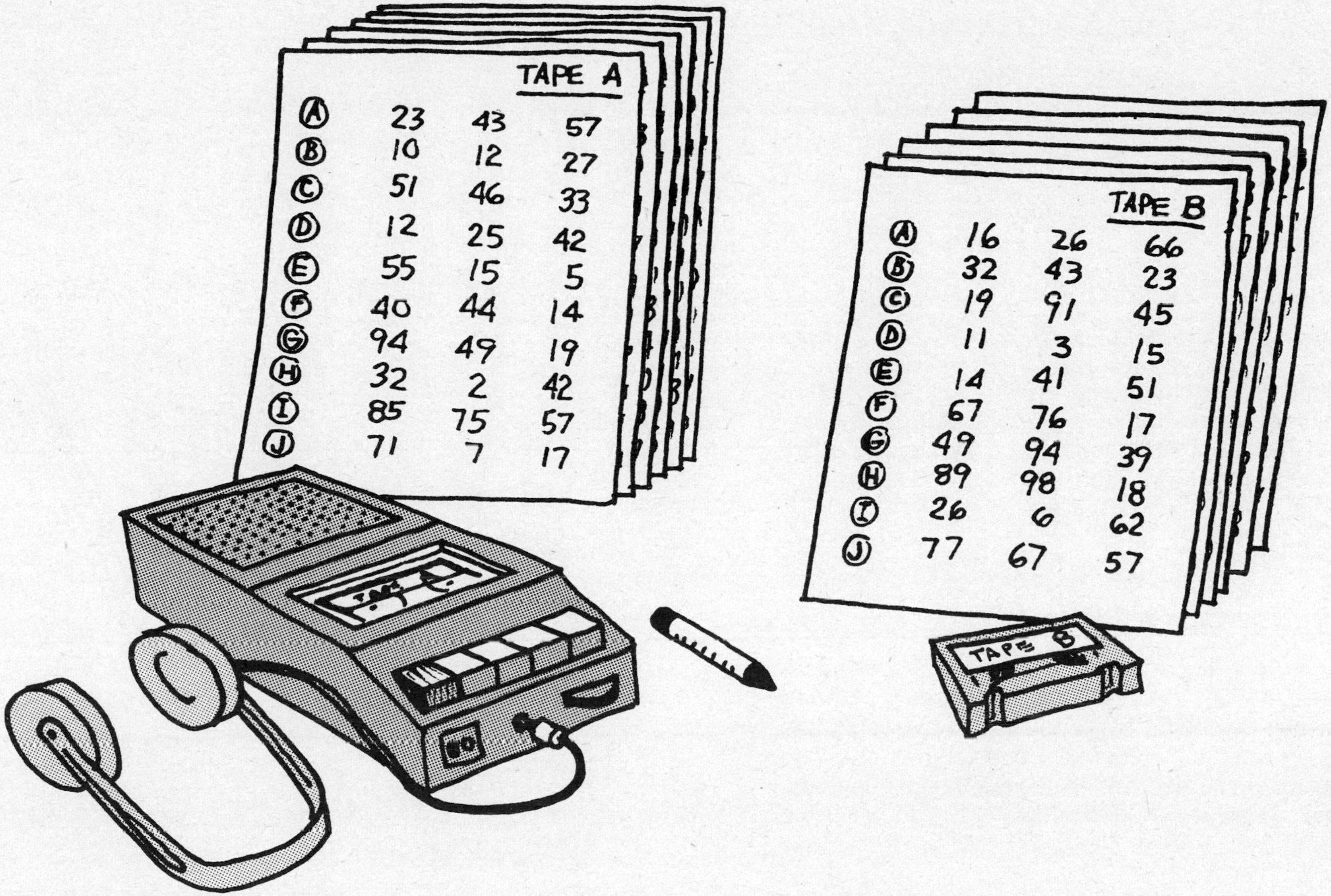
TAPE A
A 23 43 57
B 10 12 27
C 51 46 33
D 12 25 42
E 55 15 5
F 40 44 14
G 94 49 19
H 32 2 42
I 85 75 57
J 71 7 17
TAPE B
A 16 26 66
B 32 43 23
C 19 91 45
D 11 3 15
E 14 41 51
F 67 76 17
G 49 94 39
H 89 98 18
I 26 6 62
J 77 67 57
TAPE B

Place Value Center

Purpose: To provide various activities to reinforce the concept of place value.

Activity 5: Fido's Football Game

Construction

Prepare the game board on an 11" x 14" sheet of colored **tagboard,** mount on **cardboard,** and cover with clear **contact.** Duplicate a number of **score sheets** (shown on page 243). Provide a **die,** four game **markers,** and **pencils.**

Procedure

Up to four students can play. Each player has a game marker, a score sheet, and a pencil. All markers are placed at "START." The first player rolls the die, moves the number of spaces shown, and then records on his score sheet the number of hundreds, tens, or ones indicated in the circle on which he lands. The game continues until each player has five turns. Then each player adds up the points on his score card, and the student with the highest total wins.

Evaluation

The teacher may evaluate this activity by correcting the score sheets, by observation, or by participation.

START
GO BACK TO START
Name
hundreds
tens
ones
TOTAL

Time Center

Purpose: To reinforce concepts of time.

Activity 1: Time Match

Construction

Build the carrel from three 12" x 26" pieces of **tagboard,** backed with **cardboard.** Make the large pocket for cards from **tagboard.** Attach 16 **library pockets** to the carrel, drawing a clock face on each. Cover with clear contact. Hinge the carrel together with 1½" **Mystik tape.** Prepare 16 **cards** (3" x 5"), each having written on it a time corresponding to one of the clock faces.

Procedure

The child takes the cards from the large pocket and places each card in the matching library pocket.

Evaluation

This activity may be evaluated by teacher observation, or may be self-evaluating if the proper clock face is drawn on the back of each time card.

1. Take a card.
2. Find a "clock pocket" for each card.
3. Place a card in each pocket.
1:15
2:00
5:15
1:30

Time Center

Purpose: To reinforce concepts of time.

Activity 2: Clock Cards

Construction

Prepare 12 (or more) 5" x 7" clock **cards** as shown on pages 244–245. These should be **laminated,** covered with clear **contact,** or placed in **plastic sleeves.** Provide **wax marking pencils** and small squares of acrylan **carpet** for erasing.

Procedure

The child reads the sentence on each card, fills in the blank, and draws the hands on the clock to correspond with the completed sentence.

Evaluation

This activity may be evaluated by teacher observation.

①
I get up
at ____
o'clock.
②
I eat
breakfast
at ____
o'clock.
③
Recess is
at ____
ock.
I eat
lunch
at ____
o'clock.

Time Center

Purpose: To reinforce concepts of time.

Activity 3: Pinwheels

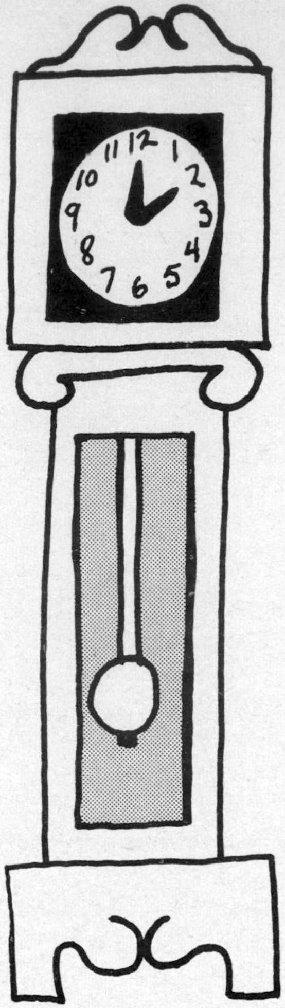

Construction

Cut six 14"-diameter **tagboard** circles, and draw 12 clock faces on each as shown. Four of the circles deal with different time concepts (times on the hour, on the half hour, quarter past the hour, and quarter to the hour); the remaining two circles provide mixed practice. Back the circles with **cardboard** and cover with clear **contact.** Take 72 wooden spring **clothespins;** on each clothespin write the time corresponding to one of the clock faces. The clothespins can be put in one large **box,** or can be divided into sets to accompany each pinwheel.

Procedure

The child chooses a wheel and clips a clothespin to each of the clock faces, so that each clothespin gives the time shown on the clock face to which it is attached.

Evaluation

This activity may be evaluated by teacher observation, or it may be made self-evaluating by writing times on the back of the wheels or drawing clock faces on the reverse side of the clothespins.

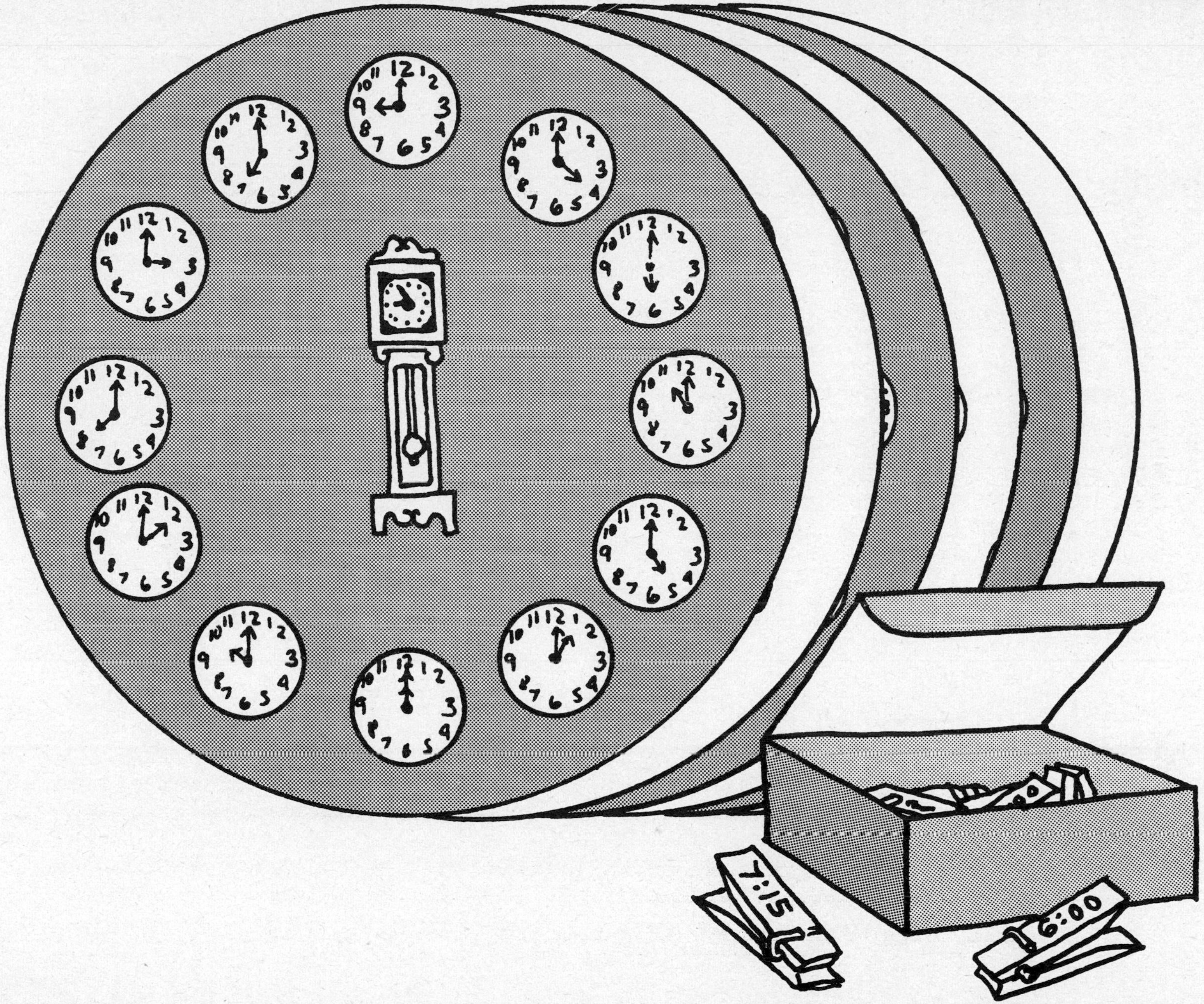
7:15
6:00

Time Center

Purpose: To reinforce concepts of time.

Activity 4: Give Me a Hand

Construction

Duplicate at least a dozen copies of the **form** on page 246. Mount each on **tagboard**, and cut the two copies apart. On each resulting card, write a time. (You can provide times on even hours and half hours with the two dozen cards; additional cards can be prepared for other times.) **Laminate** or **contact** the cards. Provide **wax marking pencils** and small squares of acrylan **carpeting** for erasing.

Procedure

The child takes a card, reads the time printed on it, and draws the hands of the clock to show that time.

Evaluation

This activity may be evaluated by teacher observation. It may be made self-evaluating by providing an answer key or by drawing clock faces with hands on the reverse side of the cards.

12
11
1
1. Take a card.
2. Read the time.
3. Draw the hands on the clock to show the time.
2:30

Time Center

Purpose: To reinforce concepts of time.

Activity 5: Race of Time

Construction

Draw the game board on a large sheet of colored **tagboard,** mount it on **cardboard** and cover with **contact.** Prepare 24 cards (3" x 4") cut from **tagboard.** Write a time on one side of each card (even hours and half hours), and draw the corresponding clock face on the other side of the card. Provide a **die** and four game **markers.** Additional game boards can be prepared with cards showing other times.

Procedure

Two to four children may play. The cards are placed in a pile, clock side up. The markers are placed at "Start." The first player picks up the top card and says the time shown by the clock. He turns the card over to check his response. If he is correct, he rolls the die and moves the number of spaces indicated. If he is not correct, he does not move on this turn. The card is returned to the bottom of the deck. Each player takes a turn, and play continues until one player wins by reaching "Finish."

Evaluation

This activity is self-evaluating, but additional evaluation can be made by teacher observation.

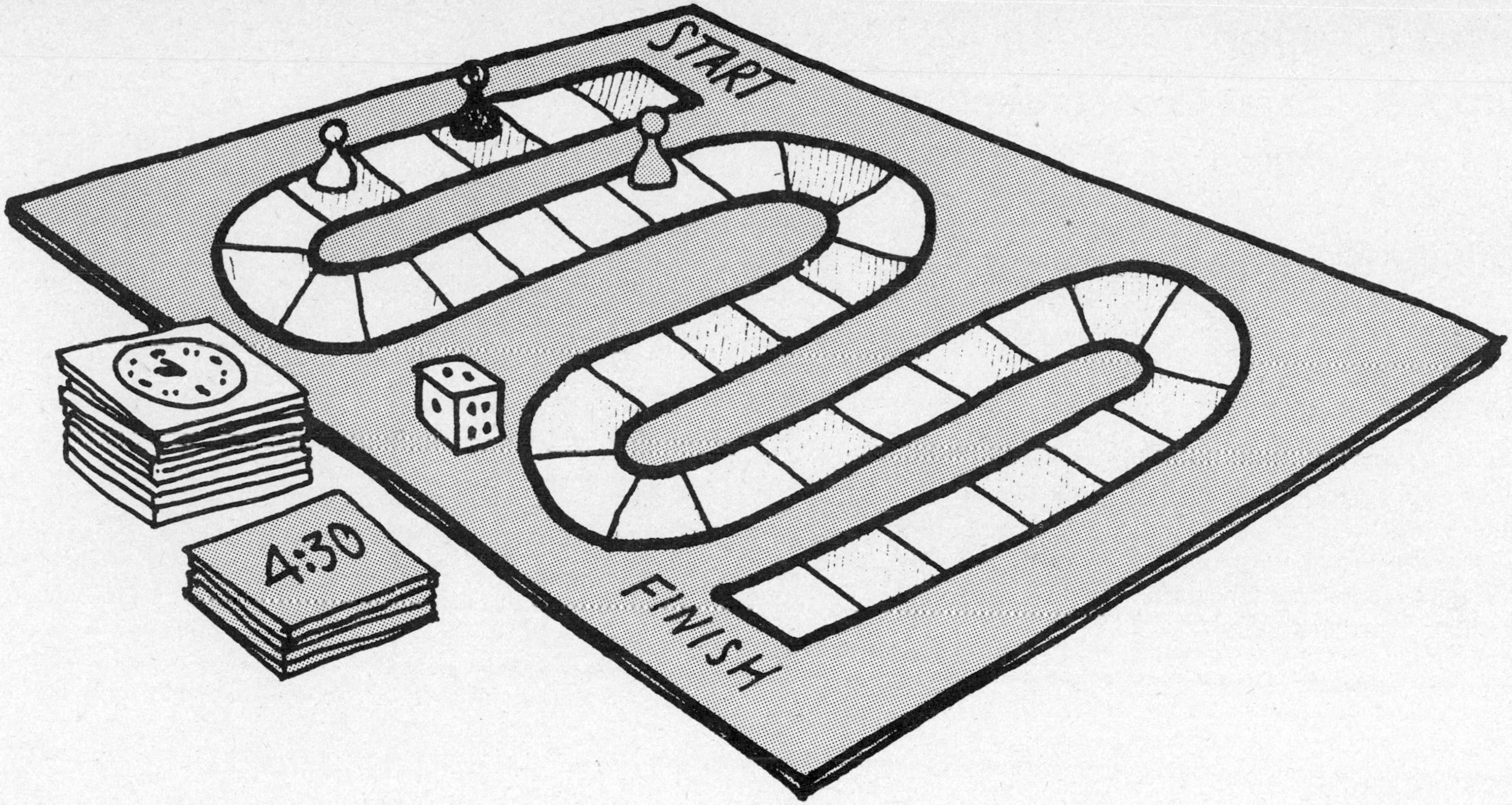

front

back

Time Center

Purpose: To reinforce concepts of time.

Activity 6: The Clockshop

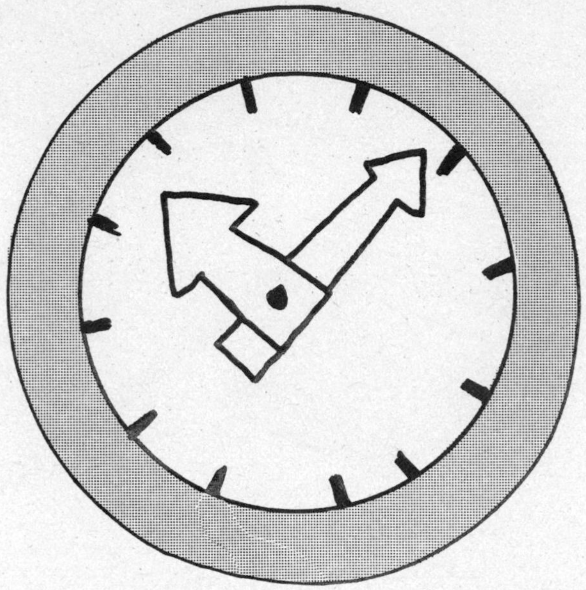

Construction

From a 9" **paper plate,** prepare a pattern with quarter-hour and center positions cut out. Prepare 4" minute hands and 2½" hour hands cut from **tagboard** (one of each kind of hand for each student). Provide one 9" **paper plate** for each student, **pencils, crayons,** and brass **paper fasteners.**

Procedure

The child uses the pattern to mark the center and quarter-hour positions on his plate. He then uses crayon to fill in the other positions and to write numerals on his clock face. He uses a pencil to punch a hole in the center of the plate, and attaches the clock hands through the hole with a paper fastener. (For younger children, it may be necessary to prepunch holes in the clock hands.) The completed clocks can be used for practice in reading time and in setting the hands to given times.

Evaluation

This activity may be evaluated through teacher observation.

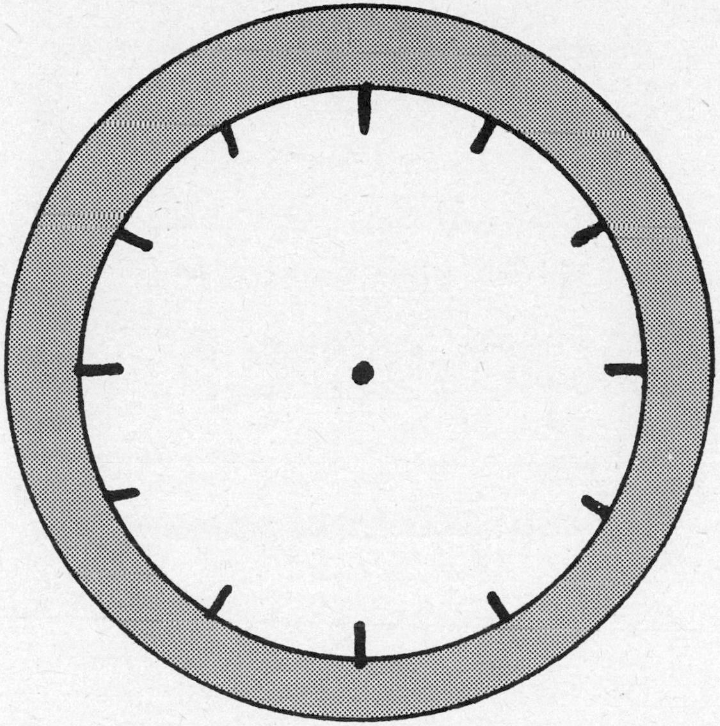

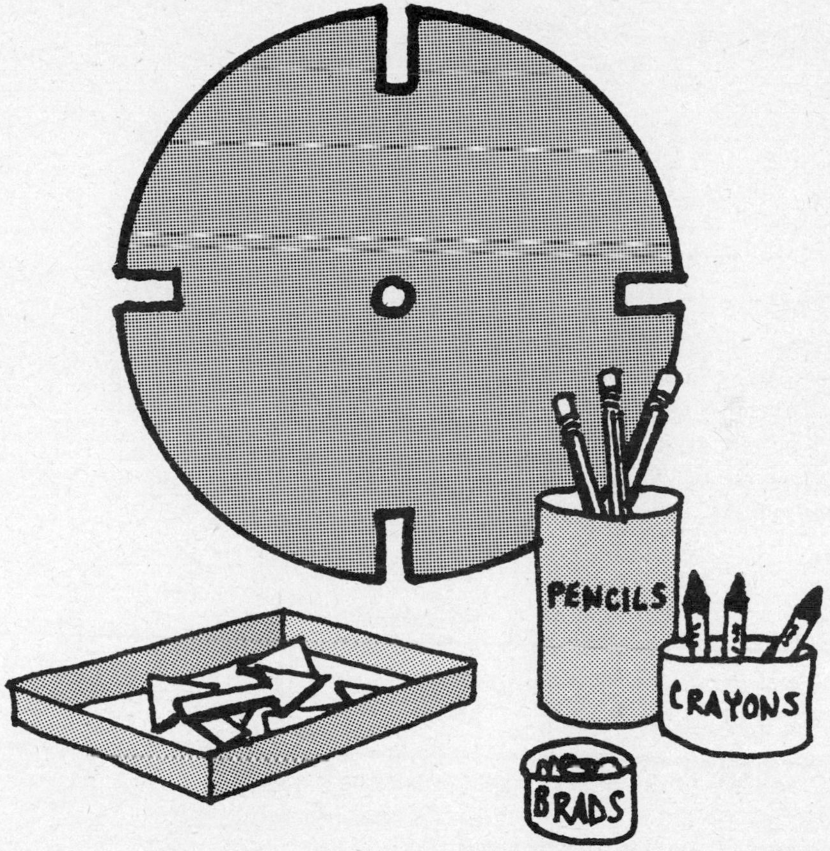
PENCILS
CRAYONS
BRADS

Time Center

Purpose: To reinforce concepts of time.

Activity 7: Time Sheets

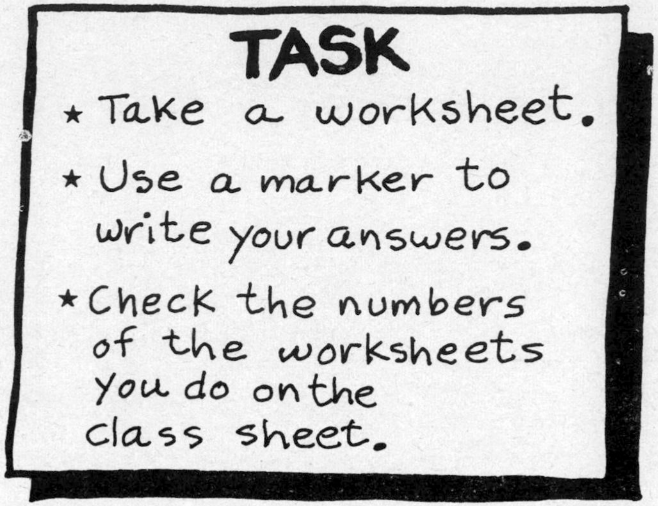

Construction

Prepare 20 to 30 **worksheets** with appropriate problems about time concepts, or obtain such worksheets from workbooks. Mount the sheets on **tagboard** and **laminate** or **contact** them, or place each in a **plastic sleeve.** Use **press-apply dots** to number the worksheets. Provide **wax marking pencils** and scraps of acrylan **carpeting** for erasing.

Procedure

The child takes a worksheet and uses the wax pencil to record his answers on it. The teacher can assign specific worksheets to meet the needs of individual students.

Evaluation

The student's work can be evaluated by teacher correction of the worksheets, or answer keys can be provided for self-evaluation.

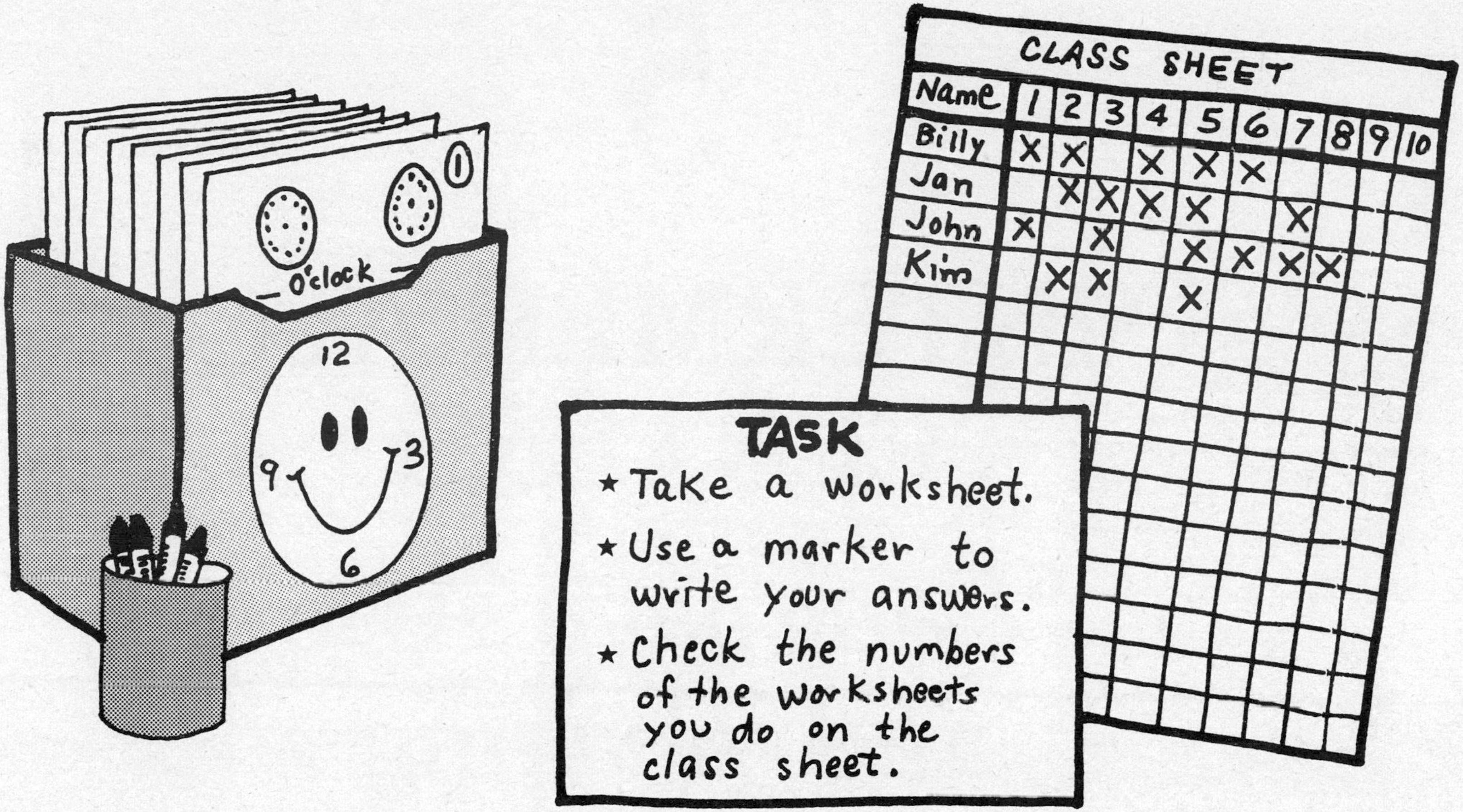
O'clock
12
3
6
9
1
CLASS SHEET
Name
1 2 3 4 5 6 7 8 9 10
Billy
Jan
John
Kim
TASK
★ Take a worksheet.
★ Use a marker to write your answers.
★ Check the numbers of the worksheets you do on the class sheet.

5

INTERMEDIATE CENTERS

Language Arts and Reading

Word Attack Skills Center

Activity 1: Phonic Dominoes
Activity 2: Prefix Game
Activity 3: Jigsaw Syllables
Activity 4: Find the Suffix
Activity 5: Accent Windows
Activity 6: 1–2–3–4 Number Game

Comprehension Skills Center

Activity 1: Riddle Match
Activity 2: Comics Sequence
Activity 3: Paragraph Sequence
Activity 4: Make the Headlines
Activity 5: Ad Concentration
Activity 6: Player Contrast
Activity 7: What's the Story
Activity 8: Question Match

Tall Tale Center

Activity 1: Viewing Station
Activity 2: Creative Writing Station
Activity 3: Story-Starter Wheels
Activity 4: Game Station
Activity 5: Art Station
Activity 6: Free Reading Station

Word Attack Skills Center

Purpose: To provide activities that reinforce word attack skills.

Activity 1: Phonic Dominoes

Construction

Prepare a set of cards made like dominoes, but bearing words instead of dots. In each word, a letter or letters spelling a sound are underlined. The examples on pages 247–248 could be used, or you can create your own. The cards can be made on **tagboard** and covered with clear **contact** for durability. Provide a **die.**

Procedure

This is a game for two players. All dominoes are turned face down. Each child draws four dominoes. Each player rolls the die; the one rolling the largest number starts. The first player puts out one domino (face up). The other player must place one domino on the board to match sounds (as numbers are matched in ordinary dominoes). The child pronounces the two words and the sound as he places the domino. If a player cannot match a sound from the dominoes he has, he must draw dominoes from the pile until he can make a match. The first player to use all the dominoes in his hand wins the game. With a larger number of dominoes, more players can join the game.

Evaluation

This activity may be evaluated through teacher observation or participation.

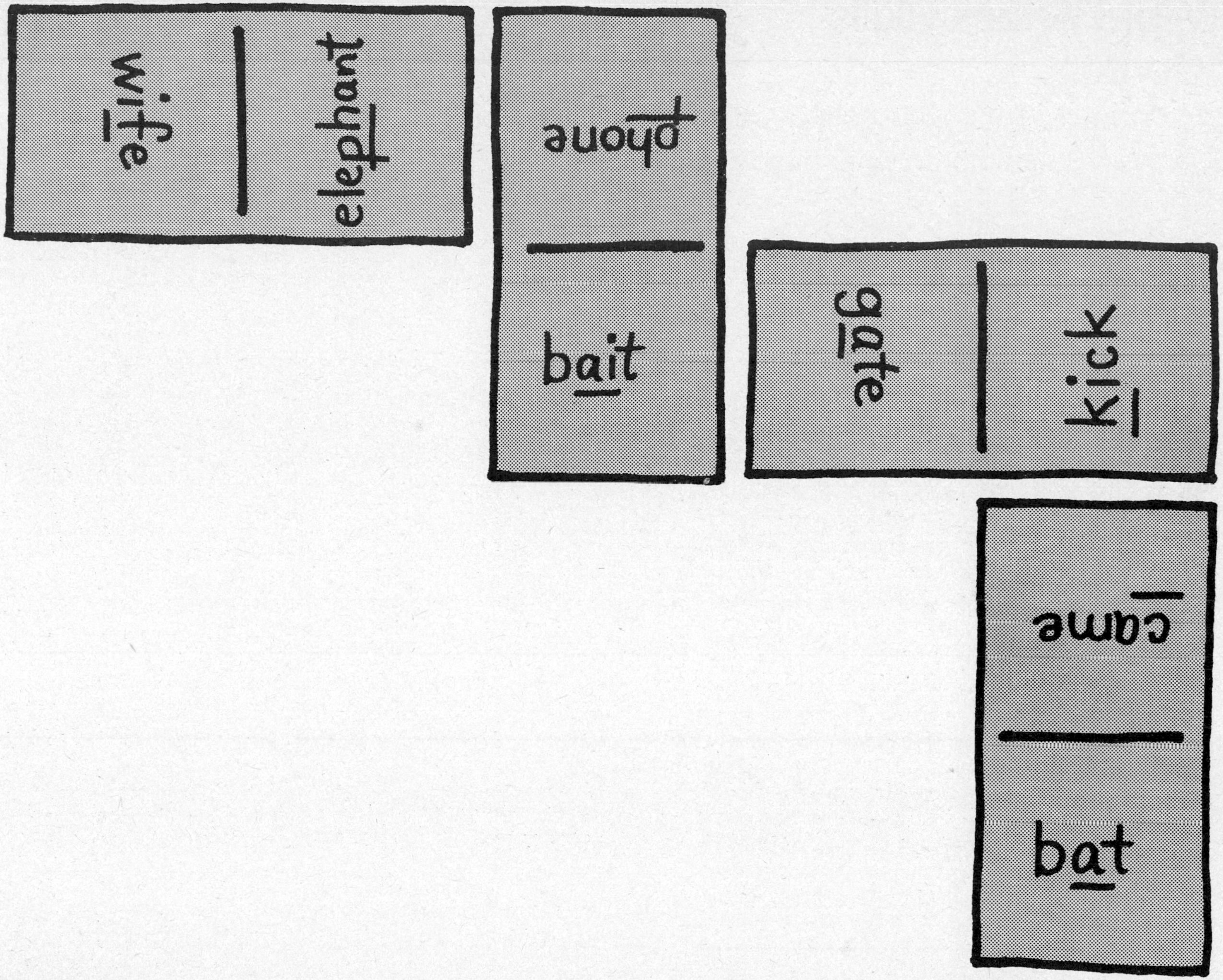
wife
elephant
phone
bait
gate
kick
came
bat

Word Attack Skills Center

Purpose: To provide activities that reinforce work attack skills.

Activity 2: Prefix Game

Construction

Make six playing boards on 9" x 12" sheets of colored **tagboard** (see page 249 for a sample board). Across the top row of each board, print four prefixes chosen from the list on this page. Cover the boards with clear **contact**. Make 62 **tagboard** cards (each 2½" x 3"). On eight of these cards, print the word "FREE." On each of the remaining cards, print one of the root words from the following list.

Procedure

Six children may play the game. Shuffle the cards and place them face down in the center of the table. Each child has a prefix board. The first player draws a card and reads the root word aloud. If he can form a word by combining the root word with one of the prefixes on his board, he says the new word aloud and places the card in the column of his board under the prefix used. If he cannot make a word, he discards the card. If he draws a "FREE" card, he may place it anywhere on his board. (He may not move the "FREE" card after it has been placed.) The first player to fill all the spaces on his board wins the game.

Evaluation

This activity may be evaluated by teacher observation or participation. Students can use a dictionary or answer key for self-evaluation. (In preparing an answer key, remember to check for root words that may be combined with two or more prefixes.)

Prefixes and Root Words for the Prefix Game

mis	sub	dis
behave	marine	like
place	topic	obey
trust	floor	connect
use	soil	color
match	total	appear
spell	culture	agree
in	**un**	**re**
justice	finished	pay
active	wise	visit
complete	happy	build
correct	friendly	open
visible	fold	fill
action	tie	paint
de	**pre**	**im**
code	shrunk	mature
rail	judge	polite
merit	historic	possible
value	test	proper
throne	paid	pure
frost	set	patient

These prefixes and root words can be combined in other ways to form words such as replace or preplace. Use a dictionary to resolve any disputes about the validity of words used in the game.

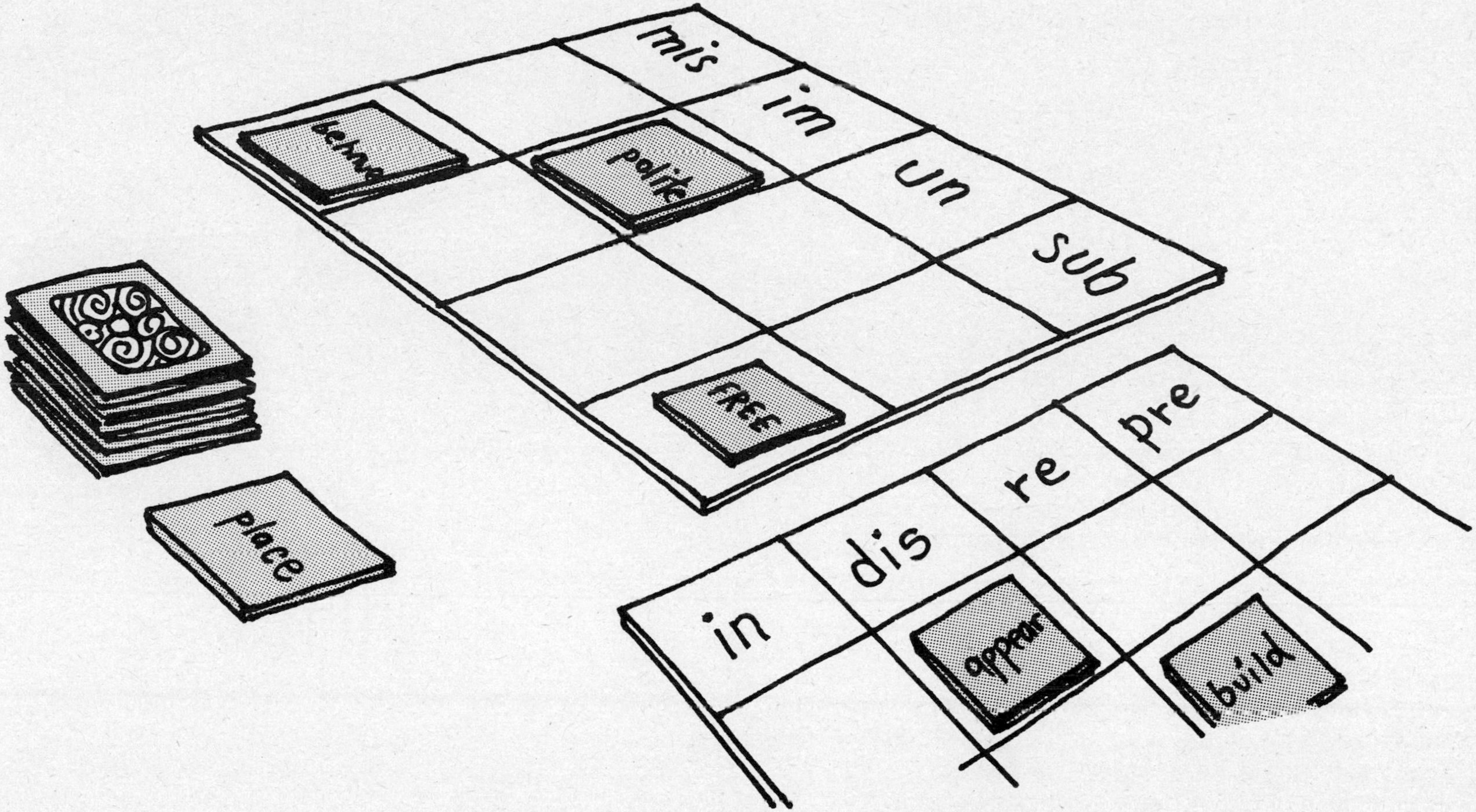
mis
im
un
sub
polite
FREE
pre
re
dis
in
appear
build
place

Word Attack Skills Center

Purpose: To provide activities that reinforce word attack skills.

Activity 3: Jigsaw Syllables

Construction

Prepare 90 **tagboard** word cards. Print a two-syllable word on each card, and cut the card between the syllables along an irregular line. Number six 5" x 7" **manila envelopes.** Put the pieces of 15 word cards into each envelope, numbering the pieces to correspond with the envelope. Provide **writing paper.**

Procedure

Each child takes an envelope and puts the puzzle pieces on the table. As he assembles each word, he writes it on a sheet of paper. The activity can be made into a game for six players, with the student who finishes his list of words first (and correctly) being the winner.

Evaluation

This activity can be evaluated by teacher observation, or by teacher correction of the word lists.

2
1
one
1
any
1
battter
1
1

Word Attack Skills Center

Purpose: To provide activities that reinforce word attack skills.

Activity 4: Find the Suffix

Construction

Fasten six **library book pockets** inside a **manila folder.** On each pocket, write one of the suffixes from the following list. Obtain 36 **cards** of a size that will fit in the pockets. On each card, write one of the root words from the list. For a typical class, you will want to prepare six folders, each with its own set of cards.

Procedure

The child takes a folder and a deck of cards. He reads each root word and places the card into a pocket for a suffix that can be combined with the root word.

Root Words and Suffixes for "Find the Suffix"

ness	**tion**	**ous**
great	collect	marvel
thick	dictate	courage
dark	elect	poison
ill	educate	danger
sad	donate	humor
mad	direct	fame

able	**ful**	**ment**
laugh	color	amuse
print	cheer	amaze
favor	help	place
avail	truth	assign
work	hand	amend
read	thank	assort

Evaluation

This activity can be evaluated by teacher observation. The activity can be self-evaluating if an answer key is provided, or if the pockets are numbered and corresponding numbers are placed on the backs of the cards. In this case, encourage students to note cases where a root word can be combined with suffixes other than the "correct" answer given; a dictionary can be used to settle any questions that arise about the validity of particular combinations.

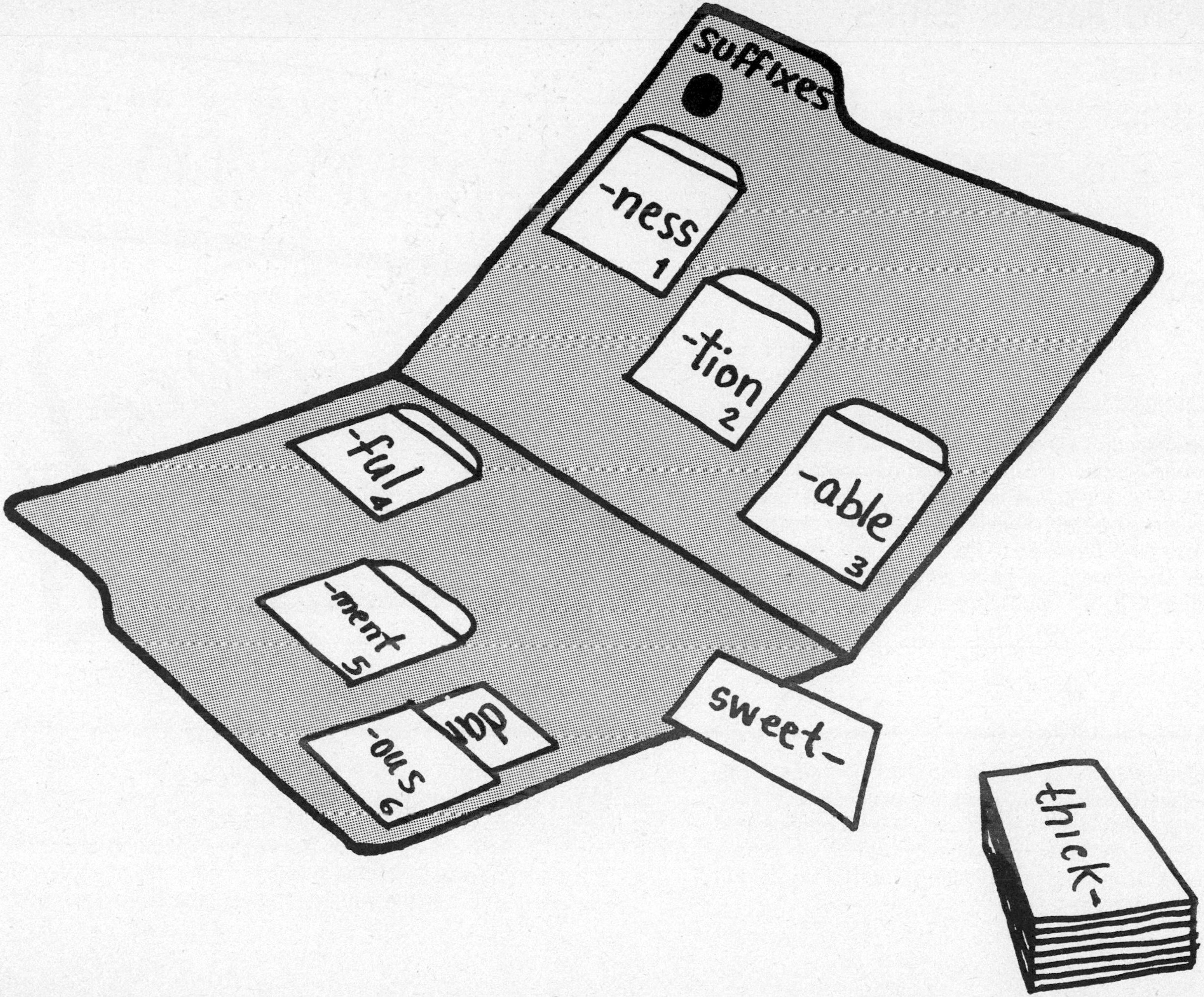
suffixes
-ness
1
-tion
2
-able
3
-ful
4
-ment
5
-ous
6
sweet-
thick-

Word Attack Skills Center

Purpose: To provide activities that reinforce word attack skills.

Activity 5: Accent Windows

Construction

Build six accent windows. Each is made from a piece of clear acetate and a piece of cardboard for the back (3½" x 5"). The window and the cardboard back are joined with Mystik tape, leaving room to slip a word strip between them. Use a marking pen to make an accent on each window. Make a large number of 3" x 8" word strips from tagboard.

Procedure

Each child takes an accent window and a word strip. He says the word and puts the word strip into the accent window so that the accent will be placed on the correct syllable. This activity can be done as a group activity (each child taking a turn) or as an individual activity.

Evaluation

This activity can be made self-evaluating by printing the word in small letters on the back of each word strip with the accent marked in its correct position.

al
low
mo
ment

Word Attack Skills Center

Purpose: To provide activities that reinforce word attack skills.

Activity 6: 1–2–3–4 Number Game

Construction

Make eight 8" x 8" **tagboard** word cards as shown, and cover them with clear **contact.** Cut thirty-two 1½" squares from each of four different colors of **tagboard.** Write the numeral "1" on all of the squares of one color, "2" on all of the squares of the second color, and so on. Make a spinner as shown from **tagboard** and a **paper fastener.**

Procedure

Eight children may play. Each takes a word card and four squares of each color. He puts a square (numeral up) over each of the words on his card. The players then take turns spinning the spinner. The player spins a number and then removes from his word card one of the squares bearing that number. He must then say the contraction uncovered and say the two words that have been combined to form that contraction. If he fails to do this correctly, he must replace the numbered square on his word card. If a player spins a number and has no squares of that number left on his card, he loses his turn. The winner is the first player who removes all of the number squares from his word card.

Evaluation

This activity may be evaluated through teacher observation or participation.

doesn't	I'd	we're	hadn't
let's	won't	we'll	isn't
we're	he's	aren't	they'll
I've	don't	she'd	you'd

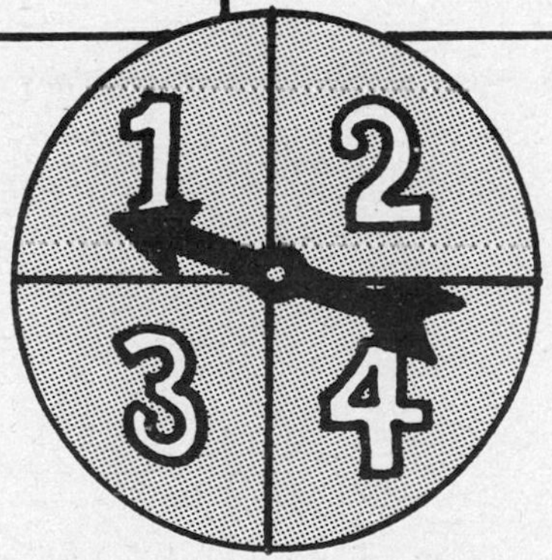

Comprehension Skills Center

Purpose: To provide experiences that reinforce comprehension skills.

Activity 1: Riddle Match

Construction

Build the carrel from two 14" x 20" pieces of colored **tagboard,** backed with **cardboard** and hinged with **Mystik tape.** Attach 18 **library book pockets** to the carrel. Write a riddle on each of the pockets. Write the answer to each riddle on a 3" x 5" **index card.** (One pocket can be used to store the answer cards.)

When is an
egg like a
gas station

Procedure

Two children can participate. One reads the riddles. The other finds the appropriate answer among the answer cards and places that card in the riddle pocket.

Evaluation

Self-evaluation of this activity is possible if the pockets are numbered and the corresponding numbers are written on the backs of the answer cards.

TASK CARD

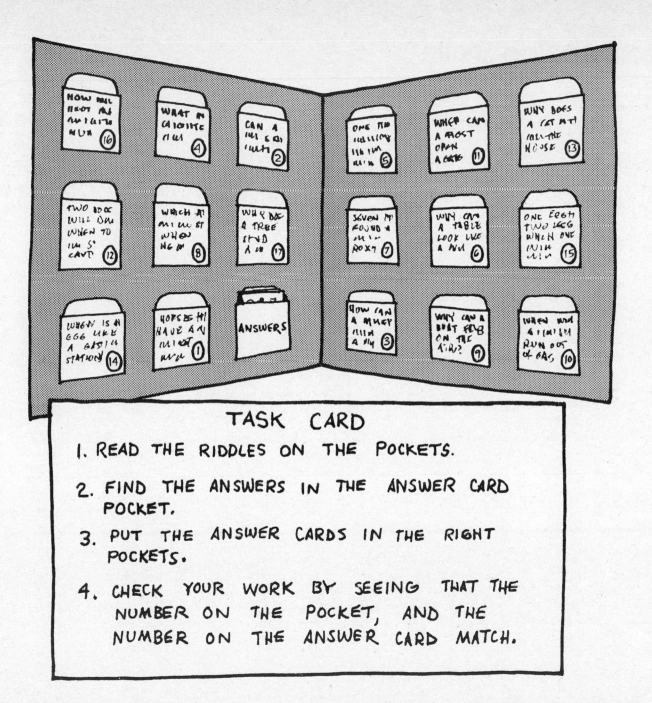

1. READ THE RIDDLES ON THE POCKETS.
2. FIND THE ANSWERS IN THE ANSWER CARD POCKET.
3. PUT THE ANSWER CARDS IN THE RIGHT POCKETS.
4. CHECK YOUR WORK BY SEEING THAT THE NUMBER ON THE POCKET, AND THE NUMBER ON THE ANSWER CARD MATCH.

Comprehension Skills Center

Purpose: To provide experiences that reinforce comprehension skills.

Activity 2: Comics Sequence

Construction

Obtain 24 **cartoon strips** from newspapers or comic books. Cut the panels of each strip apart and mount each panel on a 3" x 5" **index card.** Cover with clear **contact** for durability. Put all of the panels for each strip into a 5" x 7" **clasp envelope.** Code the cards and envelopes for easy refiling.

Procedure

The child takes an envelope and removes the cartoon panels. He arranges the panels in their original sequence.

Evaluation

The panels can be coded by putting sequential numbers on the backs of the cards, or by using a **press-apply dot** to put a symbol on each panel with an **answer key** showing the proper sequence of symbols. Thus the activity can be made self-evaluating.

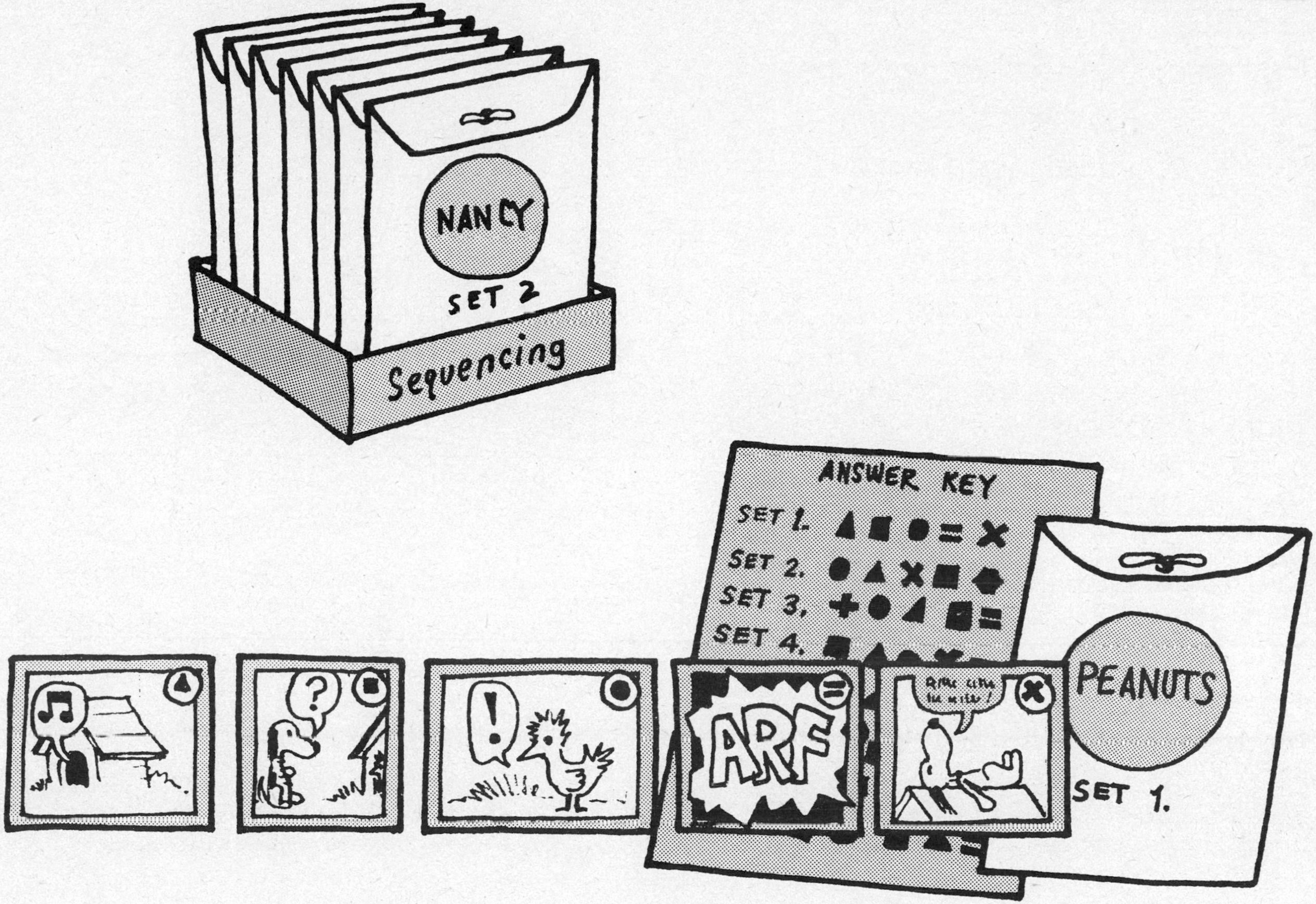
NANCY
SET 2
Sequencing
ANSWER KEY
SET 1.
SET 2.
SET 3.
SET 4.
ARF
PEANUTS
SET 1.

Comprehension Skills Center

Purpose: To provide experiences that reinforce comprehension skills.

Activity 3: Paragraph Sequence

Construction

Obtain 24 **short stories** from discarded texts, magazines, or materials written by the teacher or students. Cut apart the paragraphs of each story and mount them in scrambled sequence on a 9" x 12" piece of **tagboard.** Cover with clear **contact.** Provide **wax marking pencils** and **carpet** squares for erasing.

Procedure

The child chooses a story board, reads the paragraphs, and uses a wax pencil to number the paragraphs in their correct sequence.

Evaluation

This activity can be made self-evaluating by providing an answer key, or by indicating the correct sequence on the back of each story board.

3
1
3
1
4
2

Comprehension Skills Center

Purpose: To provide experiences that reinforce comprehension skills.

Activity 4: Make the Headlines

Construction

Obtain 24 short **newspaper articles.** Mount the article on one side of a **tagboard** sheet or **index card,** and mount the headline on the opposite side. Cover with clear **contact.** Provide **wax marking pencils** and **carpet** squares for erasing.

Procedure

The student reads the article and then writes in a headline for it. He then compares his headline with the actual headline on the back of the card.

Evaluation

This activity can be evaluated by teacher observation or be self-evaluated. In either case, the goal is to write a good headline for the article, **not** necessarily to duplicate the headline actually published on the article.

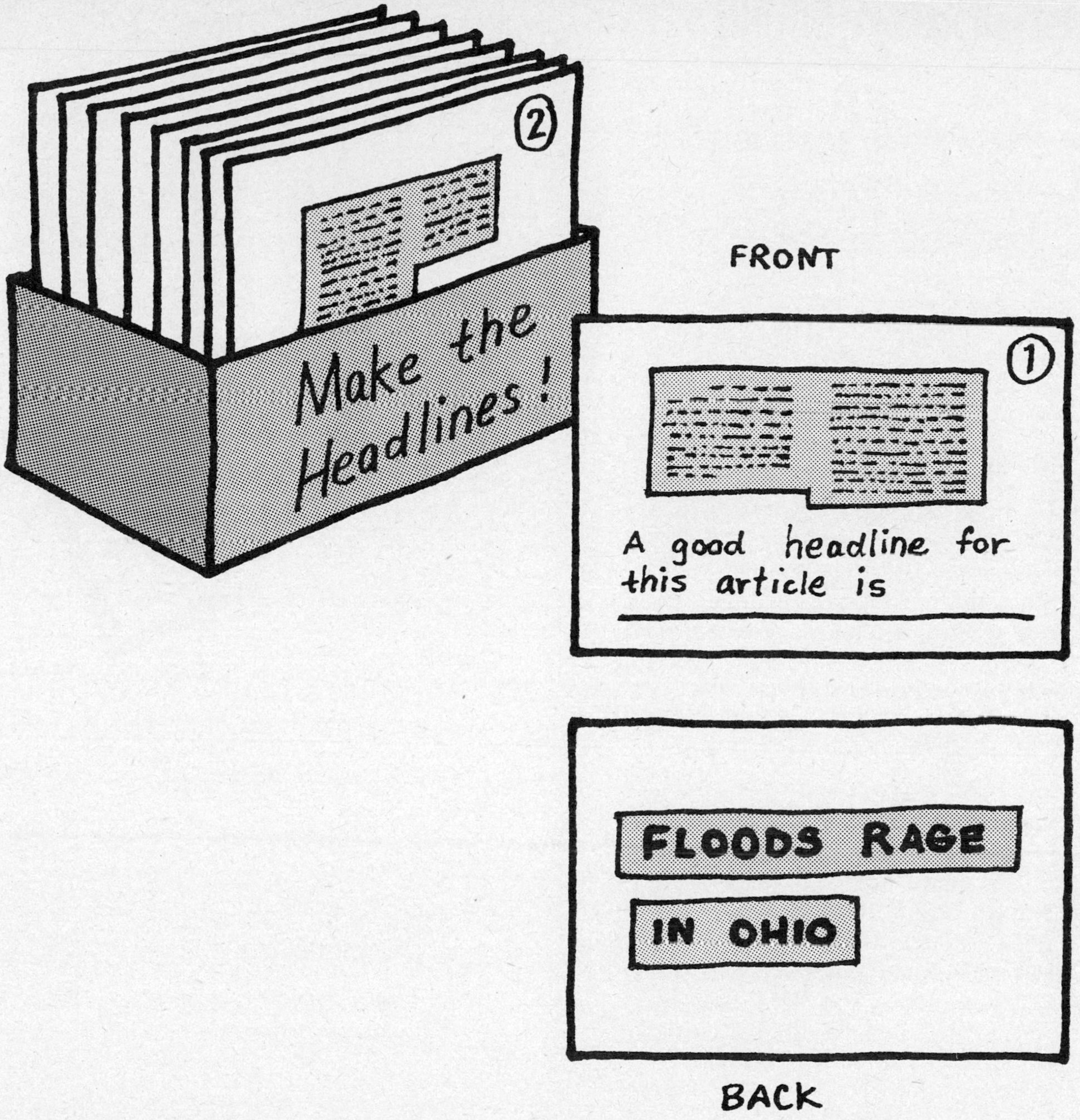

Make the Headlines!
②
FRONT
①
A good headline for this article is
FLOODS RAGE
IN OHIO
BACK

Comprehension Skills Center

Purpose: To provide experiences that reinforce comprehension skills.

Activity 5: Ad Concentration

Construction

Obtain forty 3" x 5" **index cards.** On one card paste a picture of a product or its label; on another card write or paste a slogan associated with that product. Materials can be obtained from **magazine advertisements.** In this way, prepare twenty pairs of cards. (The cards are blank on the back.) The cards may be covered with **contact** for durability.

Procedure

Two to six children can play the game. The cards are spread out face down on the table or floor. Each player in turn chooses any two cards and turns them face up. If the cards make a matched pair, the player picks them up and takes another turn. If the cards do not match, they are turned face down again in the same positions. Play continues until all cards have been removed; the player who has picked up the most cards is the winner.

Evaluation

This activity may be self-evaluated or evaluated by teacher observation or participation.

The Un-cola
7UP

VEGETABLE
SOUP
M'm! M'm! Good!

K2
Don't rub it in! Lift it out.

Comprehension Skills Center

Purpose: To provide experiences that reinforce comprehension skills.

Activity 6: Player Contrast

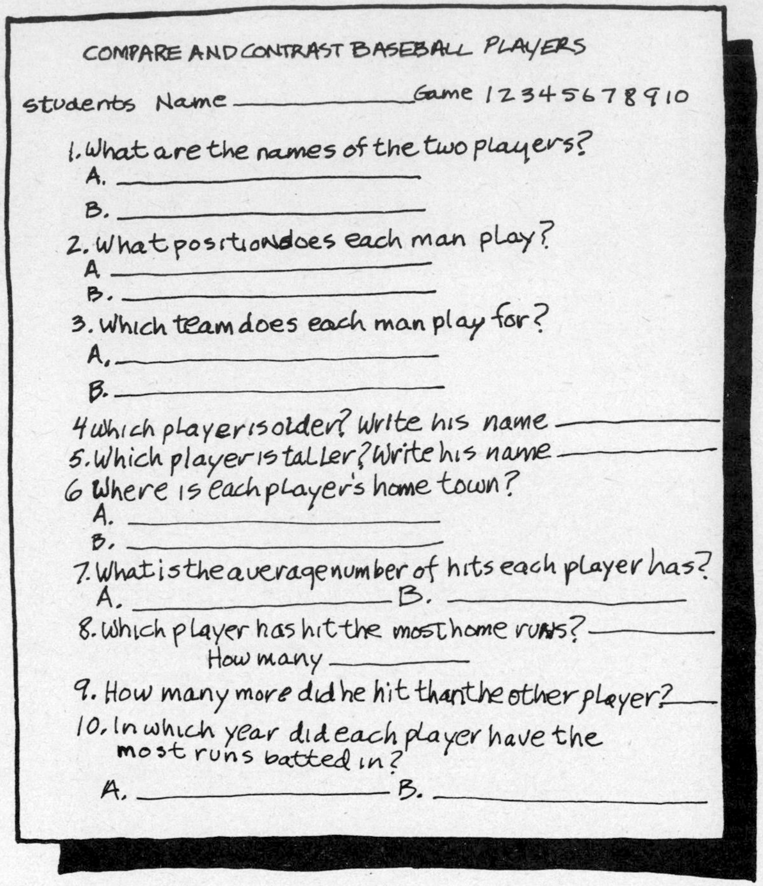
COMPARE AND CONTRAST BASEBALL PLAYERS

students Name ________ Game 1 2 3 4 5 6 7 8 9 10

1. What are the names of the two players?
A. ________
B. ________
2. What position does each man play?
A ________
B. ________
3. Which team does each man play for?
A. ________
B. ________
4 Which player is older? Write his name ________
5. Which player is taller? Write his name ________
6 Where is each player's home town?
A. ________
B. ________
7. What is the average number of hits each player has?
A. ________ B. ________
8. Which player has hit the most home runs? ________
How many ________
9. How many more did he hit than the other player? ________
10. In which year did each player have the most runs batted in?
A. ________ B. ________

Construction

Obtain 24 baseball, football, or basketball **cards**. (These can be purchased from variety stores or vending machines.) Make pockets to hold pairs of cards as shown from 5" x 8" plain **index cards,** folded and stapled 1½" from the bottom. Number each pocket and label it with the names of the two players whose cards are enclosed. Duplicate a large number of **answer sheets** from the sample given on page 250. (You will have to develop a modified answer sheet if the players are not baseball players.)

Procedure

The child chooses a pair of cards. He answers the questions on the answer sheet by studying the information printed on the cards.

Evaluation

An answer key can be provided to make this activity self-evaluating.

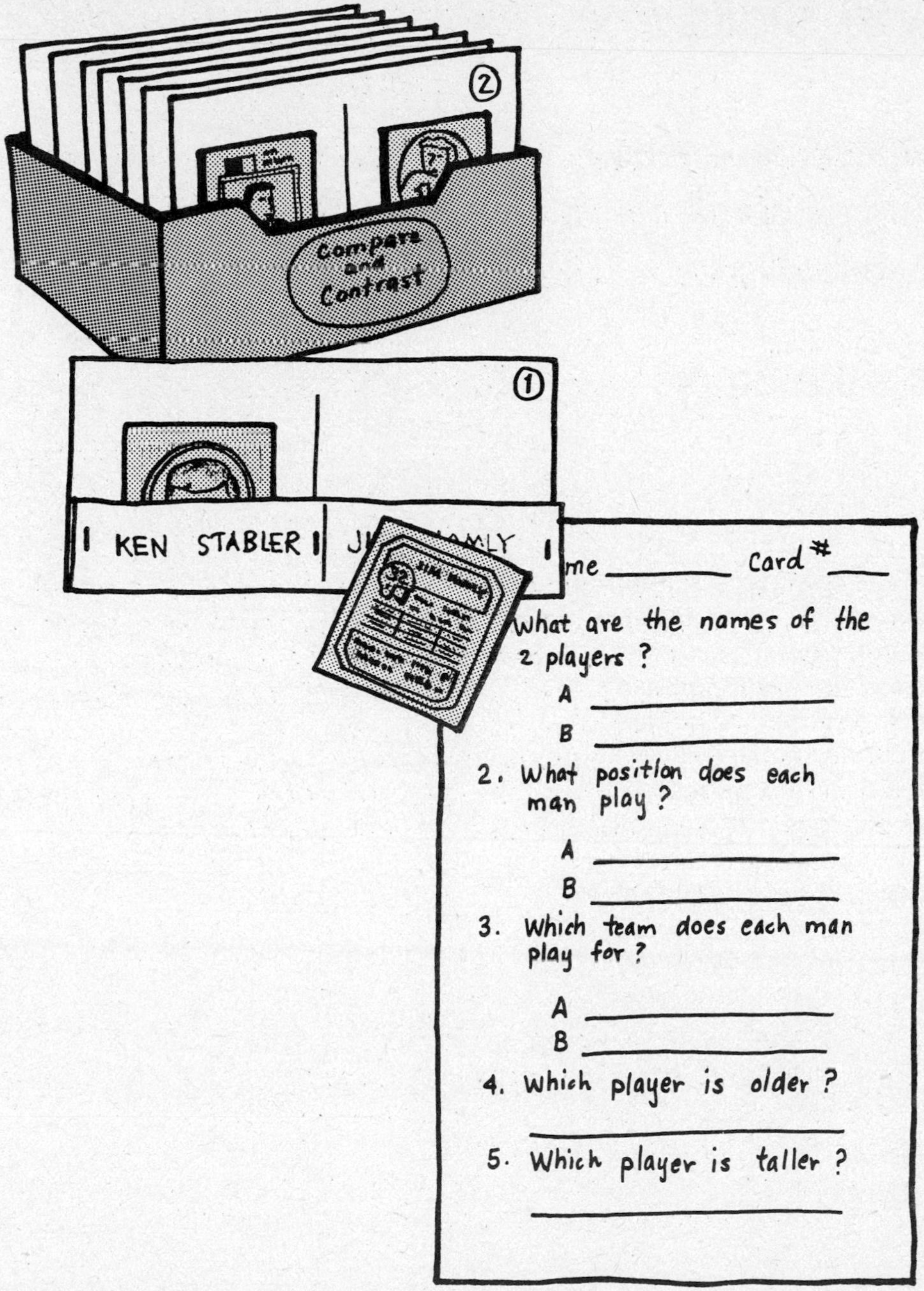

②
Compare and Contrast
①
KEN STABLER
me Card #
What are the names of the 2 players?
A
B
2. What position does each man play?
A
B
3. Which team does each man play for?
A
B
4. Which player is older?
5. Which player is taller?

Comprehension Skills Center

Purpose: To provide experiences that reinforce comprehension skills

Activity 7: What's the Story

Construction

Cut several pictures from **newspapers** and **magazines.** Mount each picture at the top of a sheet of **tagboard** or **construction paper.** On a 3" x 5" **index card,** write a paragraph describing the picture. Mount the card with **corner mounts** under the picture. Put the picture sheets in a **ring binder** or **manila folder.** Remove the paragraph cards from the pages and place them in a 5" x 7" **clasp envelope.** For a typical class, you will want to prepare about four such collections of pictures and paragraph cards (use some form of coding such as set numbers for easy refiling of cards with the proper collection of picture sheets).

Procedure

The child reads the paragraph card, finds the picture that is described, and fits the card in the corner mounts under the picture.

Evaluation

This activity can be made self-evaluating by putting codes on the back of the cards that indicate the picture with which they belong.

One day Billy thought of a way to have fun. He made a yellow kite.
Paragraph Matching
SET 1
SET 2
SET 3

Comprehension Skills Center

Purpose: To provide experiences that reinforce comprehension skills.

Activity 8: Question Match

Construction

Obtain sixty 3" x 5" **index cards.** Use thirty of them to make question cards. Each question card bears one of the following questions: WHO? WHAT? WHERE? WHEN? WHY? HOW? (Make five duplicate cards for each question.) Use the other thirty cards to make phrase cards. On five cards, write different phrases that tell "who." Make five phrase cards for each of the other questions. All of the cards have blank backs.

Procedure

Two to four children may play the game. Shuffle the deck of cards and place five cards face-up in the center of the table. If the first player can match any question card with a phrase card that answers it, he picks up that pair of cards and replaces them with two cards drawn from the deck. When he can find no more matching pairs, he draws one card from the deck. If he can find a match for it on the table, he picks up the pair and draws again. If he cannot find a match for the card he has drawn, he puts the drawn card face up with the others and the next player has a turn. If there are fewer than five cards face up when a player begins his turn, he begins by drawing enough cards to bring the total to five; he may then replace any pairs that he picks up before having to draw his first regular card from the deck. The game continues until all cards have been picked up; the player picking up the most cards is the winner.

Evaluation

This activity may be evaluated by teacher observation or participation. Each player should identify each matching pair aloud, so that students may participate in group evaluation as the game progresses.

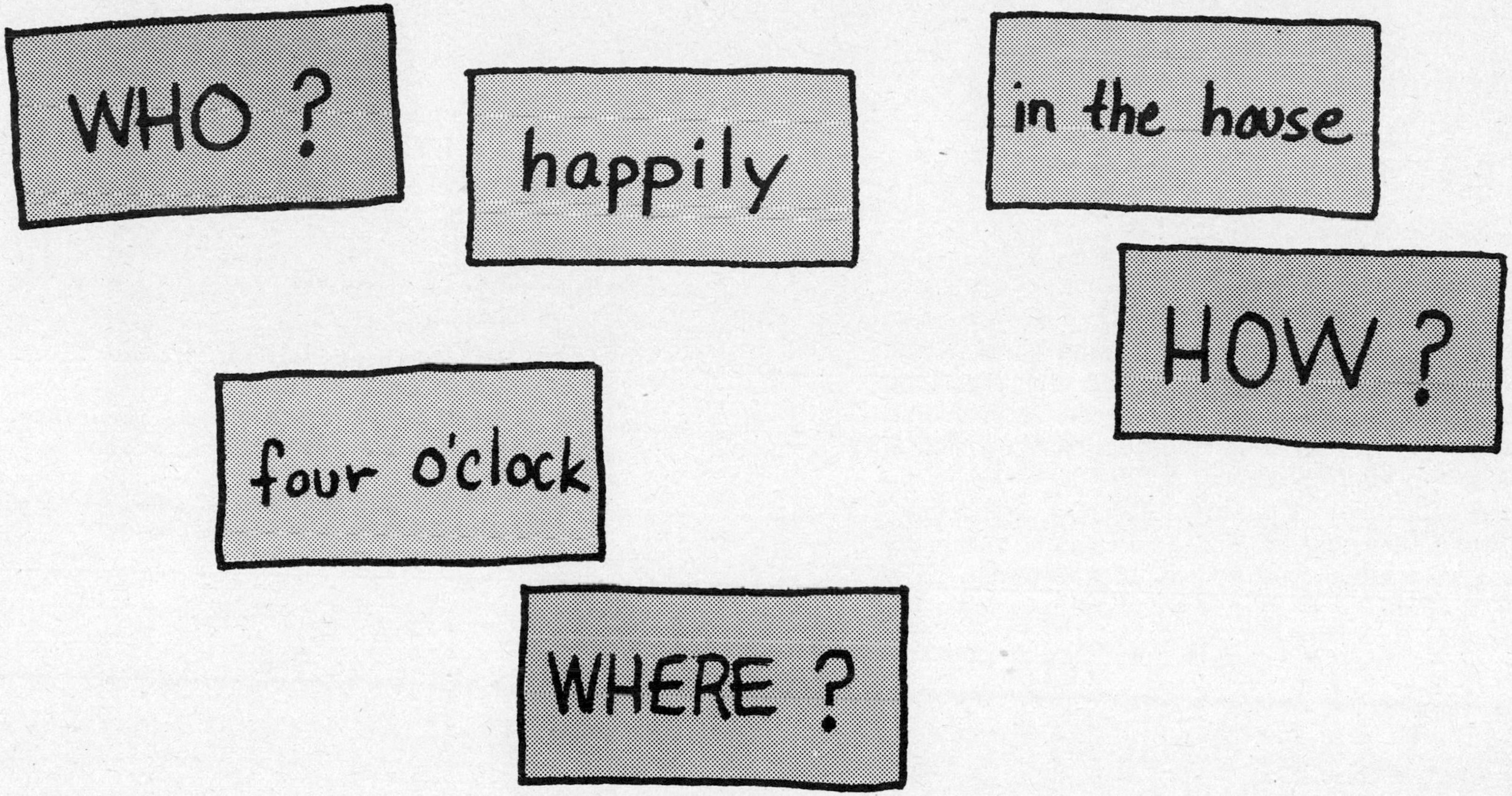
WHO ?
happily
in the house
HOW ?
four o'clock
WHERE ?

Tall Tale Center

Purpose: To provide opportunities to read and enjoy tall tales.

Activity 1: Viewing Station

TASK CARD
1. What does exaggeration mean?
2. Who was Paul Bunyan?
3. Write three examples of exaggeration in this story.

Construction

Build the carrel from an 18" x 22" piece of **cardboard** and two 11" x 18" pieces of cardboard for the sides. Use white **tagboard** to make a viewing screen on the front of the center panel. The side panels and the back of the center panel can be covered with colored **tagboard** and decorated if desired. If clear **contact** is used for durability, do not put the contact over the viewing screen. Hinge the panels with **Mystik tape.** Obtain a **filmstrip** showing a tall tale and a **filmstrip projector.** If desired, prepare **task cards** asking questions about the filmstrip. Provide **pencils** and **writing paper.**

Procedure

Children view the filmstrip. They write down answers to questions asked orally or given on task cards.

Evaluation

This activity may be evaluated through teacher observation or through correction of the written answers.

TASK CARD
1. What does exaggeration mean?
2. Who was Paul Bunyan?
3. Write three examples of exaggeration in this story.

Tall Tale Center

Purpose: To provide opportunities to read and enjoy tall tales.

Activity 2: Creative Writing Station

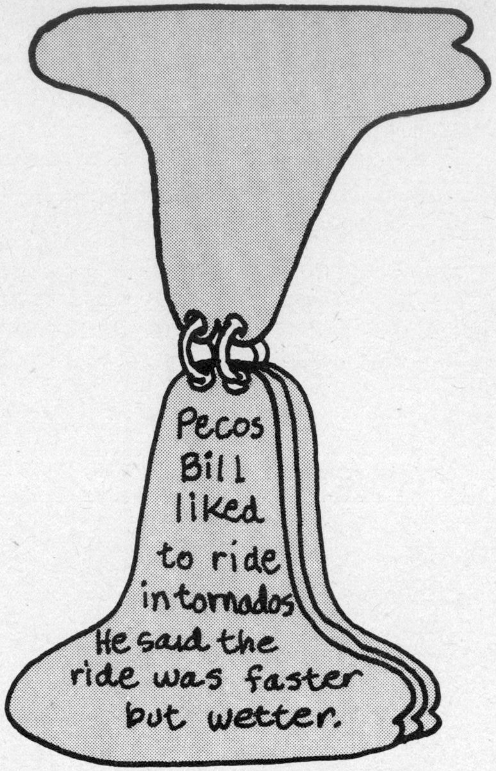

Construction

Make the carrel from **cardboard, tagboard,** and **Mystik tape.** On the left side of the carrel, provide **"story starter" cards** similar to those described for the Fairy Tale Center (see page 92) or the **"story starter" wheels** described as Activity 3 for this center. On the right side of the carrel, provide shape patterns made by mounting the pictures on pages 251–255 on heavy **cardboard** and cutting around the pictures. Provide **pencils, writing paper, construction paper, scissors,** and **paper fasteners.**

Procedure

The child writes a tall tale; if he wishes he can use a "story starter" to get an idea for his tale. He then chooses one of the shape patterns appropriate to his story and traces the pattern on sheets of writing paper. He copies his story within the shapes and cuts them out. He then makes a shaped cover for his story from construction paper, colors the picture on the cover, and fastens the book together with a paper fastener.

Evaluation

The teacher evaluates the finished stories.

Write a story
1.
TALL TALES
Shape Books

Tall Tale Center

Purpose: To provide opportunities to read and enjoy tall tales.

Activity 3: Story Starter Wheels

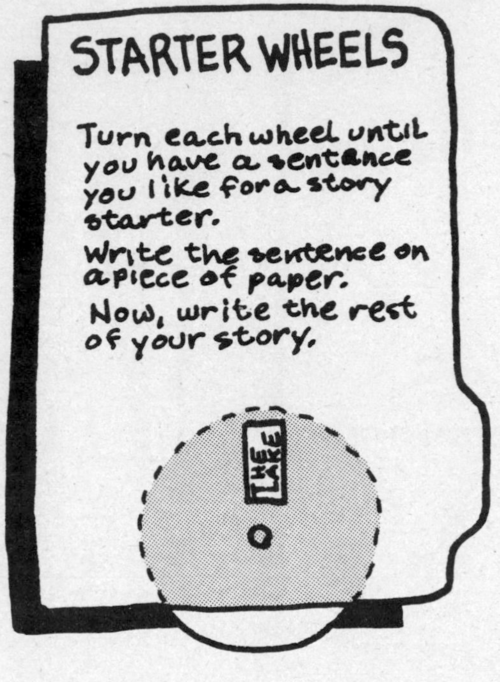

STARTER WHEELS
Turn each wheel until you have a sentence you like for a story starter.
Write the sentence on a piece of paper.
Now, write the rest of your story.
THE LAKE

Construction

In a **manila file folder,** cut three 2" x ¾" windows as shown. Cut three **tagboard** circles of 5" diameter. Use **paper fasteners** to mount the circles behind the windows in the folder as shown. Use felt-tip pen to write instructions on the folder. On the top wheel write noun phrases. On the middle wheel write verb phrases. On the last wheel write prepositional phrases and/or objects. Prepare three such folders using different words and phrases on the wheels.

Procedure

The student follows the instructions on the folder. This activity can be used as a part of the Creative Writing Station (Activity 2).

Evaluation

The teacher evaluates the activity by correcting the stories.

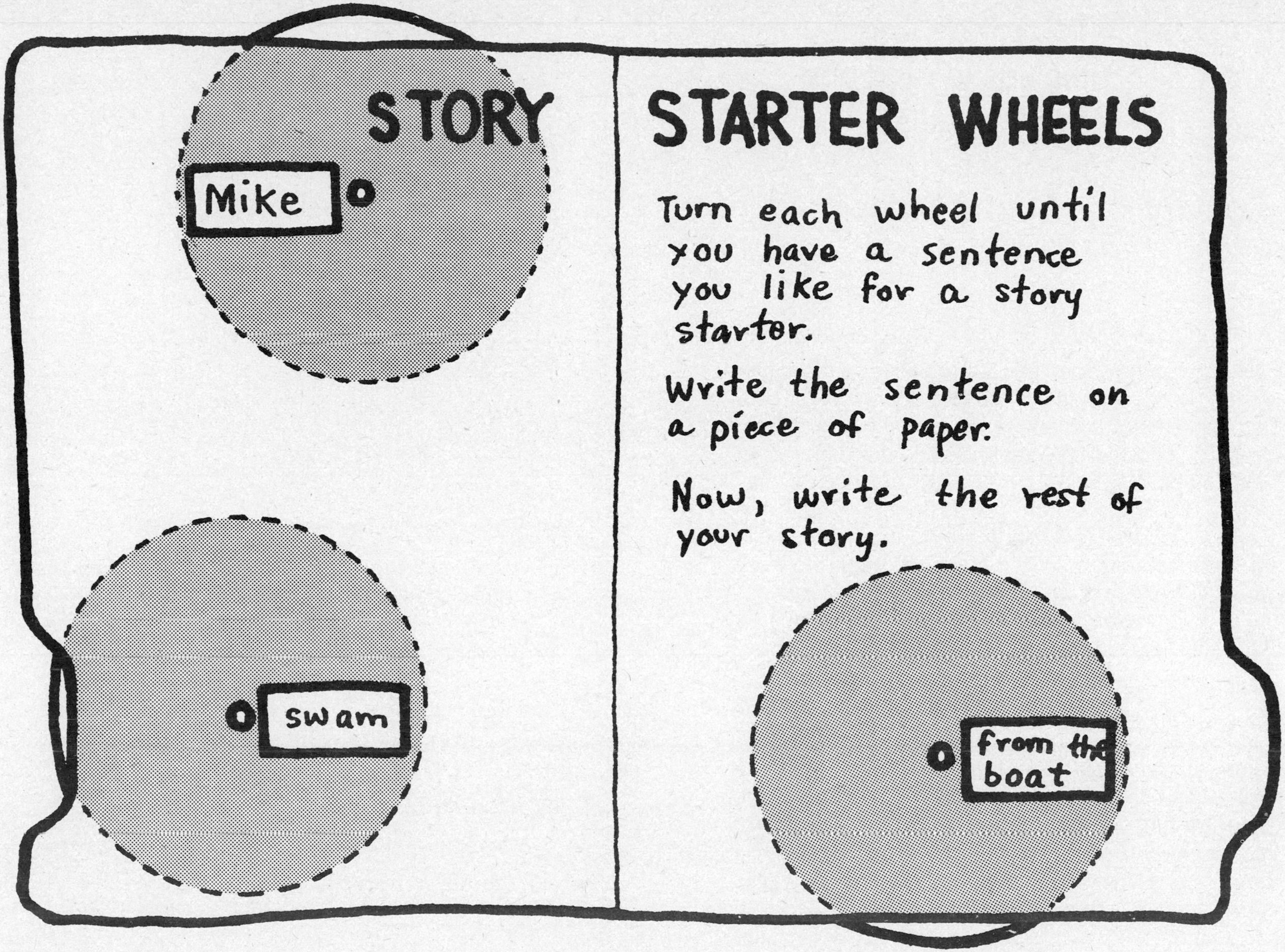
STORY STARTER WHEELS
Mike
swam
from the boat
Turn each wheel until you have a sentence you like for a story starter.
Write the sentence on a piece of paper.
Now, write the rest of your story.

Tall Tale Center

Purpose: To provide opportunities to read and enjoy tall tales.

Activity 4: Game Station

Construction

Make the game board from a large sheet of **tagboard,** backed with **cardboard** and covered with clear **contact.** Make three pocket windows as shown from **tagboard** or **construction paper.** Prepare a number of **word strips** that will slide through the pocket windows. The strips should be designed so that one word will be visible through the front window, while the definition of the word is visible through the back window. Provide a **die** and three **player markers.**

Procedure

Three students can play the game. Each inserts a word strip in his pocket window. The players roll the die to determine the order of play. The first player moves the first word into position in his window. He pronounces the word and gives its definition. If he is correct, he rolls the die and moves the corresponding number of spaces. If he is incorrect, he loses his turn. On his next turn, he will look at the next word on his strip. The first player to reach the finish line is the winner.

Evaluation

The definitions seen through the back window provide self-evaluation. Further evaluation may be made through teacher observation or participation.

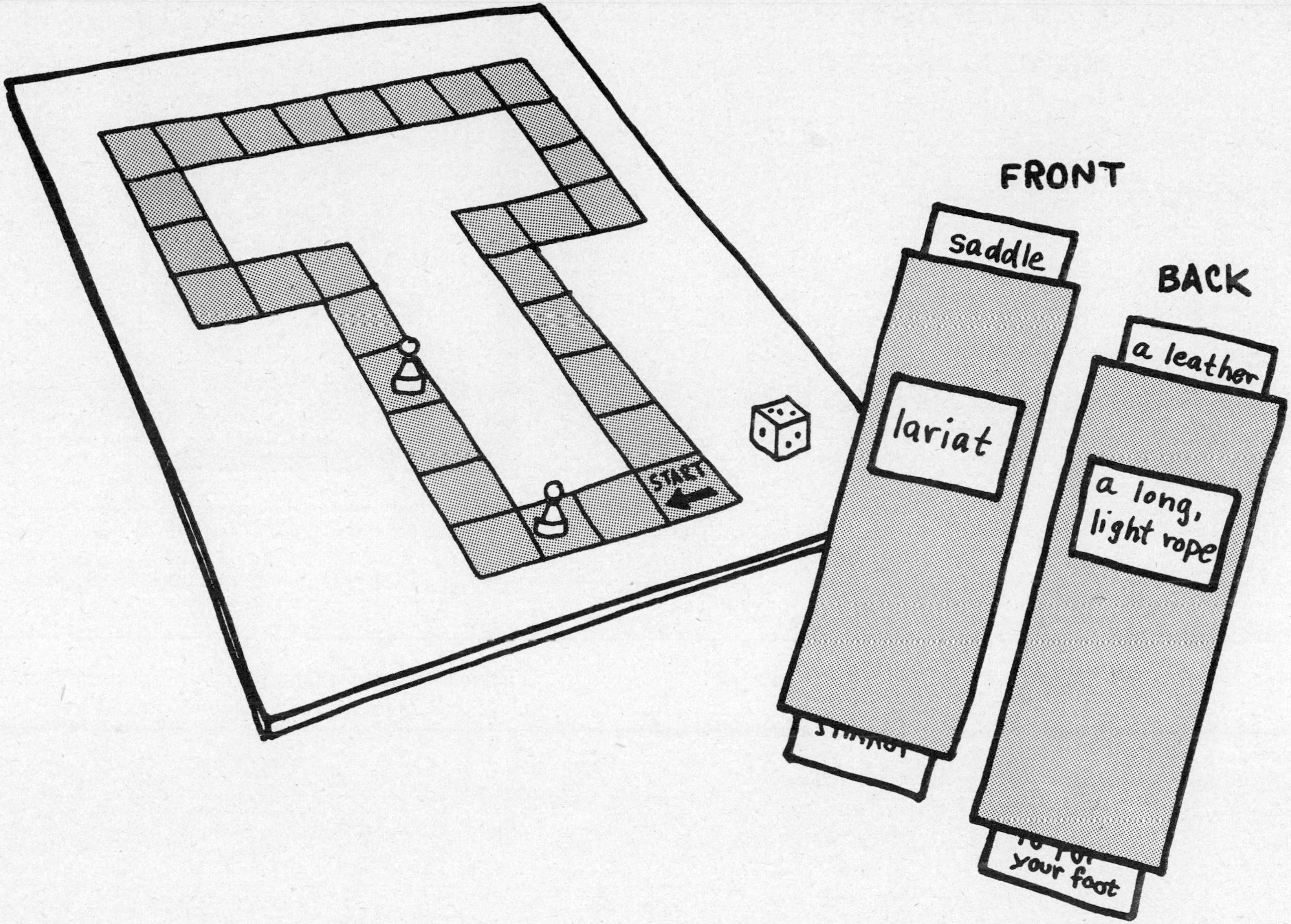
START
FRONT
saddle
lariat
BACK
a leather
a long, light rope
your foot

Tall Tale Center

Purpose: To provide opportunities to read and enjoy tall tales.

Activity 5: Art Station

Construction

Prepare a number of **task cards.** Each task card contains a brief paragraph describing a scene from a tall tale. Provide **pencils, crayons,** and **construction paper.**

Procedure

The child chooses a task card. He then draws a picture illustrating the scene described on the card.

Evaluation

Evaluation can be made through teacher observation or through study of the pictures produced.

High up on
the mountai
ART
TASK
CARDS
ONS
CRAYONS

Tall Tale Center

Purpose: To provide opportunities to read and enjoy tall tales.

Activity 6: Free Reading Station

Construction

Provide a number of **books** containing tall tales. This station can be furnished with a **table and chairs,** a comfortable **couch or chair,** or a **rug and pillows.** Do your best to provide an inviting environment for reading enjoyment.

Procedure

The child chooses a book to read.

Evaluation

No evaluation is necessary for this activity. Most of the other activities in this center serve as evaluations of the student's progress in reading tall tales.

READING
IS FUN
LAND OF OZ

6

INTERMEDIATE CENTERS

Mathematics

Multiplication Center

Activity 1: Multiplication Arrays
Activity 2: Football Practice
Activity 3: Evil Eye
Activity 4: Number Patterns
Activity 5: Light Boards

Geometry Center

Activity 1: Geoboards
Activity 2: Puzzle Station
Activity 3: Geometric Art
Activity 4: Angle Station
Activity 5: Coordinate Geometry

Metric Center

Activity 1: Equivalency Station
Activity 2: Millimetre Mouse
Activity 3: Linear Measurement Station
Activity 4: Liquid Measurement Station
Activity 5: Weighing Station

Multiplication Center

Purpose: To provide reinforcement activities for multiplication facts.

Activity 1: Multiplication Arrays

Construction

Duplicate a number of copies of the **Facts Table** on page 256. Provide these along with **construction paper,** a **box** of ½" **squares** cut from construction paper, **pencils, glue** or **paste,** and **yarn.** Prepare a **task card** or poster as shown.

Procedure

The child makes a 45-page booklet and decorates the cover. He pastes a copy of the Facts Table inside the front cover. On the pages of the booklet he makes arrays for the multiplication facts, marking off each fact on the table as he completes the corresponding array. Several days will be needed to complete this activity.

Evaluation

The activity can be evaluated by teacher observation of the booklets and by tests covering the multiplication facts.

TASK CARD

- Make a multiplication scrapbook. Paste a "facts table" on the inside cover to keep track of your progress.
- Make arrays for the facts from 2×2 to 10×10. You will need 45 pages.
- Your page that shows 2×3=6 will also show that 3×2=6. See the sample scrapbook at the station.
- Decorate the cover of your book.

Multiplication Center

Purpose: To provide reinforcement activities for multiplication facts.

Activity 2: Football Practice

Construction

Prepare a deck of at least 48 **problem cards;** each card has a multiplication problem on one side and the answer on the other side. Prepare a game board as shown on colored **tagboard;** the dashed rectangles shown should be the size of the problem cards. Use **pictures** of football players cut from magazines to decorate the board. Mount the board on **cardboard** and cover with clear **contact.** Provide a pair of **dice.**

Procedure

Two to six children may play the game. Deal all the problem cards out (problem side up) onto the spaces on the board (there should be at least four cards on each space). The first player rolls the dice, adds the numbers shown on the two dice, and takes the top problem card from the stack with that number. For example, if he rolls two and one on the dice, he takes a card from stack 3. The child reads the problem aloud and gives the answer. If he is correct, he keeps the card. If his answer is incorrect, the card is returned to the bottom of the stack from which it came. The next player then has a turn. If there are no cards left in the stack whose number a player rolls, that player loses his turn. The game ends when all cards have been removed from the board; the player with the most cards wins.

Evaluation

This activity is self-evaluating; answers are on the backs of the problem cards.

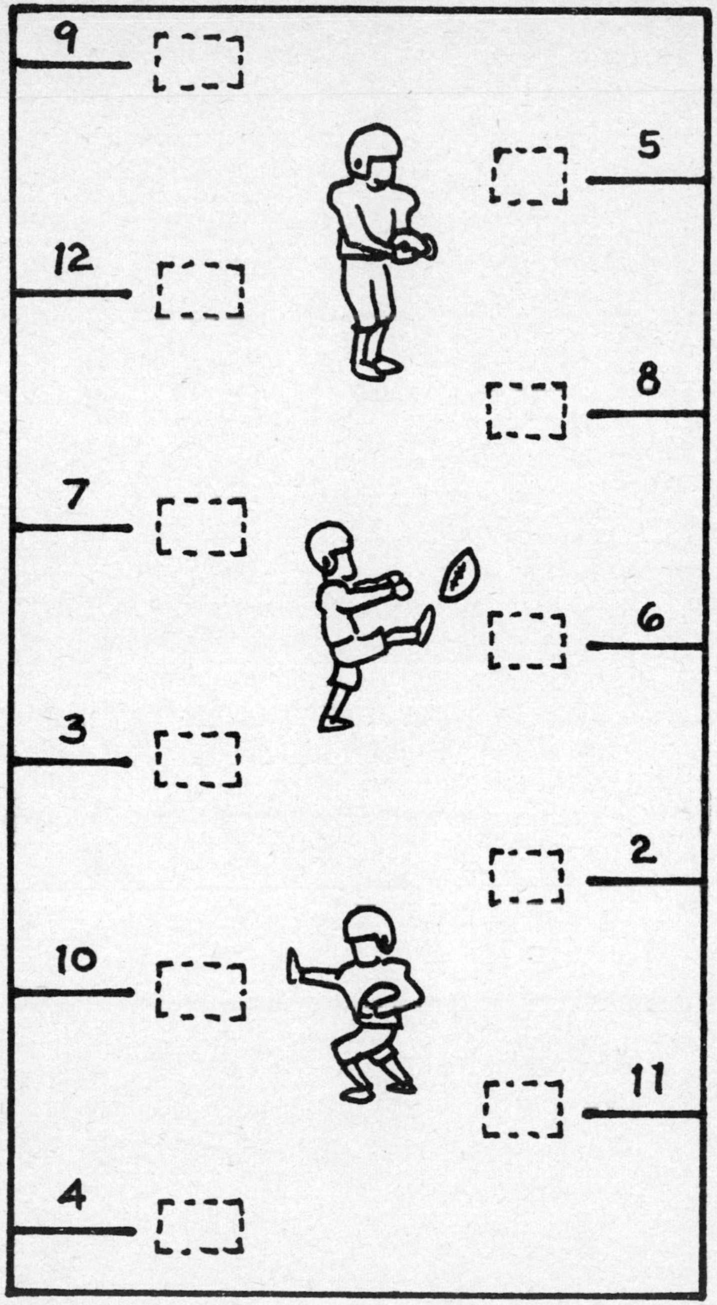
9
5
12
8
7
6
3
2
10
11
4

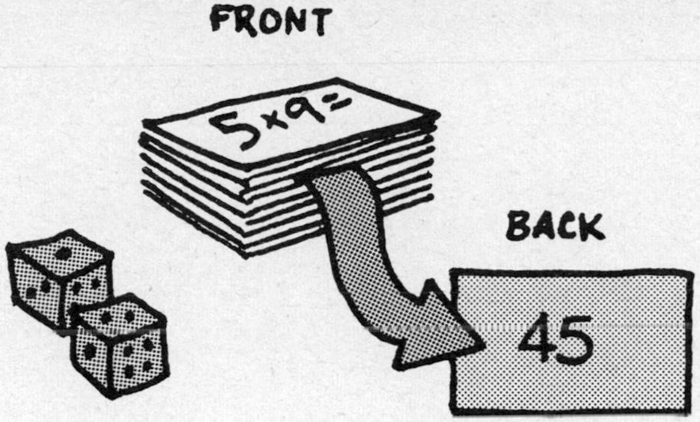
FRONT
5×9=
BACK
45

Multiplication Center

Purpose: To provide reinforcement activities for multiplication facts.

Activity 3: Evil Eye

Construction

Use the pattern on page 258 to make the spinner board from **cardboard** or **tagboard.** Cut two spinner arms from **tagboard** and attach with **paper fasteners** or **brads.** Prepare a number of copies of the **score sheet** shown on page 257.

Procedure

Any number of players may participate. Each player has a score sheet. Someone spins the two spinners; the numbers indicated form a multiplication problem. For example, if one spinner stops at 6 and the other at 9, the problem is 6 x 9 = ? Each player records the problem and the answer on his score sheet. Seven double spins (seven problems) make up a game. Any player may choose to drop out at any time after the first problem, but he must announce this before the next spin. At the end of the game, each player adds up the problem answers to find his score; he does not include any problems after the point where he dropped out. If the spinner stops at the Evil Eye, all players who have not dropped out receive a score of zero for that game, and the game is over. Three games are played. All players are back in the game for the first spin of a new game. After the three games, players compute their grand total score. The highest score wins.

Evaluation

The group can check the score sheet of the winner for mistakes. Evaluation can also be made through teacher observation.

EVIL
EYE
9
2
8
3
7
4
6
5
9
8
3
7
4
6
5

Multiplication Center

Purpose: To provide reinforcement activities for multiplication facts.

Activity 4: Number Patterns

Construction

Duplicate the **grid patterns** on pages 259 and 260. For each student, you will need nine copies of the numbered pattern and nine copies of the blank pattern. Provide **construction paper, scissors, paste,** and **paper fasteners.**

Procedure

On a blank grid pattern, the child counts out a number pattern from left to right and from top to bottom, marking each square in the pattern. For example, if he is working on the pattern of 9s, he counts 1, 2, 3, 4, 5, 6, 7, 8, 9, and marks the ninth square with an X. He then begins again with 1 on the next square. When he has finished, the child cuts out each of the squares he has marked. He then pastes the blank pattern over a numbered pattern and labels the page with the number pattern he has used. He repeats the process for each number pattern from 2s through 10s. He then makes covers from construction paper and binds his patterns together in a booklet.

Evaluation

This activity is self-evaluating, because if the work is correct the multiplication table for the number will be given by the numbers showing through the holes cut in the pattern.

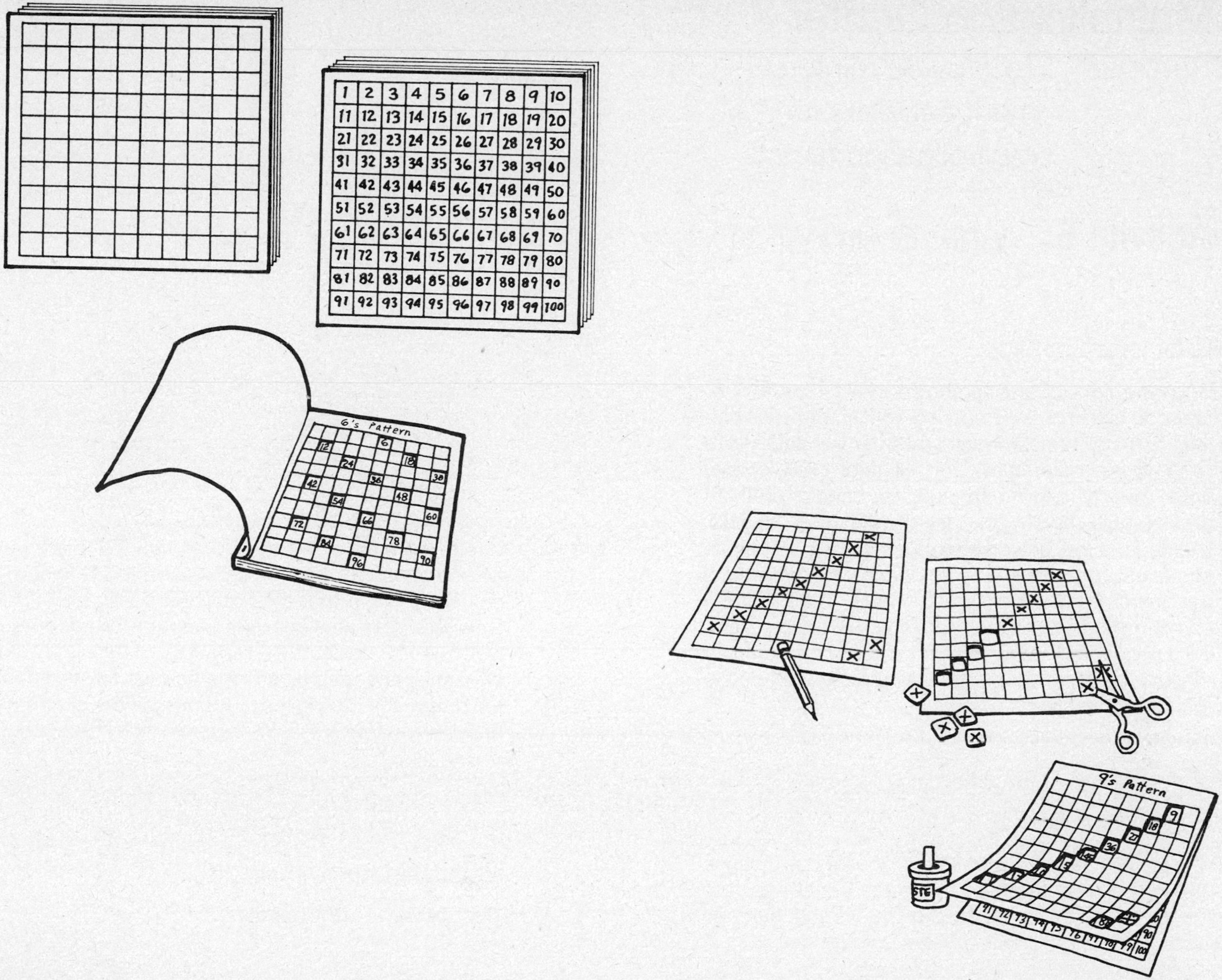
1 2 3 4 5 6 7 8 9 10
11 12 13 14 15 16 17 18 19 20
21 22 23 24 25 26 27 28 29 30
31 32 33 34 35 36 37 38 39 40
41 42 43 44 45 46 47 48 49 50
51 52 53 54 55 56 57 58 59 60
61 62 63 64 65 66 67 68 69 70
71 72 73 74 75 76 77 78 79 80
81 82 83 84 85 86 87 88 89 90
91 92 93 94 95 96 97 98 99 100
6's Pattern
9's Pattern

Multiplication Center

Purpose: To provide reinforcement activities for multiplication facts.

Activity 5: Light Boards

Construction

Build the light board as shown in a 24" x 24" x 6" **plywood box.** You will need a 6-volt lantern-type **battery,** a 6-volt panel-mount **light bulb,** insulated **wire** (#12 single conductor), ten **alligator clips,** twenty **bolts,** twenty **acorn-cap nuts,** a **handle** (cabinet drawer pull), and twenty **file-drawer label holders.** Duplicate a set of **worksheets** containing ten multiplication problems. In the holders on the left side of the board, put the problem numbers. In the holders on the right side, put the problem answers in scrambled sequence. Then "wire" the back of the board so that the wire from each problem number is clipped to the correct answer.

Procedure

The student takes a worksheet, does the problems, and writes his answers on the sheet. He then goes to the light board to check his work. He touches one wire to the problem number, the other to the answer he has chosen. If his answer is correct, the light will come on. (Note that the light board can easily be "rewired" and new answers inserted for each new worksheet. If desired, worksheets can be eliminated by putting the problems in the holders on the left of the board and having the student work the problems on writing paper.)

Evaluation

This activity is self-evaluating.

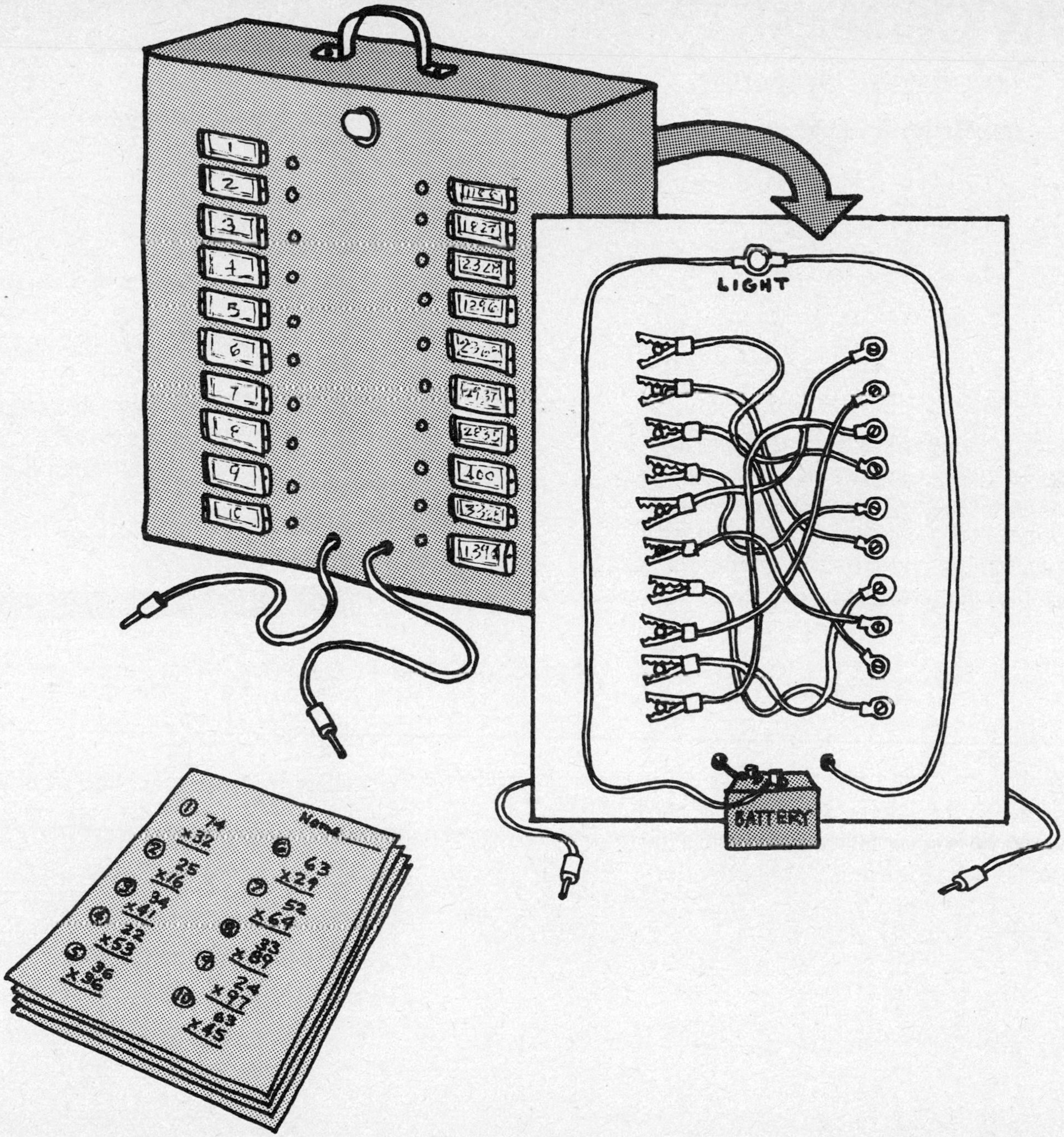
LIGHT
BATTERY

Geometry Center

Purpose: To provide activities relating to geometry.

Activity 1: Geoboards

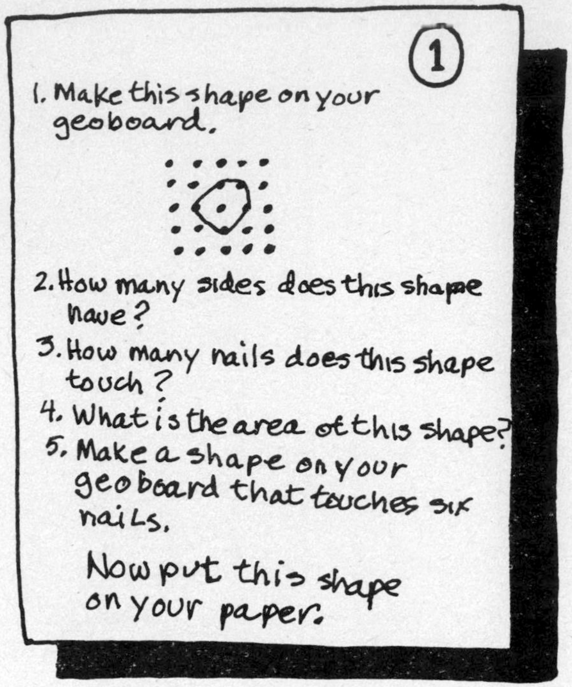
1
1. Make this shape on your geoboard.
2. How many sides does this shape have?
3. How many nails does this shape touch?
4. What is the area of this shape?
5. Make a shape on your geoboard that touches six nails.
Now put this shape on your paper.

Construction

Make six geoboards using a 1" x 6" **pine board,** cutting off six-inch lengths. Use twenty-five **nails** for each board, hammering them in about halfway as shown in the illustration. (They should be one inch apart, forming a square inch pattern.) Provide a supply of **rubber bands, paper,** and **pencils.**

Procedure

The child follows the directions on the task card (samples provided on pages 261–263), writing answers to the questions on the blank paper provided.

Evaluation

This activity may be evaluated by teacher correction of the written answers, or may be self-evaluated if answer keys are provided on the backs of the task cards.

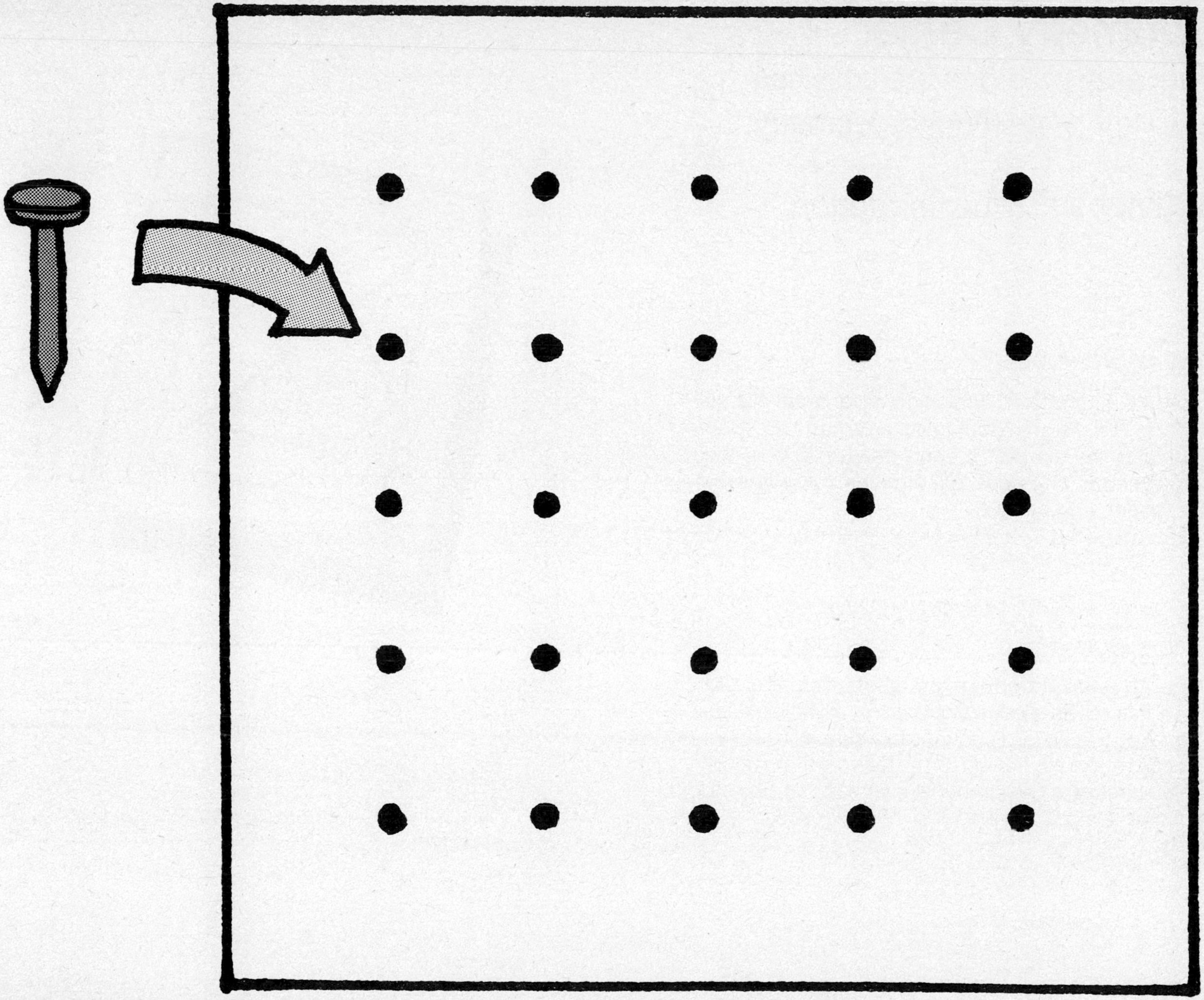

Geometry Center

Purpose: To provide activities relating to geometry.

Activity 2: Puzzle Station

Construction

Duplicate a number of copies of the **tangram puzzle** on page 264. Prepare four **task cards** (labeled "Can you make this shape?"), each bearing one of the shapes shown on pages 265 and 266. Provide **scissors, paper,** and **pencils.**

Procedure

The child takes a copy of the tangram puzzle and cuts it into seven pieces along the straight lines. He then takes a task card and tries to arrange the seven pieces to make the design on the task card. The child can also make a design of his own with the pieces, trace the design, and add it to the collection of task cards.

Evaluation

This activity may be evaluated through teacher observation.

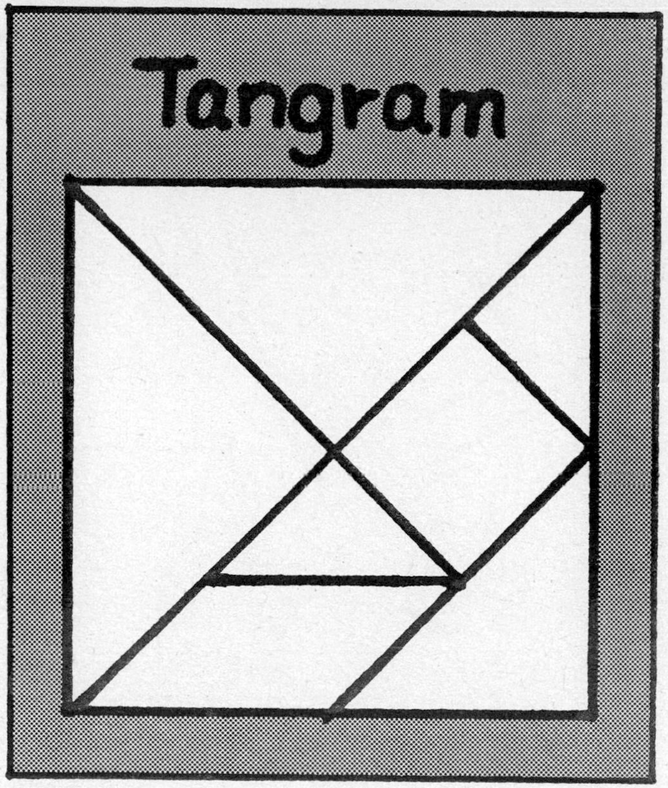
Tangram

Can you make these shapes?

Geometry Center

Purpose: To provide activitics relating to geometry.

Activity 3: Geometric Art

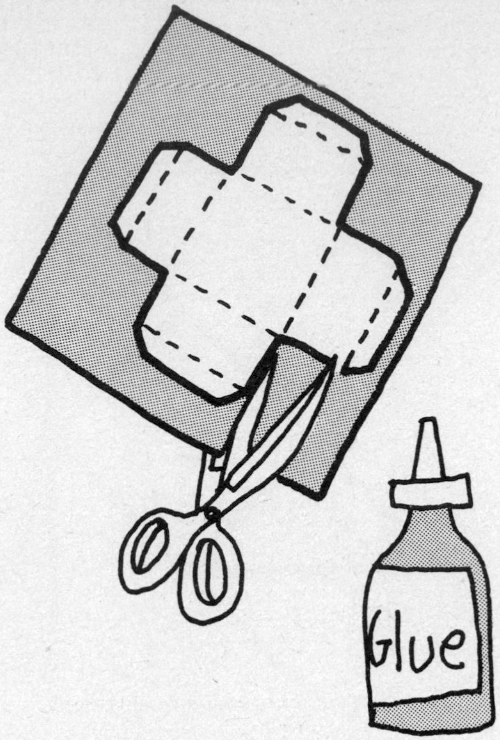

Construction

Duplicate a number of copies of the patterns shown on pages 267 and 268 on **construction paper**. Provide **scissors, glue,** and **crayons.**

Procedure

The student takes one of the patterns, colors it, and cuts out the shape along the solid lines. He then folds along the dashed lines and glues the tabs to make a solid geometric shape.

Evaluation

The student evaluates his own success in constructing the shape.

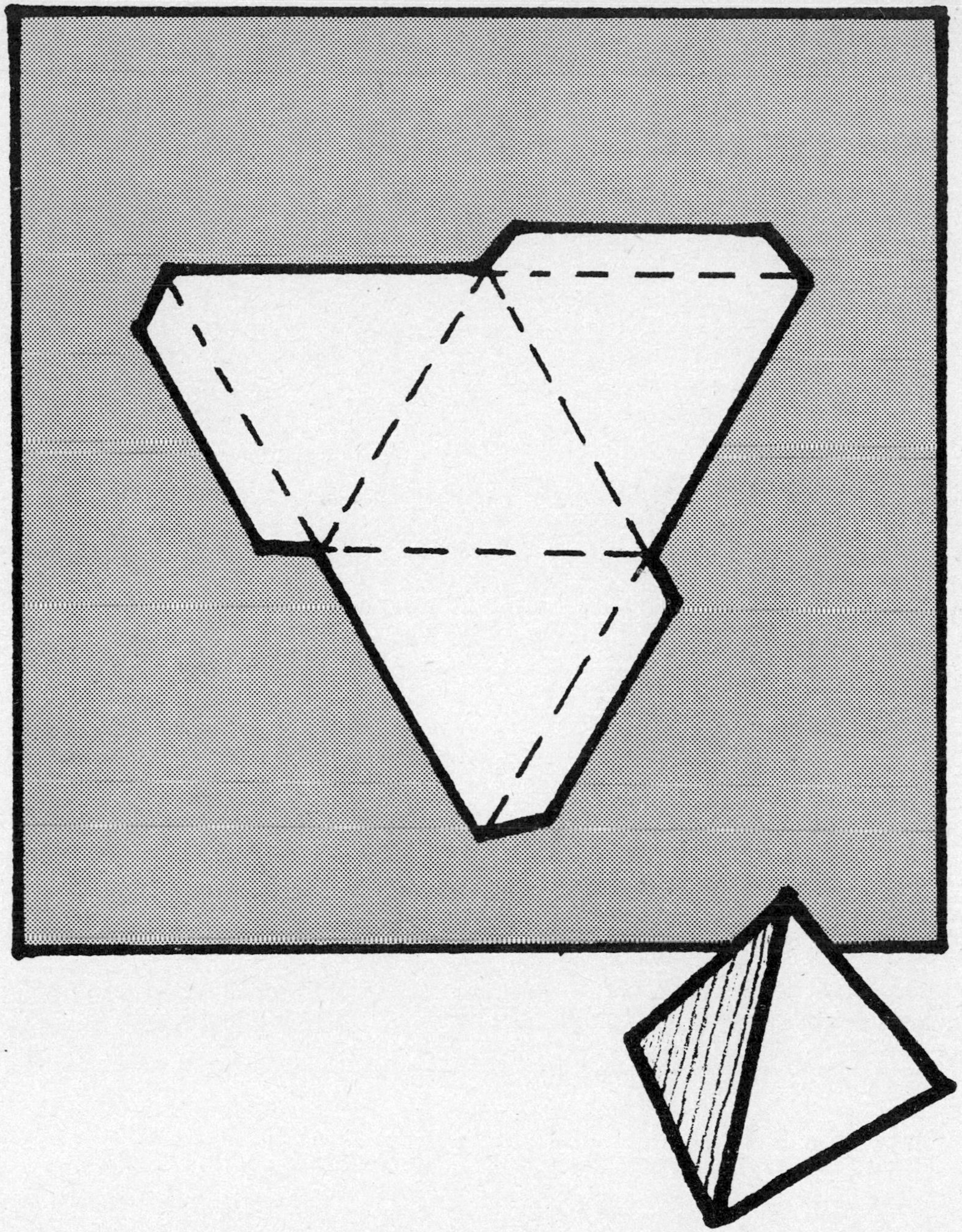

Geometry Center

Purpose: To provide activities relating to geometry.

Activity 4: Angle Station

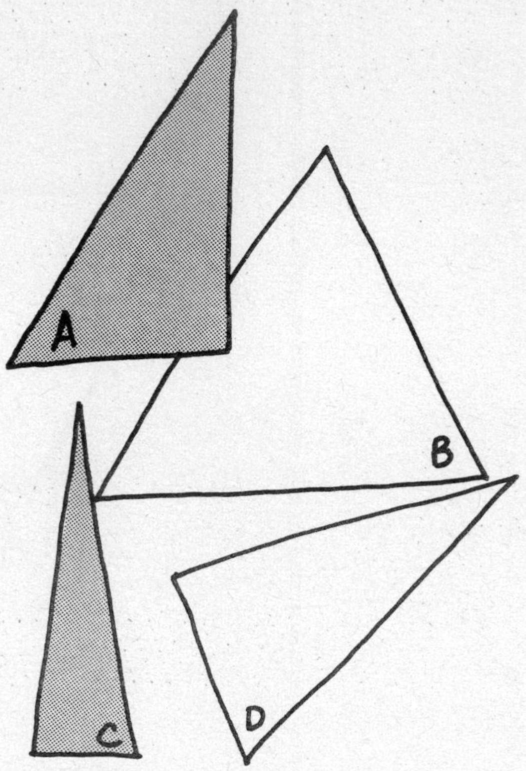

Construction

Duplicate the angle figures shown on pages 269 and 270 on **construction paper,** so that you have at least six complete sets of the eight figures (each set on a different color paper). Put each set of angles in a 9" x 12" **clasp envelope** and label the envelope by the color of the figures inside. Prepare a series of **task cards** asking questions about the angles. Provide paper, protractors, and **pencils.**

Procedure

Each child takes an envelope with a complete set of the eight figures. He chooses a task card, writing his answers to the questions on a sheet of paper.

Evaluation

This activity can be self-evaluating if answer keys are given on the backs of the task cards.

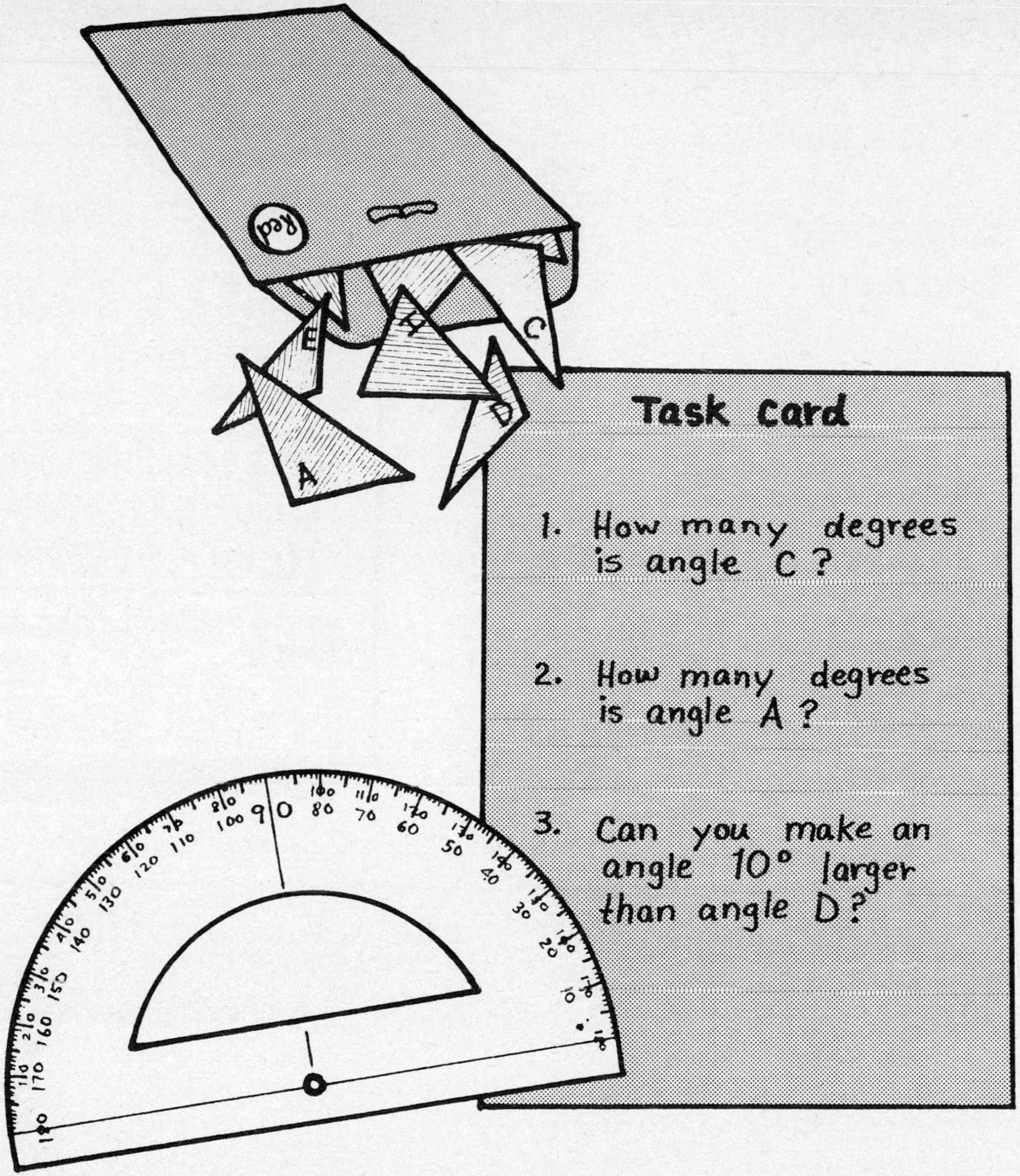
Red
E
C
D
A
Task Card
1. How many degrees is angle C?
2. How many degrees is angle A?
3. Can you make an angle 10° larger than angle D?

Geometry Center

Purpose: To provide activities relating to geometry.

Activity 5: Coordinate Geometry

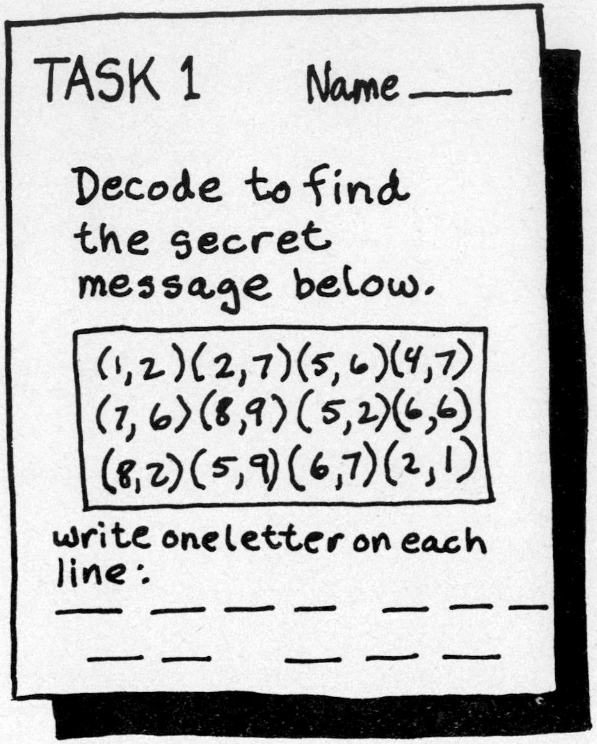

Construction

On sheets of **tagboard,** prepare six grids marked as shown. Cover with clear **contact.** Prepare a series of **task cards** containing secret messages encoded by giving the coordinates of each letter on the grid. For example:

(1,2) (2,7) (5,6) (4,7) | (7,6) (8,9) (5,2) | (6,6) (8,2) | (5,9) (6,7) (2,1)

Decoded, the message reads "MATH CAN BE FUN." Provide **pencils** and **paper.**

Procedure

The child takes a coordinate grid and a task card. He decodes the message and writes it on the paper. As a variation, he can encode secret messages of his own for classmates or the teacher to read.

Evaluation

This activity is self-evaluating.

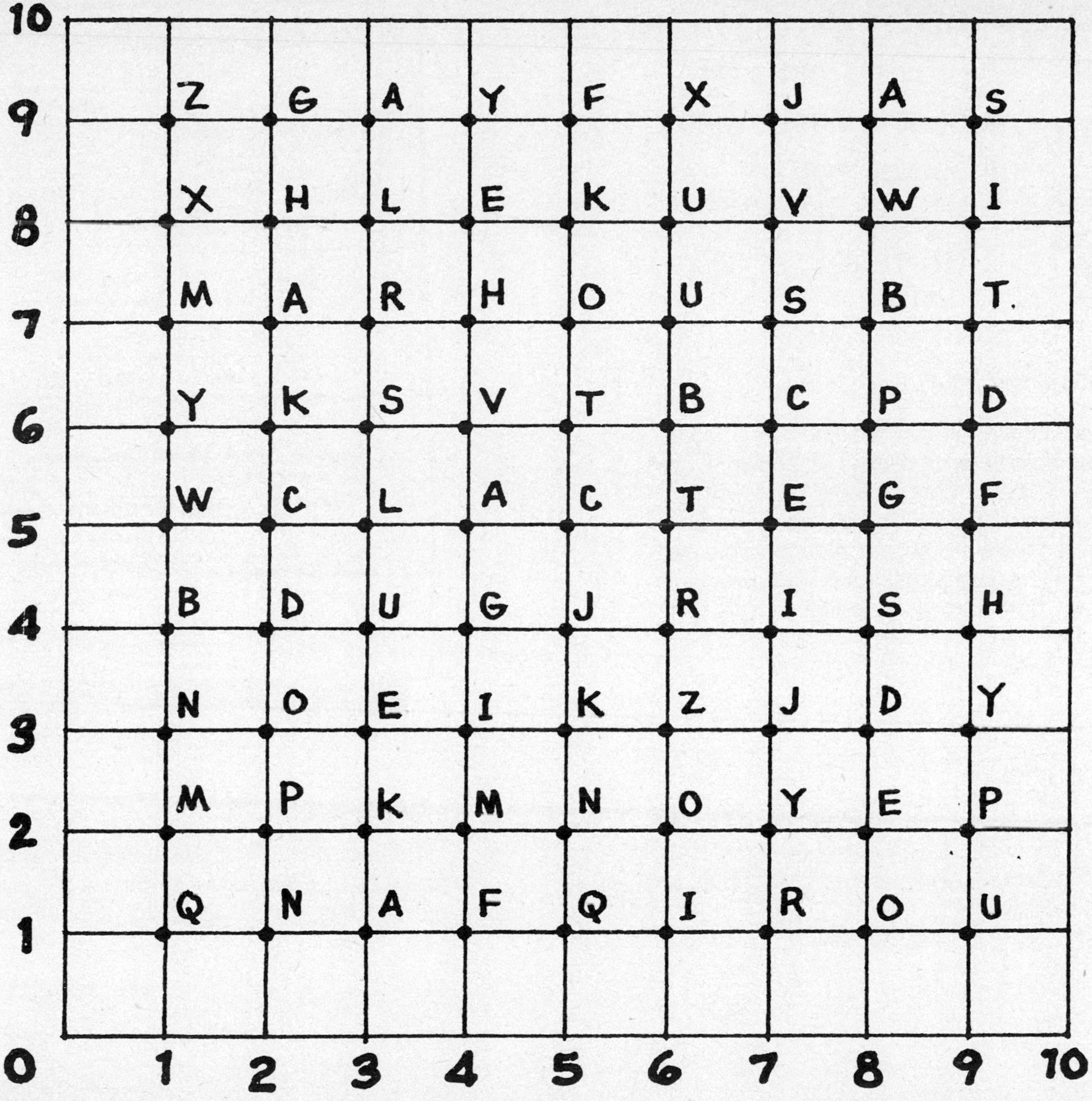
10
Z G A Y F X J A S
9
X H L E K U V W I
8
M A R H O U S B T.
7
Y K S V T B C P D
6
W C L A C T E G F
5
B D U G J R I S H
4
N O E I K Z J D Y
3
M P K M N O Y E P
2
Q N A F Q I R O U
1
0 1 2 3 4 5 6 7 8 9 10

Metric Center

Purpose: To provide reinforcement activities in metric measurement.

Activity 1: Equivalency Station

Construction

Prepare a wall chart as shown. On nine 3" x 5" cards, write the metric units and prefixes as shown. Cover each card with clear **contact** and put a strip of **magnetic tape** on the back. Use a strip of magnetic paper to make the board shown, with spaces to attach the cards. Prepare a task card with general instructions and duplicate a series of various worksheets (see the sample on page 271).

Procedure

The student first sets up the magnetic board for reference, using the wall chart as a source of information. He then selects a worksheet and writes his answers on it.

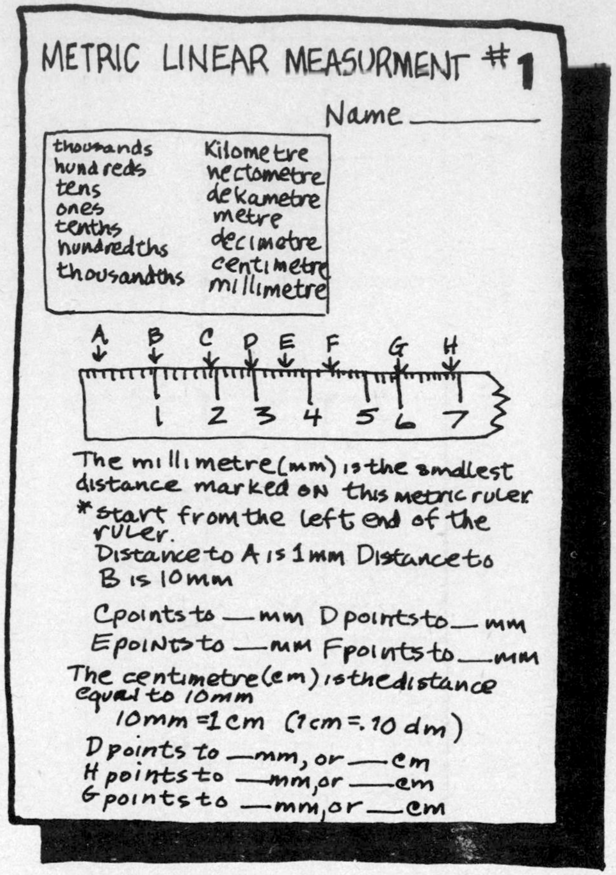

Evaluation

This activity can be evaluated through teacher correction of worksheets, or can be self-evaluated if answer keys are provided.

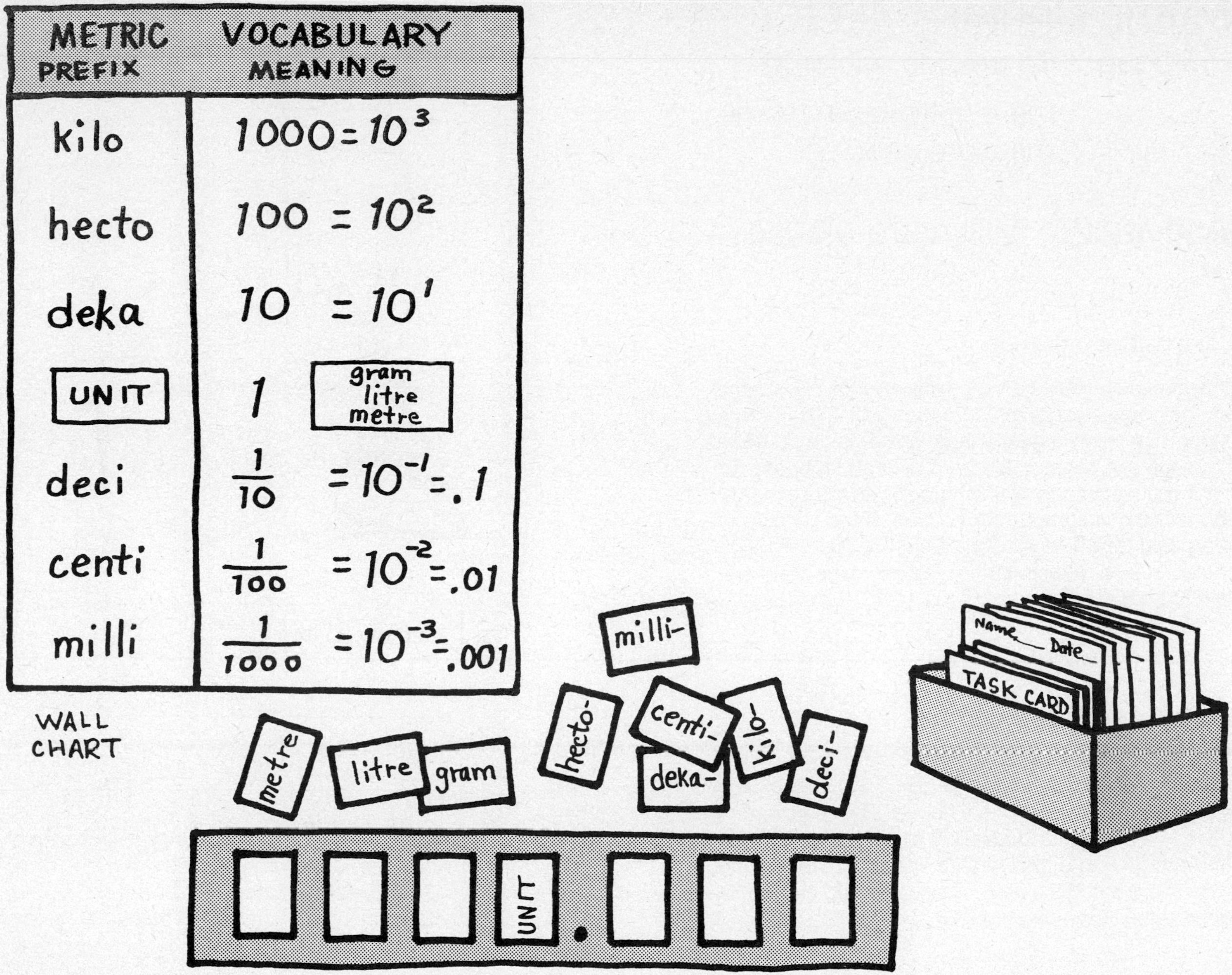
METRIC VOCABULARY
PREFIX
MEANING
kilo
1000 = 10^3
hecto
100 = 10^2
deka
10 = 10^1
UNIT
1
gram
litre
metre
deci
1/10 = 10^-1 = .1
centi
1/100 = 10^-2 = .01
milli
1/1000 = 10^-3 = .001
WALL CHART
milli-
metre
litre
gram
hecto-
centi-
deka-
kilo-
deci-
UNIT
Name___ Date___
TASK CARD

Metric Center

Purpose: To provide reinforcement activities in metric measurement.

Activity 2: Millimetre Mouse

Construction

Prepare the **bulletin board display** as shown (patterns for the houses are given on pages 272–278). Attach a short strip of **magnetic tape** in the circle on each house. Make seven mice from colored **tagboard.** To each mouse, attach a tail of **string** or **yarn** cut to one of the lengths written on the houses. Attach a strip of **magnetic tape** to the back of each mouse. Provide **metric rulers, paper, string, tailless mice,** and **unlabeled houses.**

Procedure

The student takes a mouse from the pocket on the bulletin board, measures its tail, and places the mouse "in" the appropriate house. After placing the mice in the proper houses, the student can cut a tail and attach it to a new mouse, measure the tail and write the length on a new house, and add his mouse and house to the display.

Evaluation

This activity can be evaluated by teacher observation, by students checking each other's work, or by color-coding or labeling the mice on the back for self-evaluation.

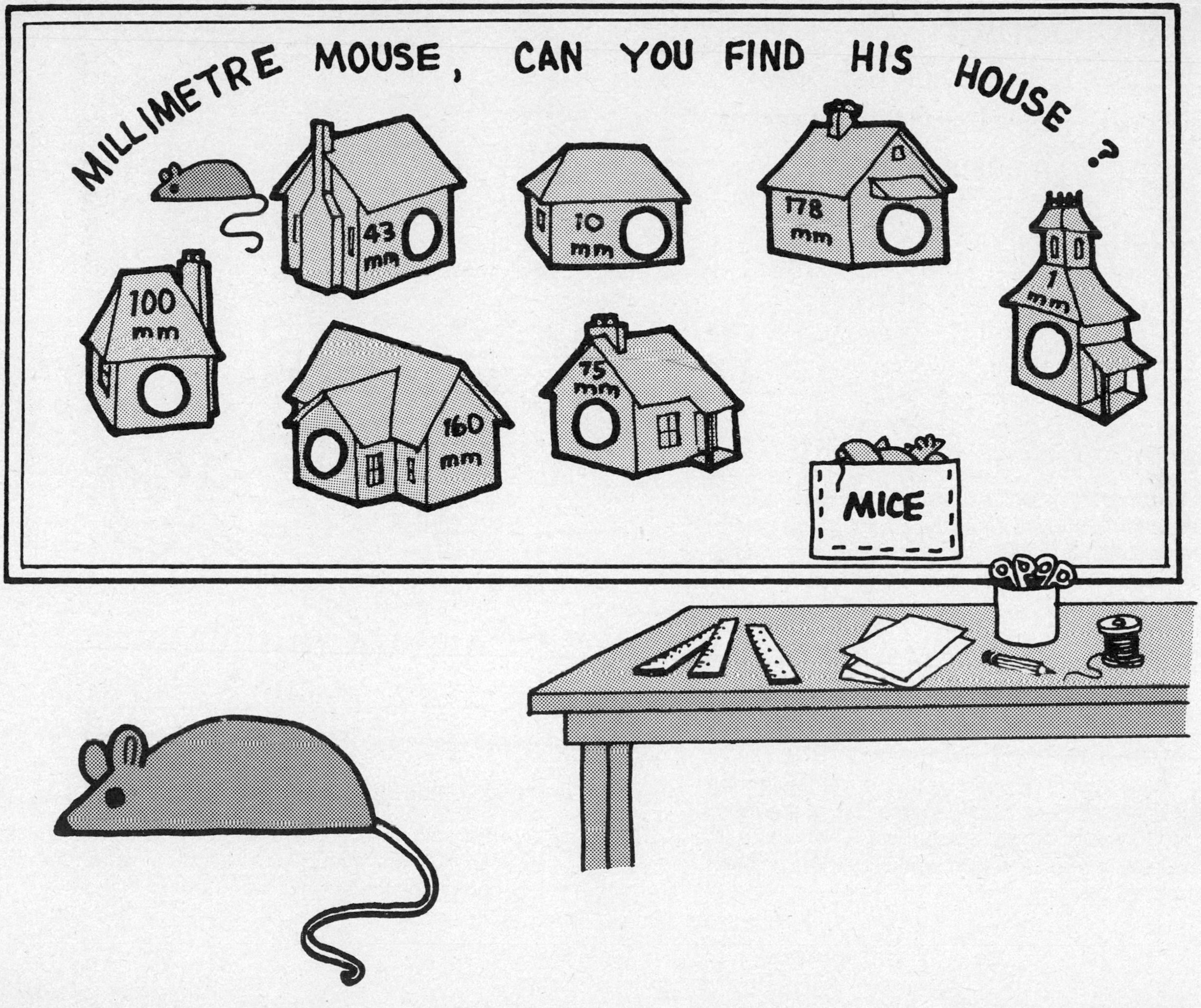
MILLIMETRE MOUSE, CAN YOU FIND HIS HOUSE ?
43 mm
10 mm
178 mm
100 mm
1 mm
75 mm
160 mm
MICE

Metric Center

Purpose: To provide reinforcement activities in metric measurement.

Activity 3: Linear Measurement Station

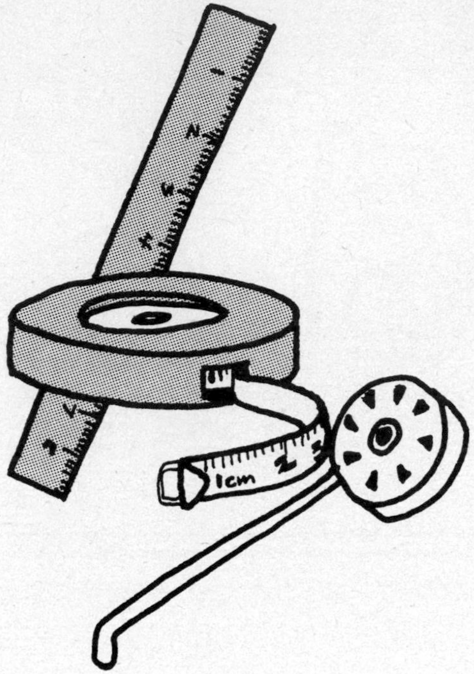

Construction

Duplicate several copies of various **worksheets** such as the sample shown. Place the copies of each worksheet in a **manila folder.** Provide **tools** for metric measurement (sticks, rulers, wheels, and so on).

Procedure

The child selects a worksheet and completes the suggested activities. You can use one of the many record-keeping devices suggested elsewhere to provide a record of which worksheets have been completed by each child.

Evaluation

This activity can be evaluated by giving a test on the use of linear metric measurements when the child completes the activity.

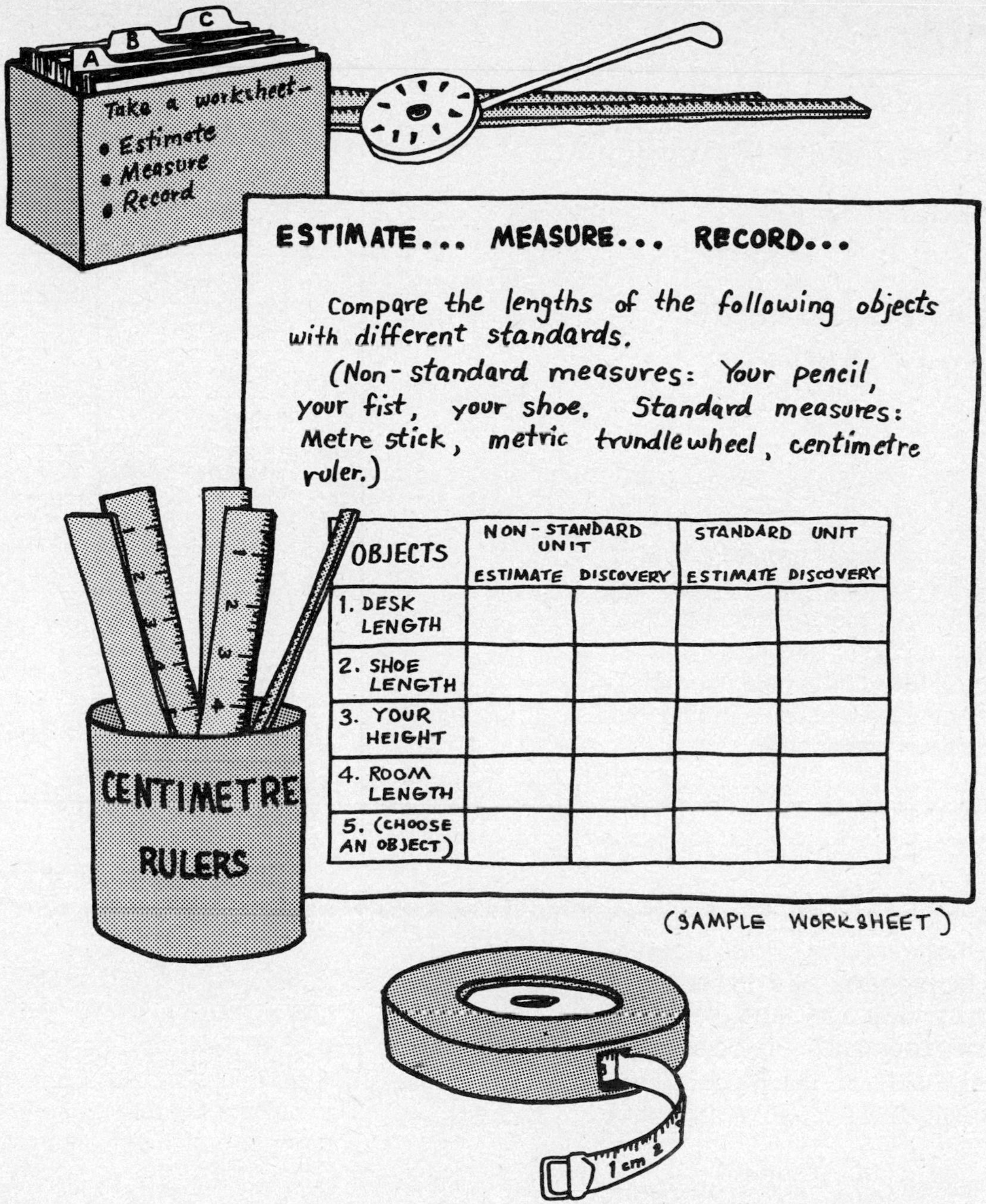

ESTIMATE... MEASURE... RECORD...

Compare the lengths of the following objects with different standards.

(Non-standard measures: Your pencil, your fist, your shoe. Standard measures: Metre stick, metric trundlewheel, centimetre ruler.)

OBJECTS	NON-STANDARD UNIT		STANDARD UNIT	
	ESTIMATE	DISCOVERY	ESTIMATE	DISCOVERY
1. DESK LENGTH				
2. SHOE LENGTH				
3. YOUR HEIGHT				
4. ROOM LENGTH				
5. (CHOOSE AN OBJECT)				

(SAMPLE WORKSHEET)

Metric Center

Purpose: To provide reinforcement activities in metric measurement.

Activity 4: Liquid Measurement Station

Construction

This station should be constructed around a **sink** or equivalent facility. Provide various **metric measuring containers** (plastic medicine cups, medicine bottles, plastic measuring cups, a plastic litre flask, and so on). Prepare a number of **task cards** (see example), giving instructions for activities that will acquaint the student with the metric liquid measures.

Procedure

The student selects a task card and follows its directions. Task cards can be prepared as worksheets, or the student can write his answers on separate paper. (Worksheets covered with contact or plastic sleeves, to be marked with wax pencils, would be appropriate; dittoed worksheets may not survive the moist environment.)

LIQUID MEASUREMENT #1

Name ________________

Estimate . . . Measure . . . Record . . .

A.

CONTAINERS	STANDARD UNIT ESTIMATE	STANDARD UNIT DISCOVERY
1. GLASS		
2. COKE BOTTLE		
3. PAN		
4. BUCKET		

B. How many millilitres in 1 litre ?

____

How did you find out ?

____

____

C. How many millilitres in 1 centilitre ?

____

D. How many centilitres in 1 decilitre ?

____

E. How many decilitres in a litre ?

____

(SAMPLE WORKSHEET)

Evaluation

This activity can be evaluated by teacher observation or correction of worksheets.

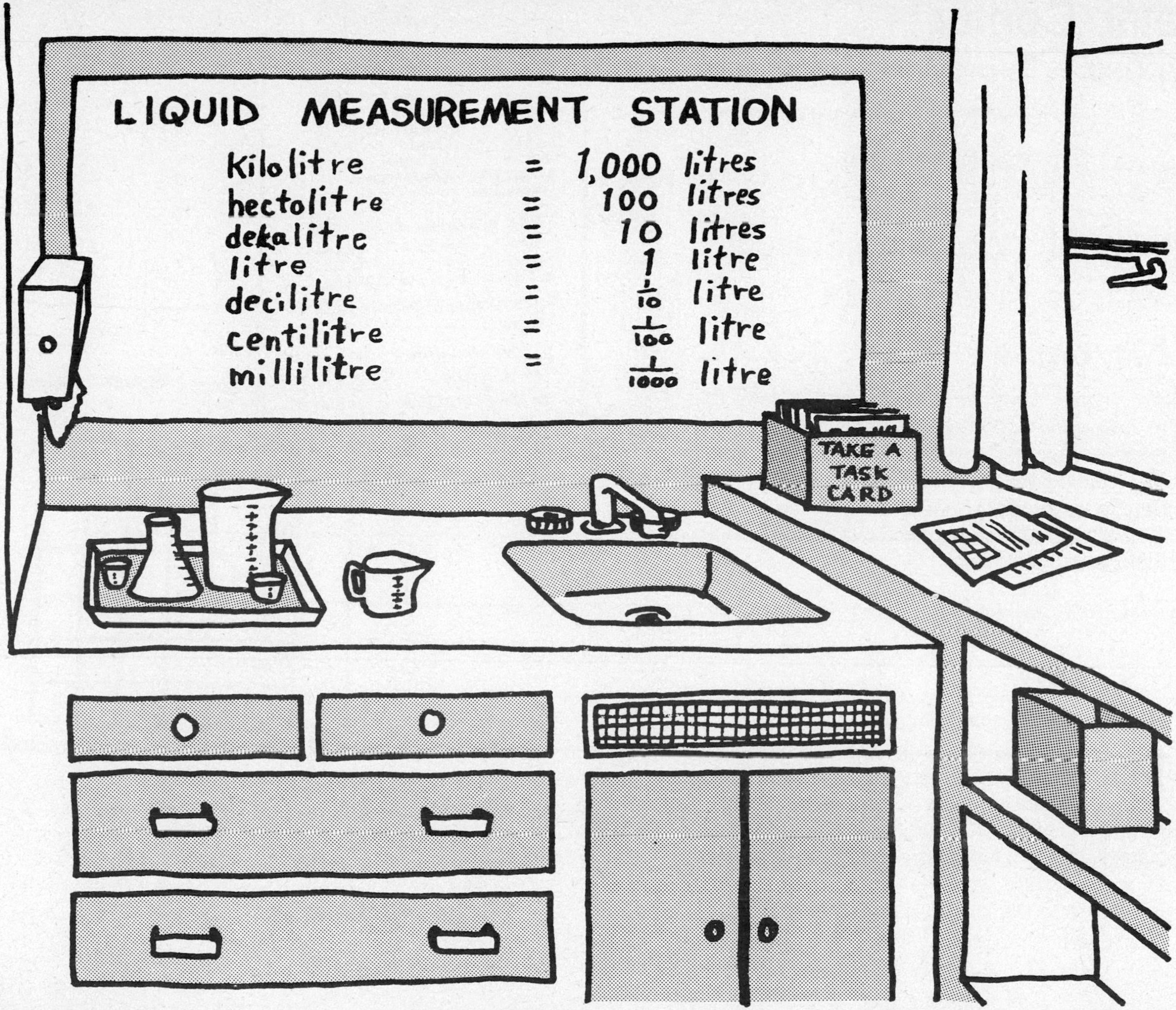
LIQUID MEASUREMENT STATION
Kilolitre = 1,000 litres
hectolitre = 100 litres
dekalitre = 10 litres
litre = 1 litre
decilitre = 1/10 litre
centilitre = 1/100 litre
millilitre = 1/1000 litre
TAKE A TASK CARD

Metric Center

Purpose: To provide reinforcement activities in metric measurement.

Activity 5: Weighing Station

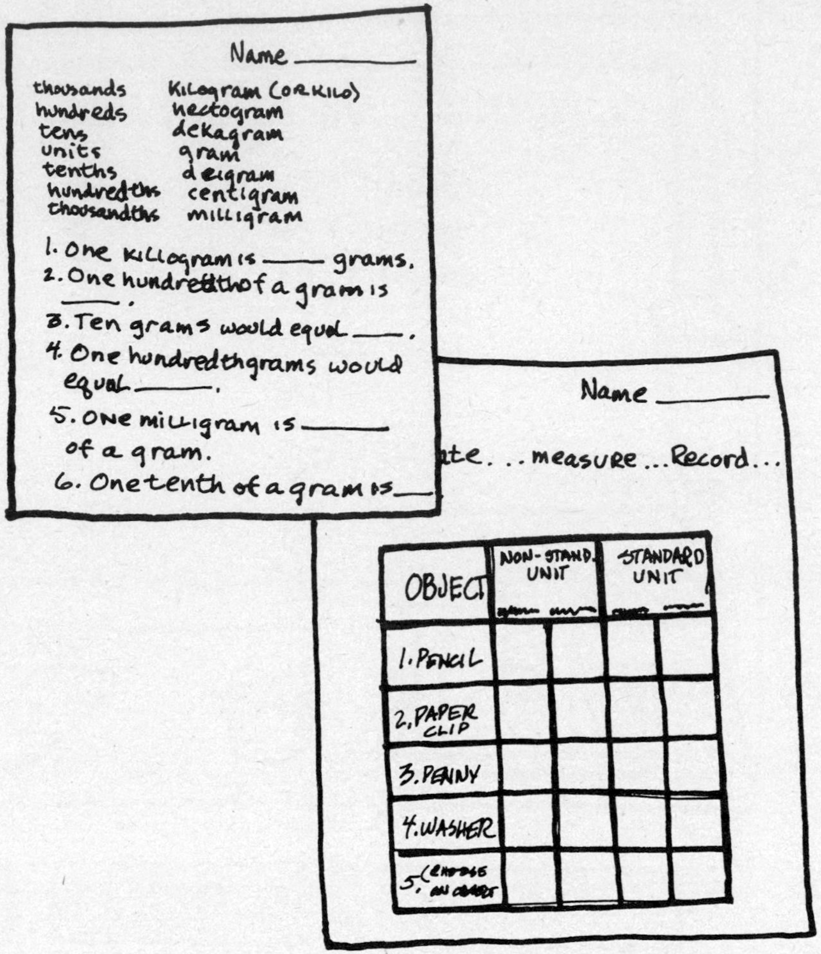

Construction

Prepare a series of duplicated worksheets (see examples on pages 279 and 280). Provide a scale, a set of metric weights, and puzzle packages (small boxes containing nails, paper clips, washers, and so on). Identify each package with a letter. A wall chart and some kind of record-keeping system will be useful additions to the station.

Procedure

The student selects a worksheet and follows the instructions on it. In the record-keeping system illustrated here, the student makes a slash mark on the Station Chart when he takes a worksheet; he turns the slash mark into an X when he finishes the worksheet, and puts it into the "Correction" box. When the teacher corrects the worksheet, she puts it in the "Return" box and fills in the square on the chart.

Evaluation

This activity can be evaluated by teacher correction of the worksheets.

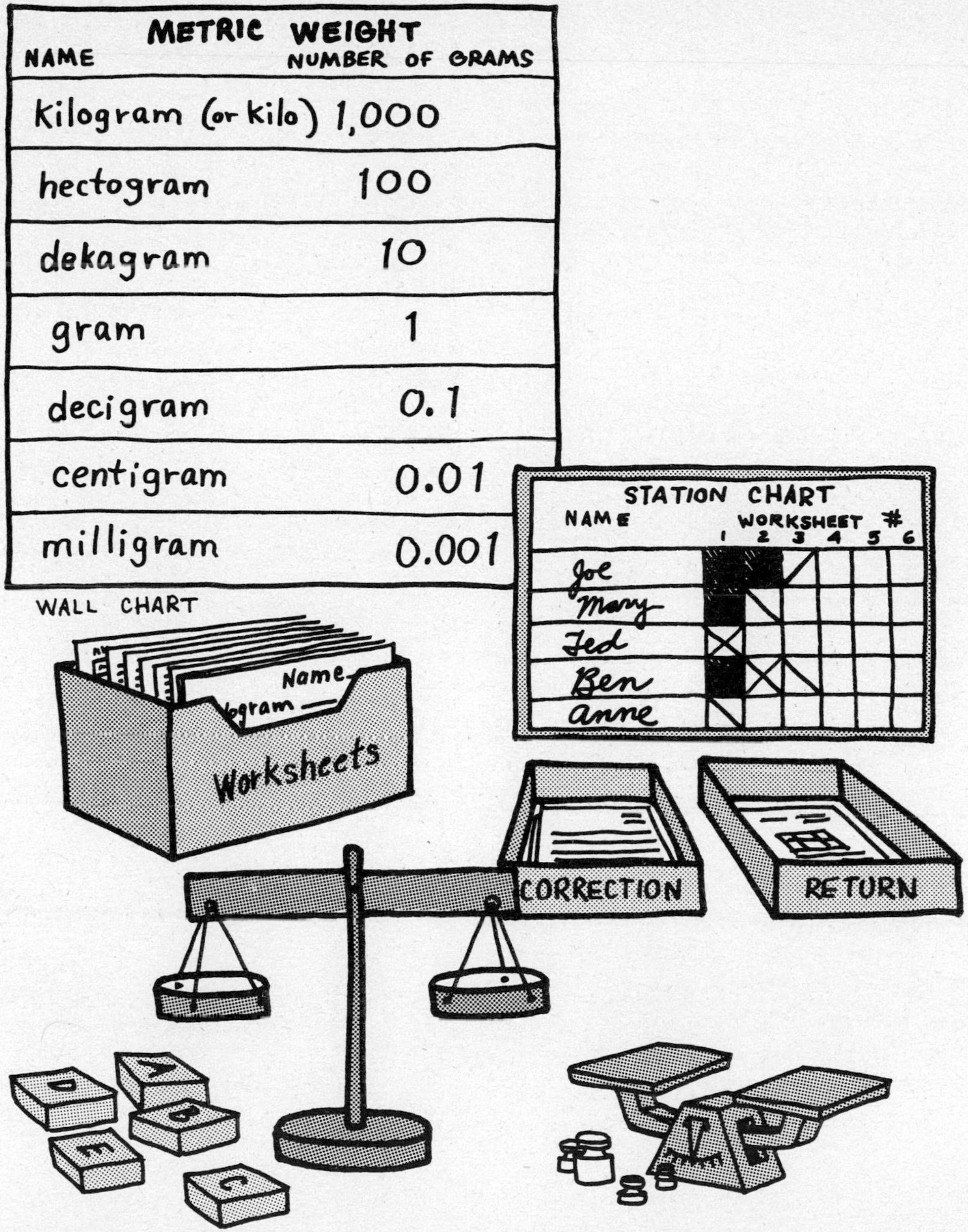
METRIC WEIGHT
NAME
NUMBER OF GRAMS
kilogram (or kilo) 1,000
hectogram 100
dekagram 10
gram 1
decigram 0.1
centigram 0.01
milligram 0.001
WALL CHART
STATION CHART
NAME
WORKSHEET #
1 2 3 4 5 6
Joe
Mary
Ted
Ben
anne
Name
Worksheets
CORRECTION
RETURN

TEAR SHEETS

For instructions see page 26

Name ________________ Task ________________

Color an apple as you finish each task.

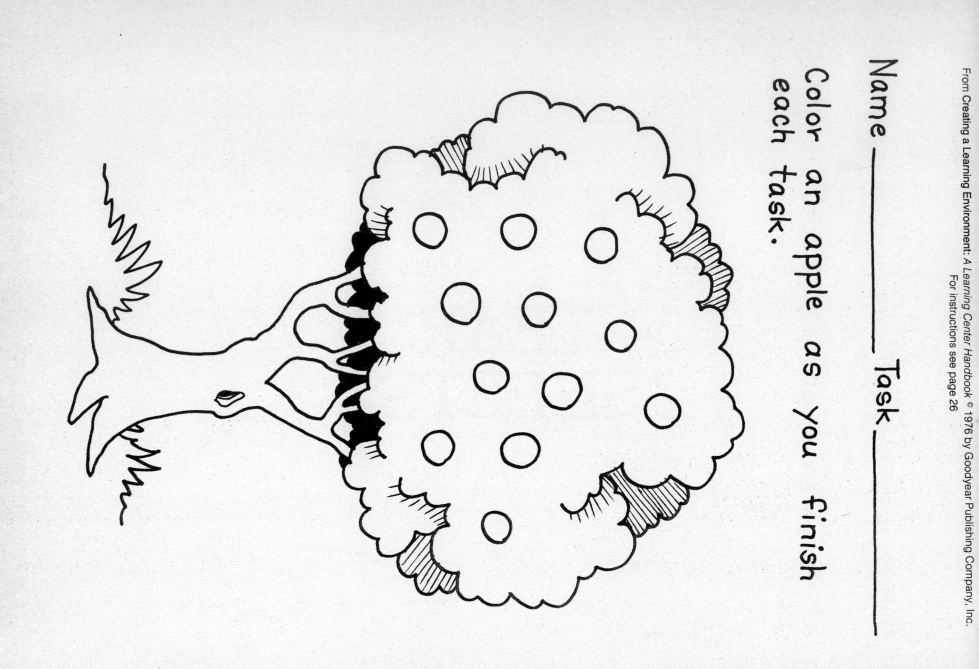

For instructions see page 26

Name ______________ Task ______________

Color a ball as you finish each task.

For instructions see page 26

Name ______________ Task ____________________

Color a candle on the birthday cake as you finish each task.

For instructions see page 26

Name______________ Task ______________

How many fish can you catch?

Color a fish as you finish each task.

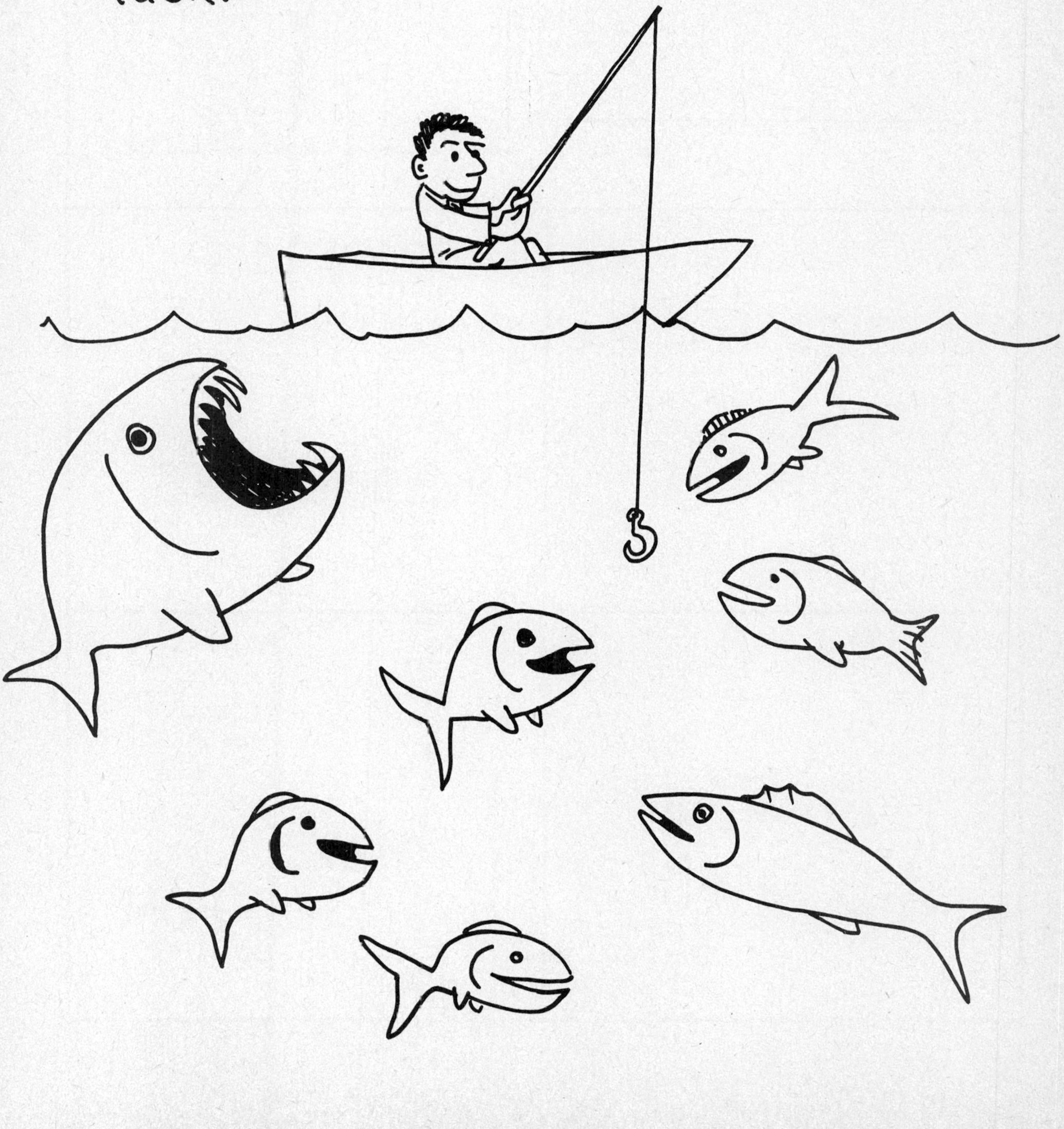

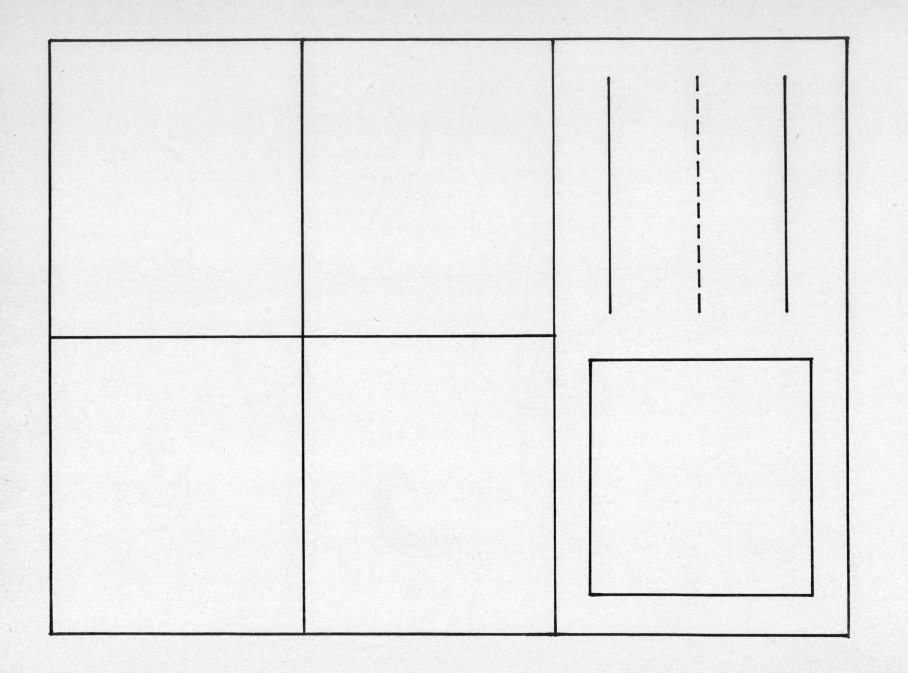

For instructions see page 38

For instructions see page 50

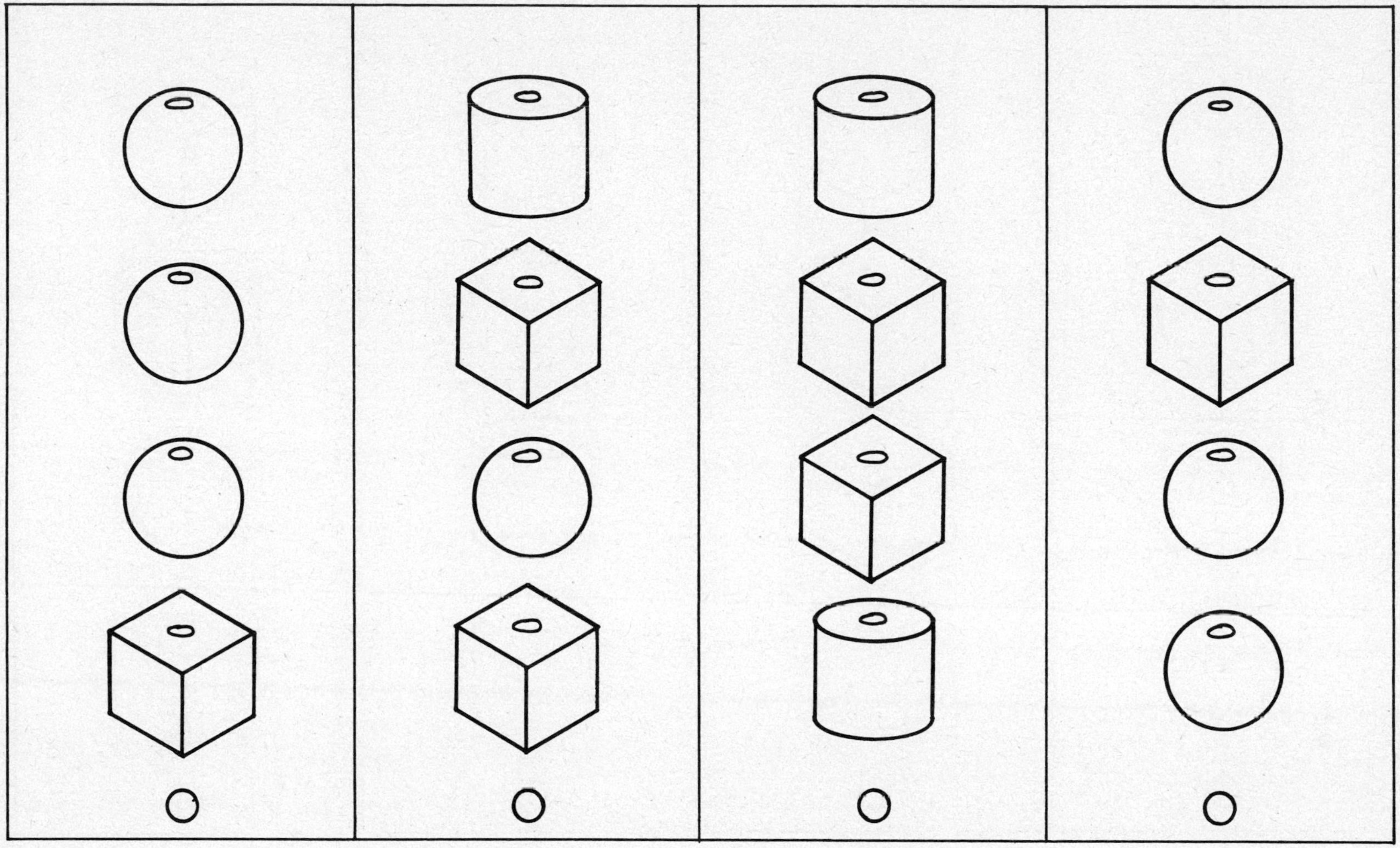

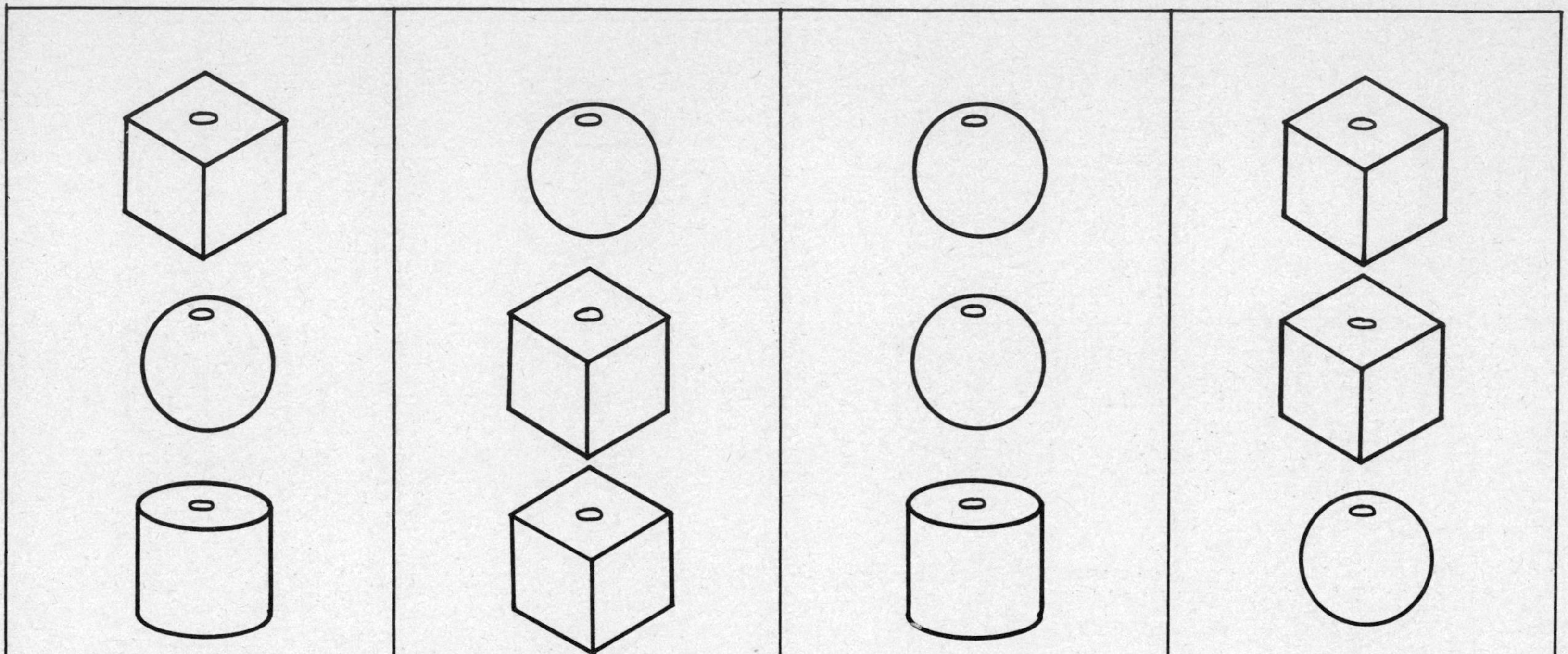

For instructions see page 50

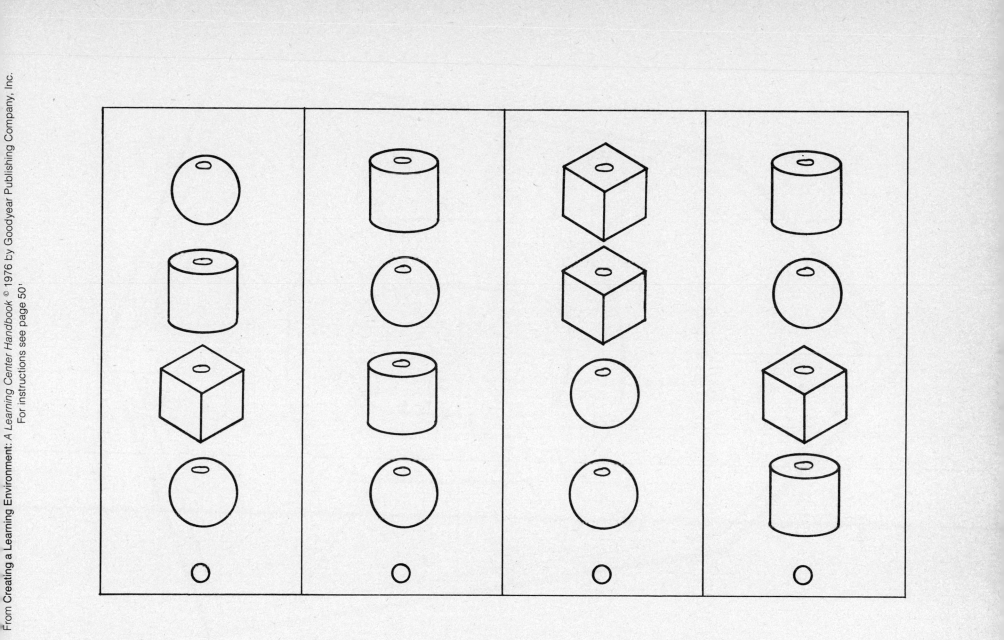

For instructions see page 50'

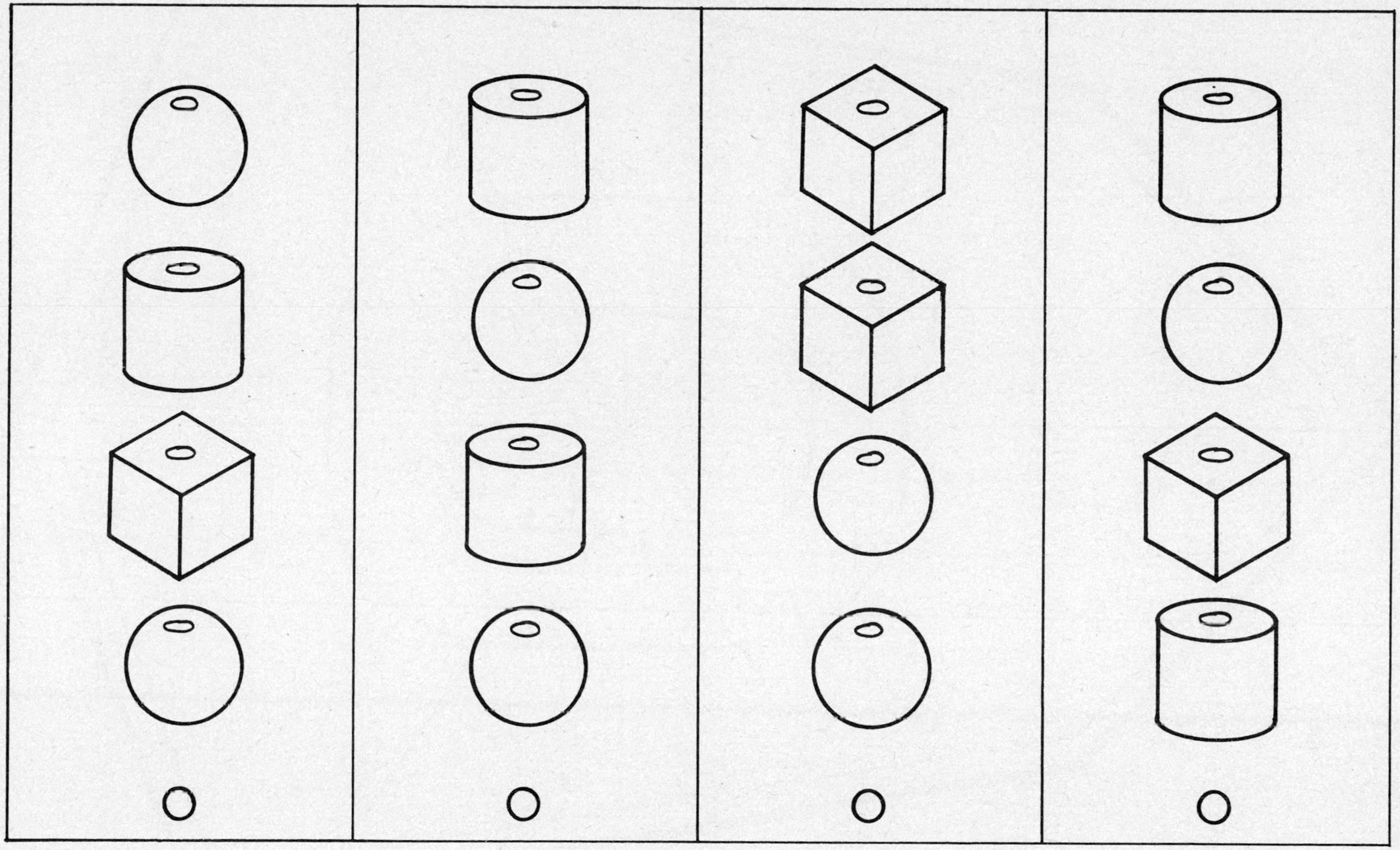

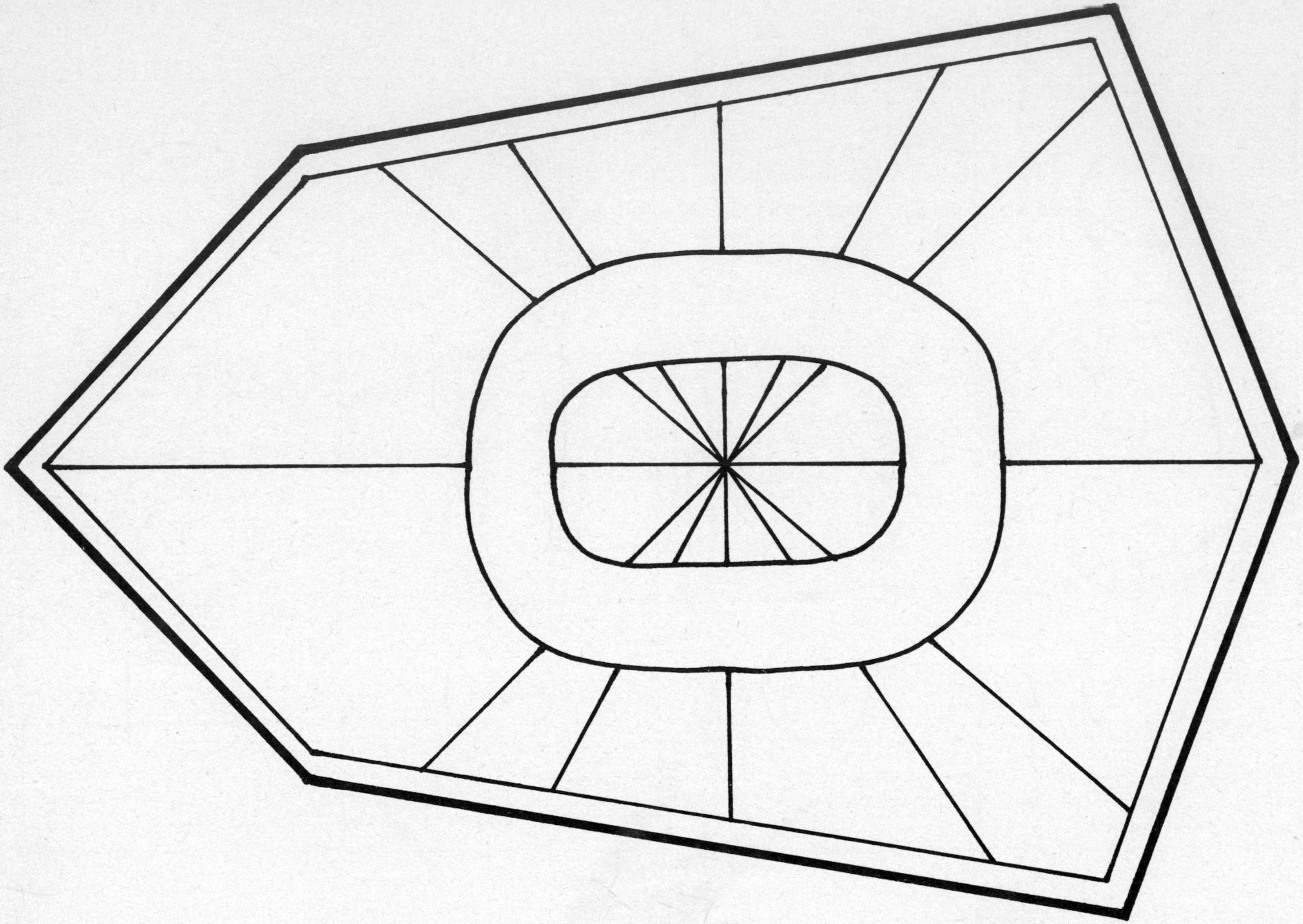

For instructions see page 58

For instructions see page 58

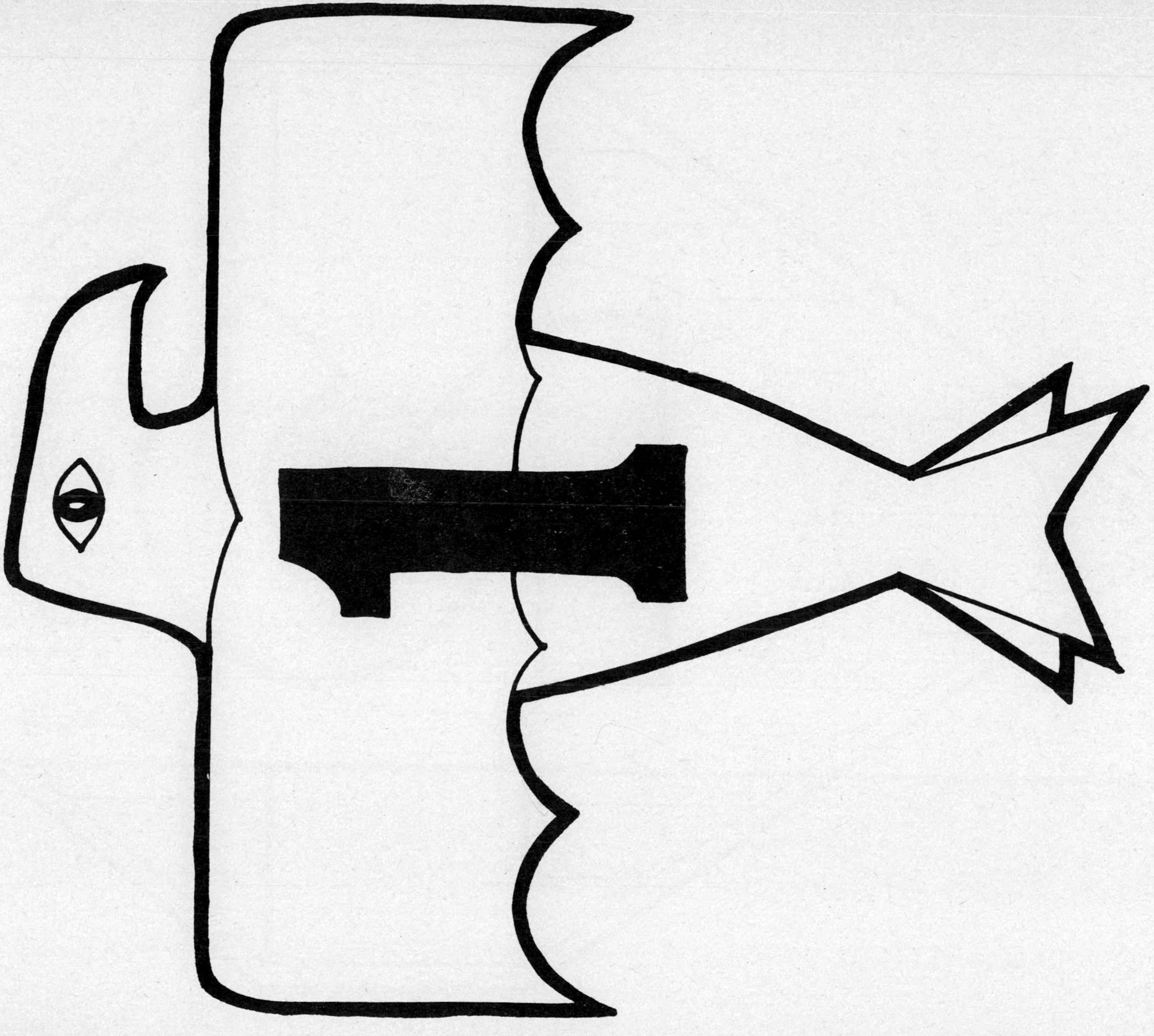

For instructions see page 58

For instructions see page 58

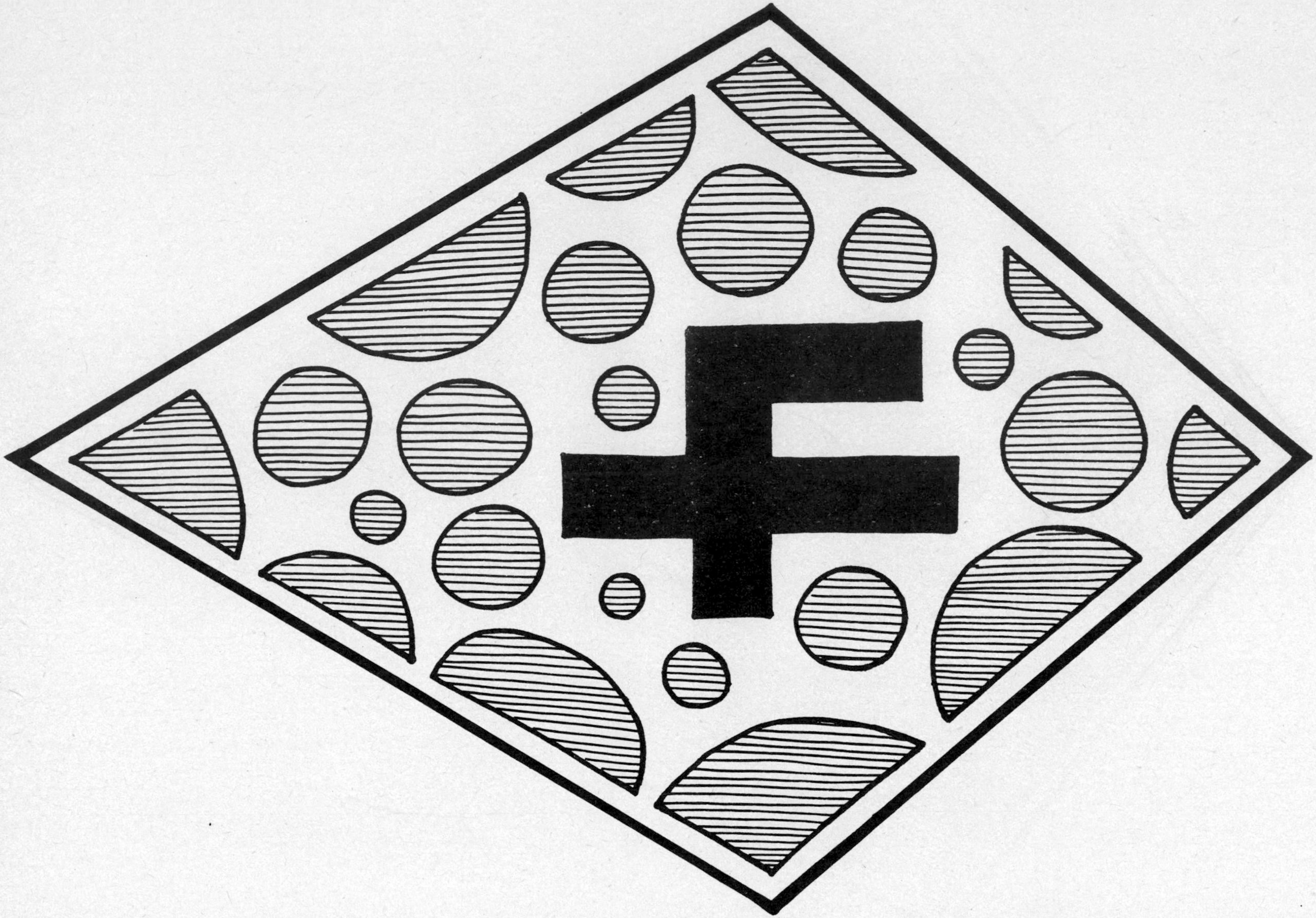

For instructions see page 58

For instructions see page 58

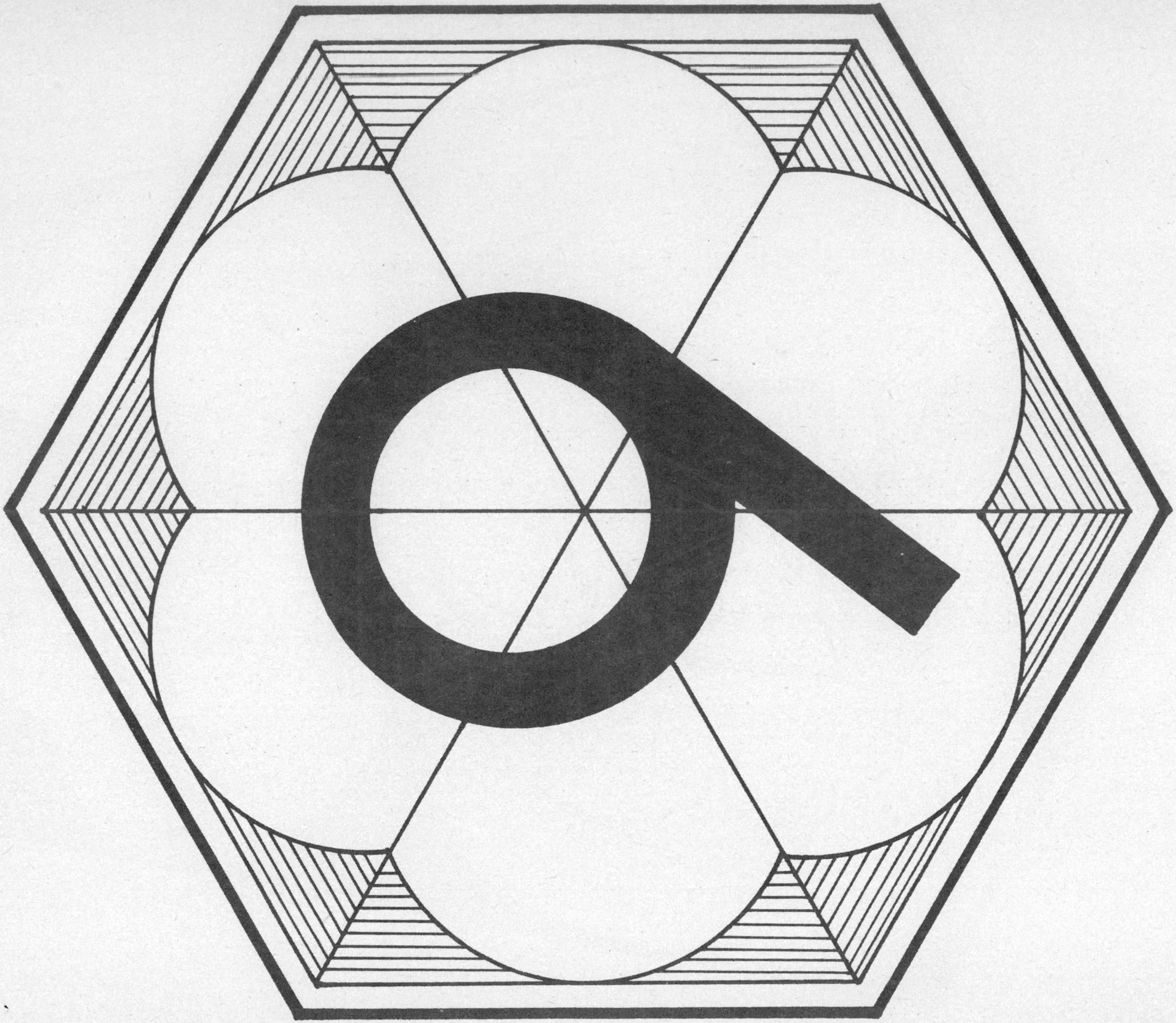

For instructions see page 58

For instructions see page 58

For instructions see page 58

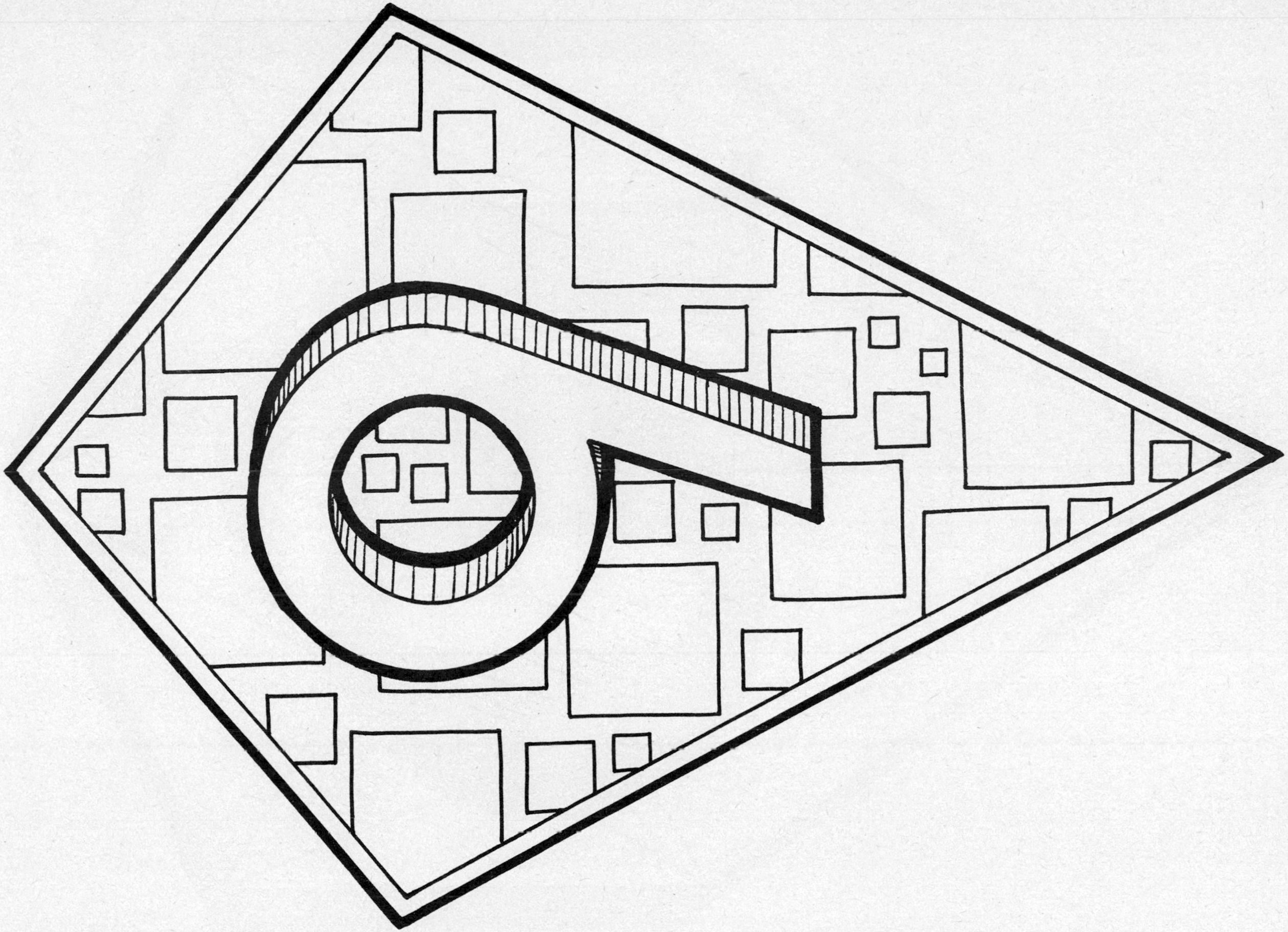

For instructions see page 58

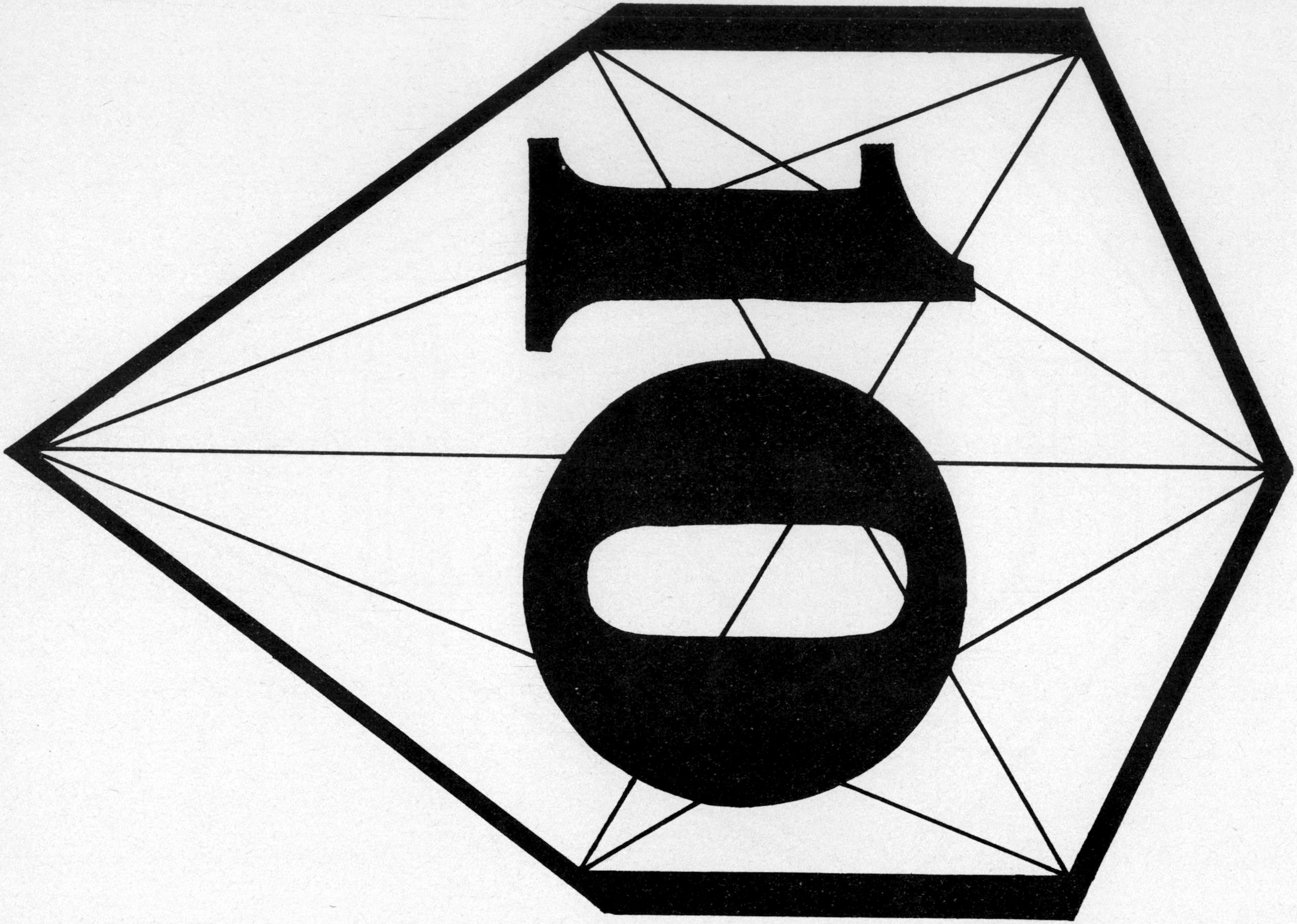

For instructions see page 58

For instructions see page 64

For instructions see page 64

My Words

Name ________________

________ ________ ________

________ ________ ________

________ ________

1. ________________________________
2. ________________________________
3. ________________________________
4. ________________________________
5. ________________________________
6. ________________________________
7. ________________________________
8. ________________________________

For instructions see page 66

PLAYER 1		PLAYER 2		PLAYER 3	
1.		1.		1.	
2.		2.		2.	
3.		3.		3.	
4.		4.		4.	
5.		5.		5.	
6.		6.		6.	
7.		7.		7.	
8.		8.		8.	
9.		9.		9.	
10.		10.		10.	
TOTAL		TOTAL		TOTAL	

For instructions see page 72

For instructions see page 72

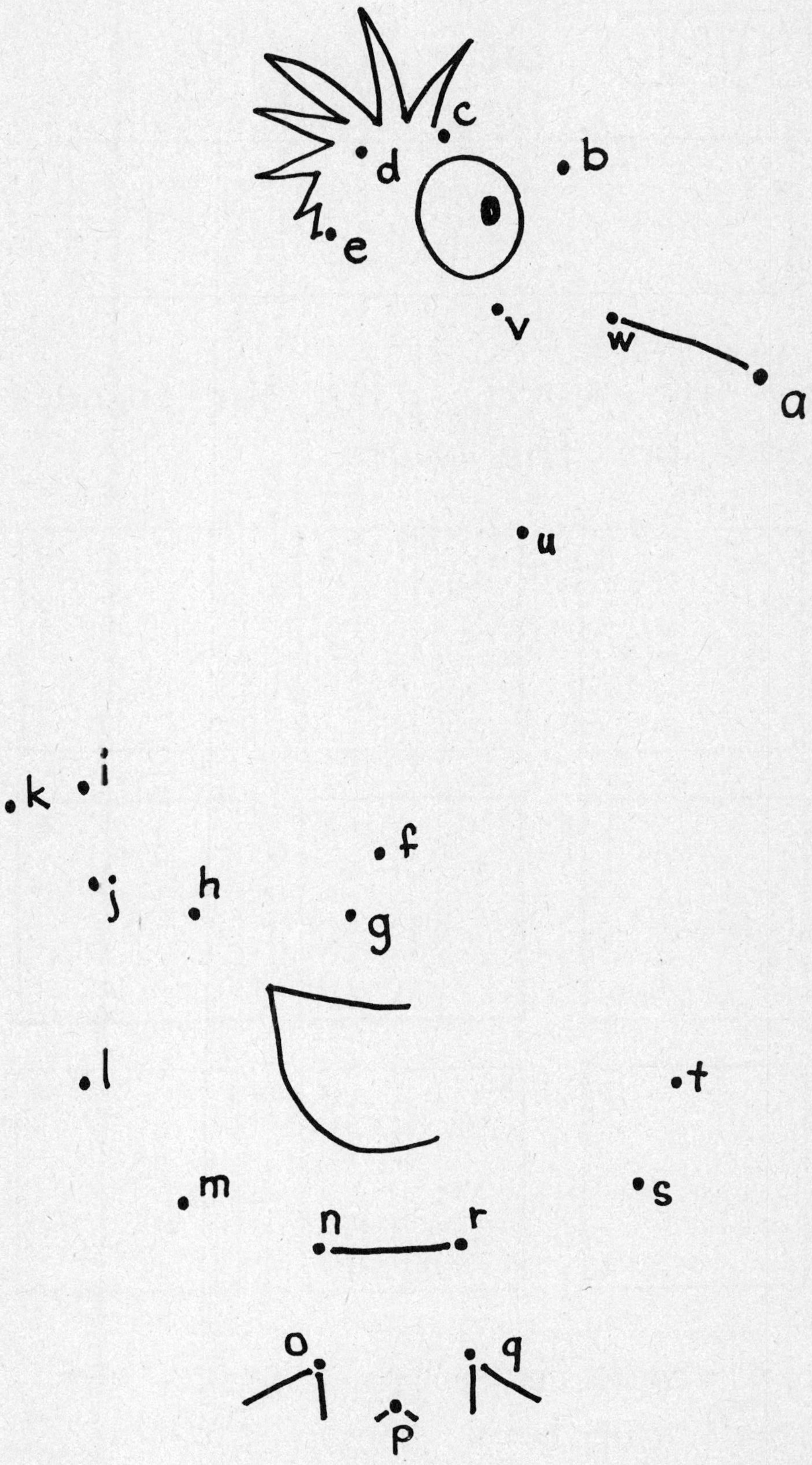

For instructions see page 78

HARD or Soft

Say the word. Put the correct sound on the word.

1	2	3
4	5	6
7	8	9

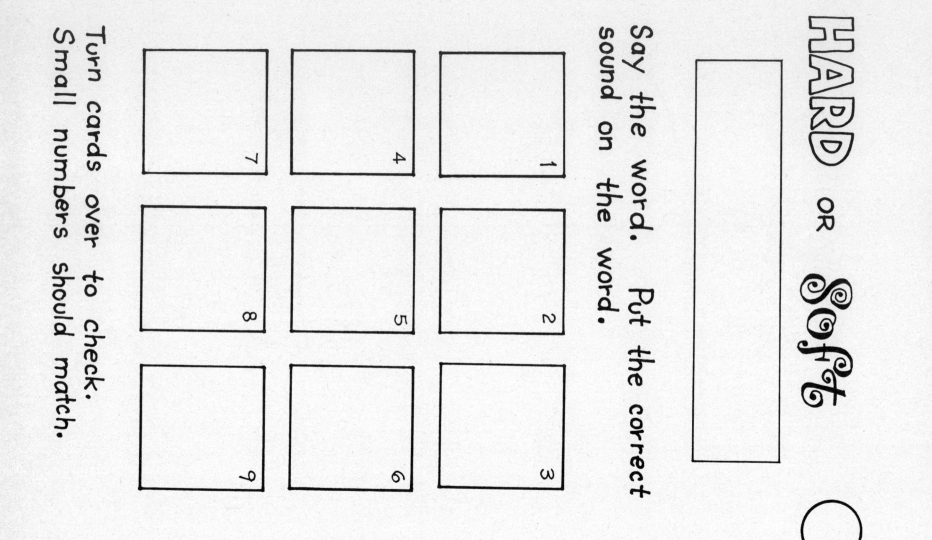

Turn cards over to check.
Small numbers should match.

For instructions see page 88

Sample Instructions for Task Cards (to be written on castle-shaped forms)

TASK CARD #1 — Don't forget your name!!

You will need: paper
pencil

Put the vocabulary words in alphabetical order.

Pick 6 words. Write each word in a sentence.

Put paper in folder.

TASK CARD #2 — Don't forget your name!!

An antonym is a word having the opposite meaning of another word.

Example: hot cold

You will need: paper
pencil

Pick 6 vocabulary words. Write an antonym for the words you choose.

Put paper in folder.

For instructions see page 88

Sample Instructions for Task Cards (to be written on castle-shaped forms)

TASK CARD #3 — Don't forget your name!!

You will need: paper
pencil

Use the vocabulary words.

A noun is a person, place, or thing.

List all the nouns from the "fairy tale" vocabulary list.

Draw a picture of 3 of the words you listed.

Have a friend check your work. Then put in folder.

Don t forget your name!!

Task Card #4

An adjective is a word that describes a noun.

Example: happy dog

You will need: paper
pencil

Choose 8 nouns from the vocabulary list. Write an adjective that describes each noun.

Put paper in folder.

For instructions see page 88

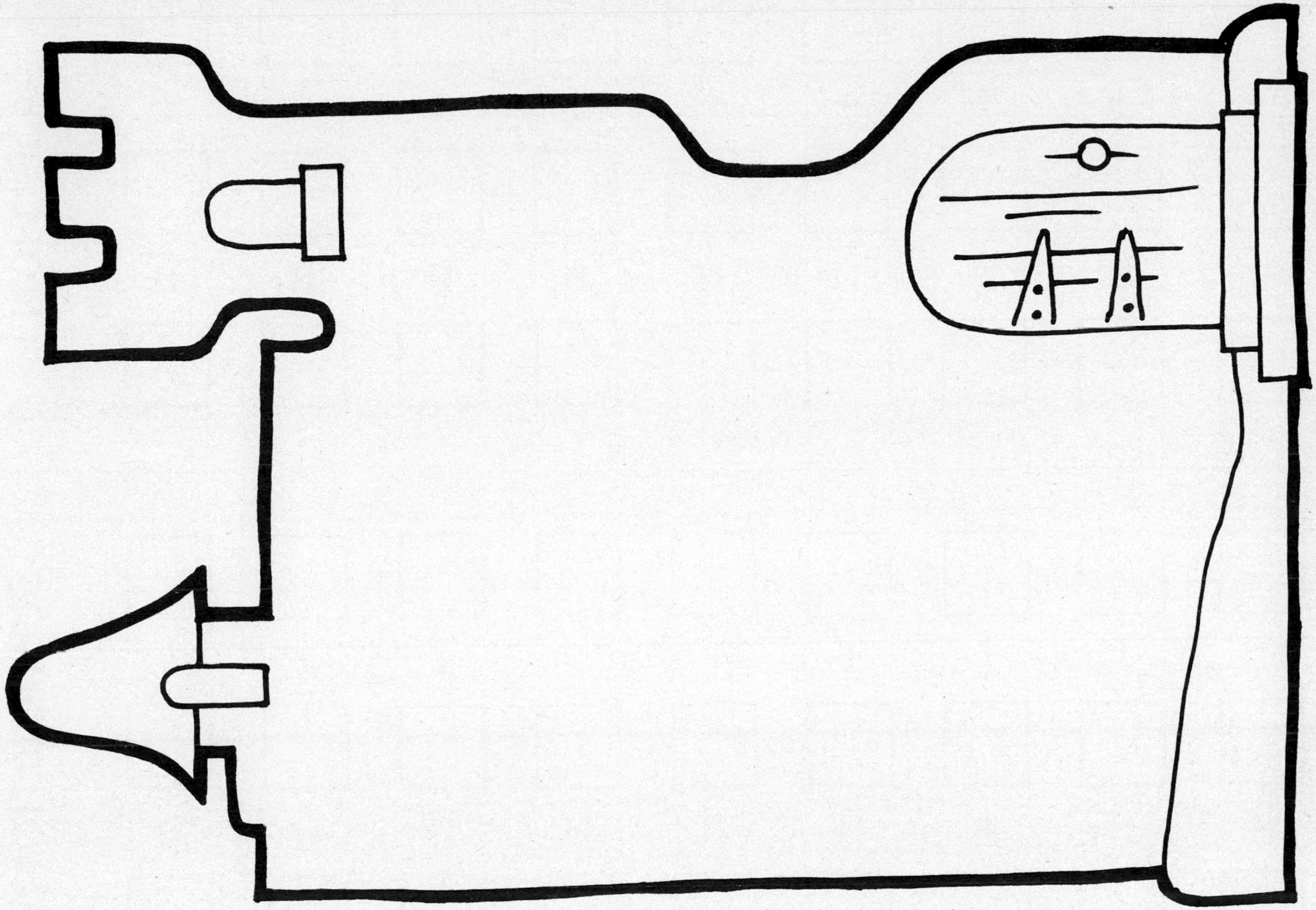

For instructions see page 104

ADDITION	SUBTRACTION
□ + □ = □	□ − □ = □
□ + □ = □	□ − □ = □
□ + □ = □	□ − □ = □
□ + □ = □	□ − □ = □
□ + □ = □	□ − □ = □
□ + □ = □	□ − □ = □
□ + □ = □	□ − □ = □
□ + □ = □	□ − □ = □
□ + □ = □	□ − □ = □

For instructions see page 110

For instructions see page 114

For instructions see page 120

Name ____________________

	hundreds	tens	ones
1			
2			
3			
4			
5			

____
TOTAL

For instructions see page 124

I get up
at

____

O'Clock.

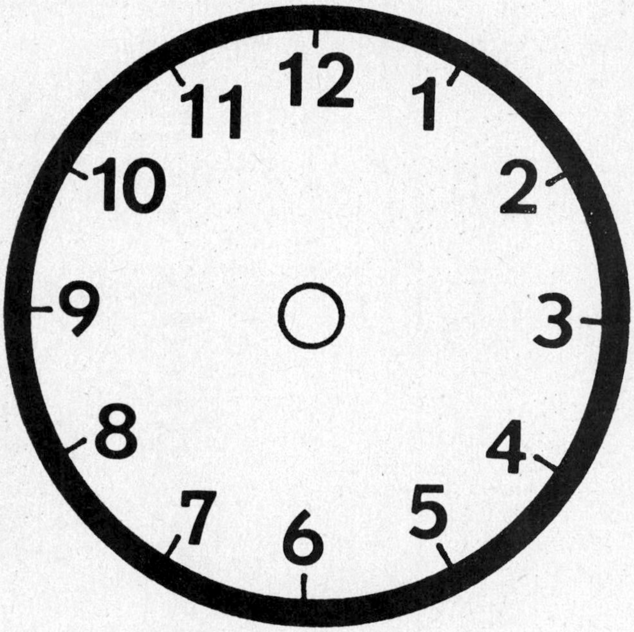

I eat lunch
at

____

O'Clock.

For instructions see page 124

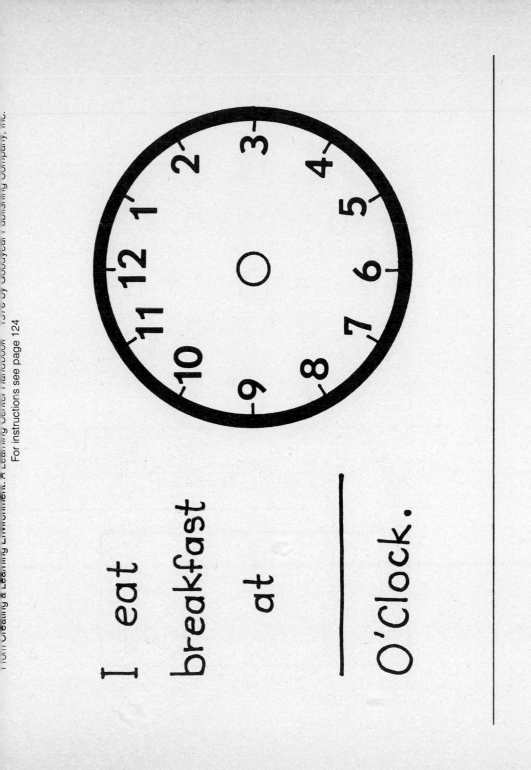

I eat
breakfast
at
____
O'Clock.

Recess
is at
____
O'Clock.

For instructions see page 128

For instructions see page 138

feet	get	float
ran	stand	hand
phone	red	roar
fix	elephant	wife
fed	ghost	boat
bed	head	note

For instructions see page 138

kid	day	rag	graph
came	kite	kiss	can
set	dough	plate	bat
coat	kind	bait	stay
fence	bet	no	ant
gate	fail	mail	fat

For instructions see page 140

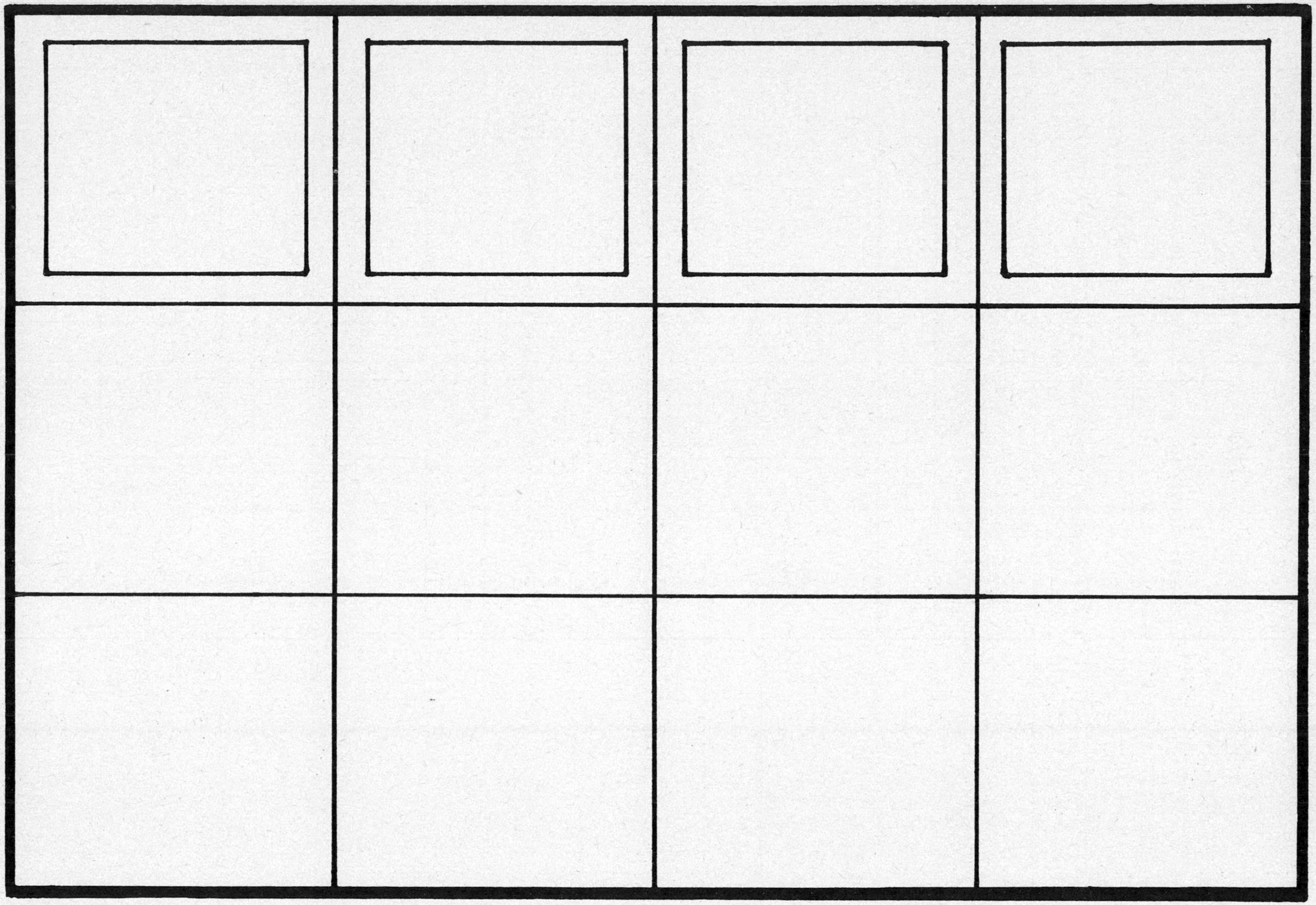

For instructions see page 160

COMPARE AND CONTRAST BASEBALL PLAYERS

Student's Name ______________________ Game 1 2 3 4 5 6 7 8 9 10

1. What are the names of the two players?

   A. ______________________

   B. ______________________

2. What position does each man play?

   A. ______________________

   B. ______________________

3. Which team does each man play for?

   A. ______________________

   B. ______________________

4. Which player is older? Write his name. ______________________

5. Which player is taller? Write his name. ______________________

6. Where is each player's hometown?

   A. ______________________

   B. ______________________

7. What is the average number of hits each player has?

   A. ______________ B. ______________

8. Which player has hit the most home runs? ______________________

   How many? ______________

9. How many more did he hit than the other player? ______________

10. In which year did each player have the most runs batted in?

   A. ______________ B. ______________

For instructions see page 168

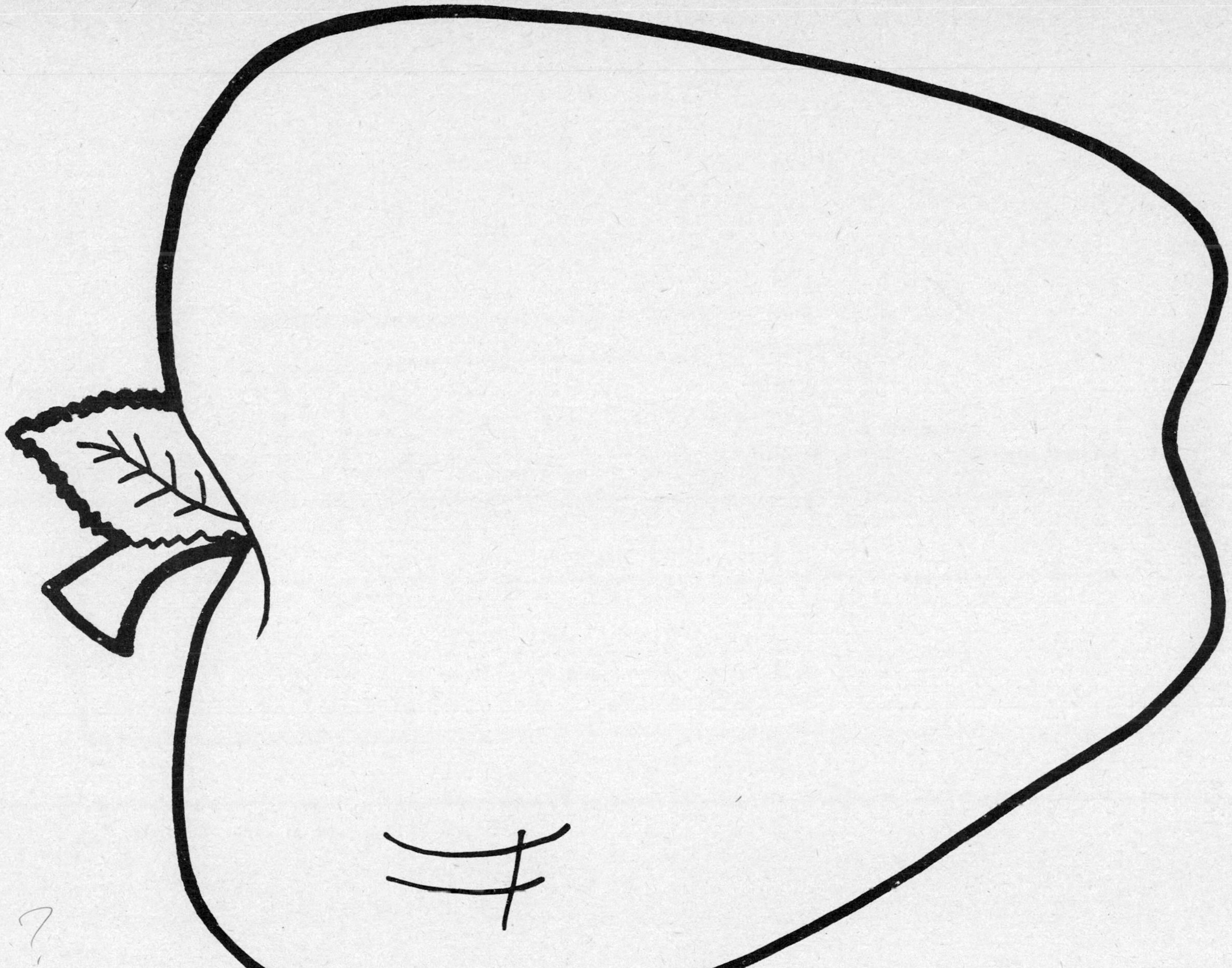

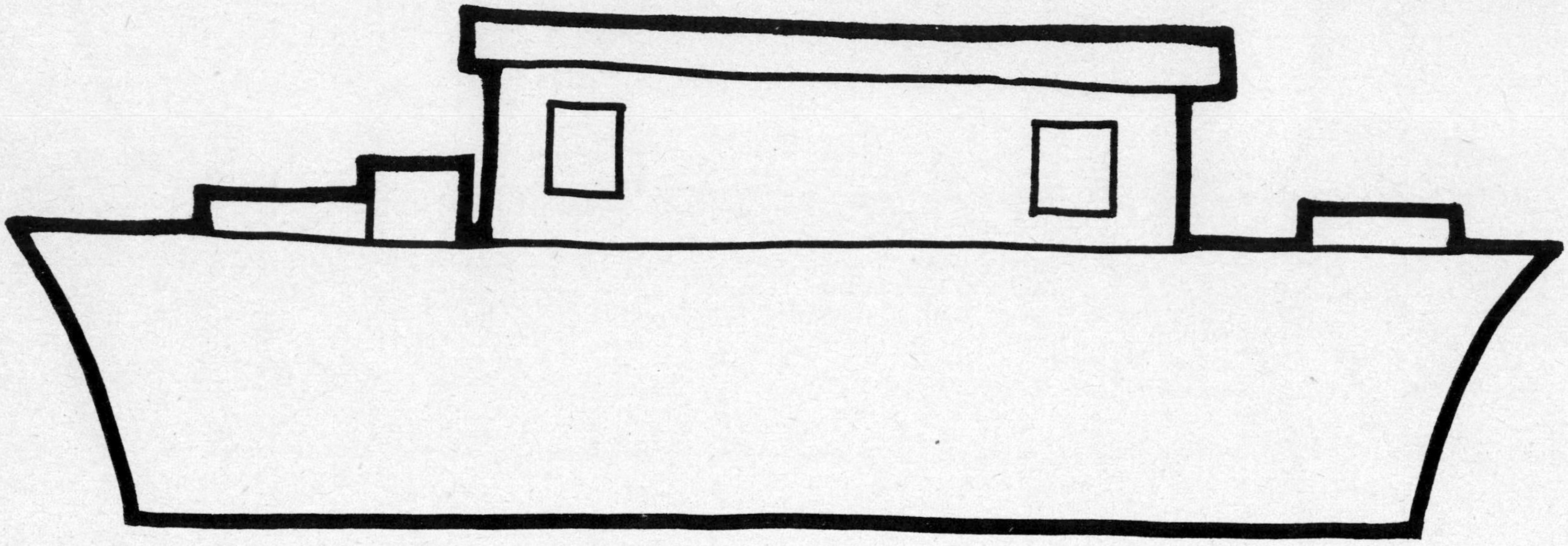

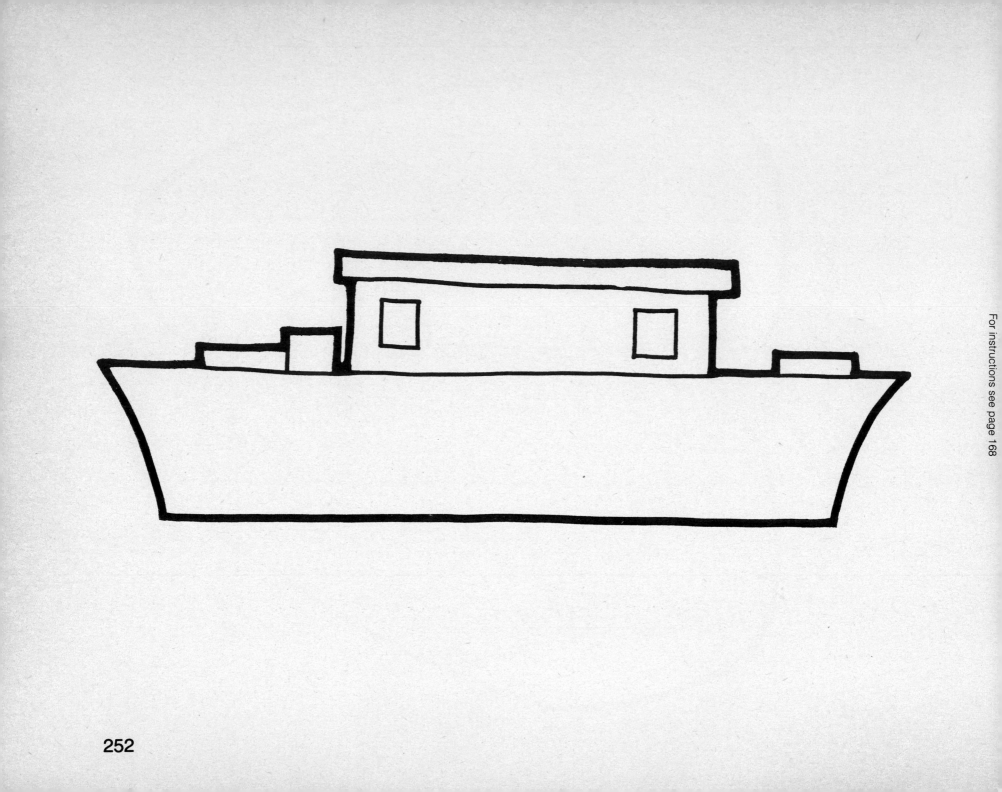

For instructions see page 168

For instructions see page 168

For instructions see page 168

For instructions see page 168

For instructions see page 180

Mark off each fact as you show it in your scrapbook.

Name ______________

X	2	3	4	5	6	7	8	9	10
2	4	•	•	•	•	•	•	•	•
3	6	9	•	•	•	•	•	•	•
4	8	12	16	•	•	•	•	•	•
5	10	15	20	25	•	•	•	•	•
6	12	18	24	30	36	•	•	•	•
7	14	21	28	35	42	49	•	•	•
8	16	24	32	40	48	56	64	•	•
9	18	27	36	45	54	63	72	81	•
10	20	30	40	50	60	70	80	90	100

For instructions see page 184

Evil Eye Score Sheet

NAME ___________________________

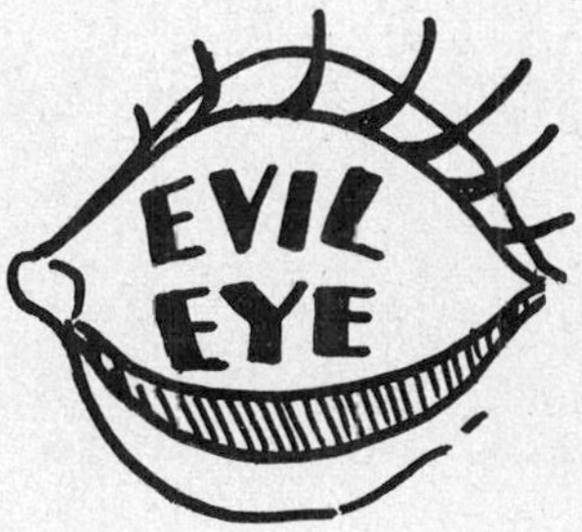

GAME #1

1. ____ x ____ = ____
2. ____ x ____ = ____
3. ____ x ____ = ____
4. ____ x ____ = ____
5. ____ x ____ = ____
6. ____ x ____ = ____
7. ____ x ____ = ____

Game Total = ____

GAME #2

1. ____ x ____ = ____
2. ____ x ____ = ____
3. ____ x ____ = ____
4. ____ x ____ = ____
5. ____ x ____ = ____
6. ____ x ____ = ____
7. ____ x ____ = ____

Game Total = ____

GAME #3

1. ____ x ____ = ____
2. ____ x ____ = ____
3. ____ x ____ = ____
4. ____ x ____ = ____
5. ____ x ____ = ____
6. ____ x ____ = ____
7. ____ x ____ = ____

Game Total = ____

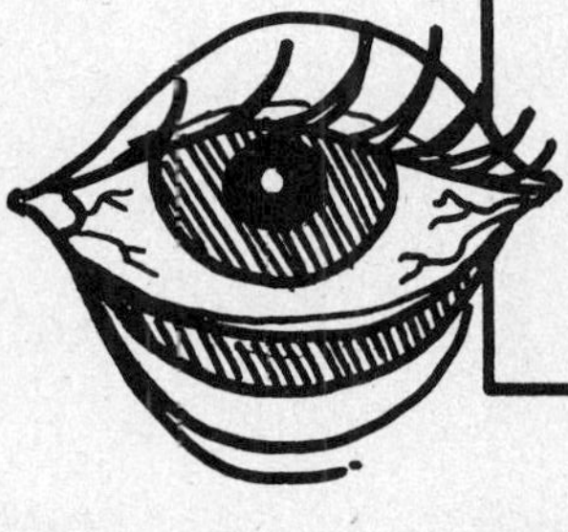

GAME TOTALS

	SCORE
Game #1	________
Game #2	________
Game #3	________
GRAND TOTAL	________

For instructions see page 184

For instructions see page 186

1	2	3	4	5	6	7	8	9	10
11	12	13	14	15	16	17	18	19	20
21	22	23	24	25	26	27	28	29	30
31	32	33	34	35	36	37	38	39	40
41	42	43	44	45	46	47	48	49	50
51	52	53	54	55	56	57	58	59	60
61	62	63	64	65	66	67	68	69	70
71	72	73	74	75	76	77	78	79	80
81	82	83	84	85	86	87	88	89	90
91	92	93	94	95	96	97	98	99	100

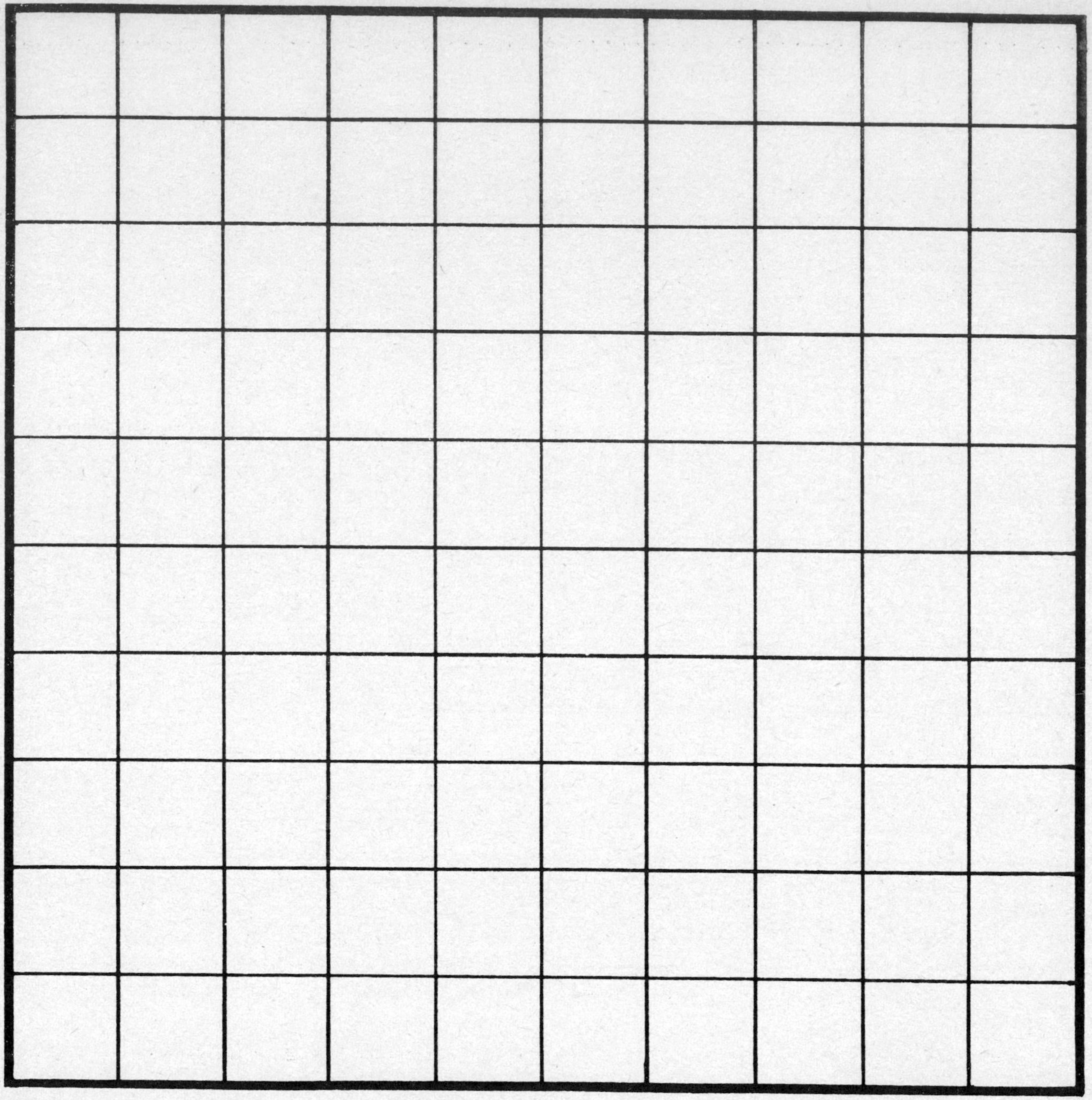

For instructions see page 186

For instructions see page 190

1

1. Make this shape on your geoboard.

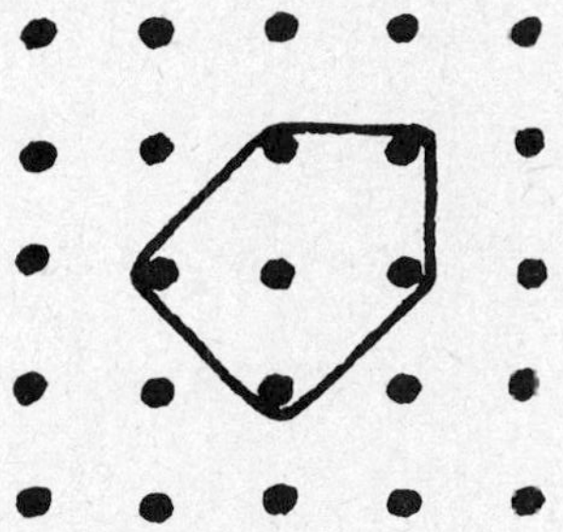

2. How many sides does this shape have?

3. How many nails does this shape touch?

4. What is the area of this shape?

5. Make a shape on your geoboard that touches six nails.

   Now put this shape on your paper.

For instructions see page 190

2

1. Make this shape on your geoboard.

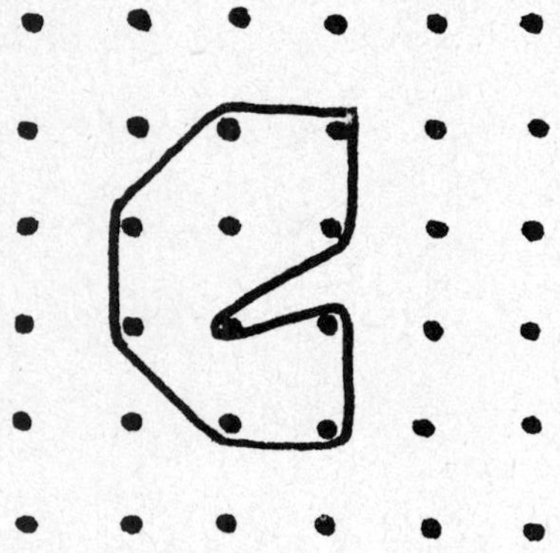

2. How many sides does this shape have?

3. How many nails does this shape touch?

4. What is the area of this shape?

5. Can you move one side to make the area ½ square unit larger?

6. Draw the new shape on your paper.

For instructions see page 190

(3)

1. Make a shape on your geoboard that has an area of 6 square units.

2. How many units long is your shape?

3. How many units wide is your shape?

4. What is the perimeter of your shape?

5. Make your shape have a perimeter of 8".

6. Draw your new shape on your paper.

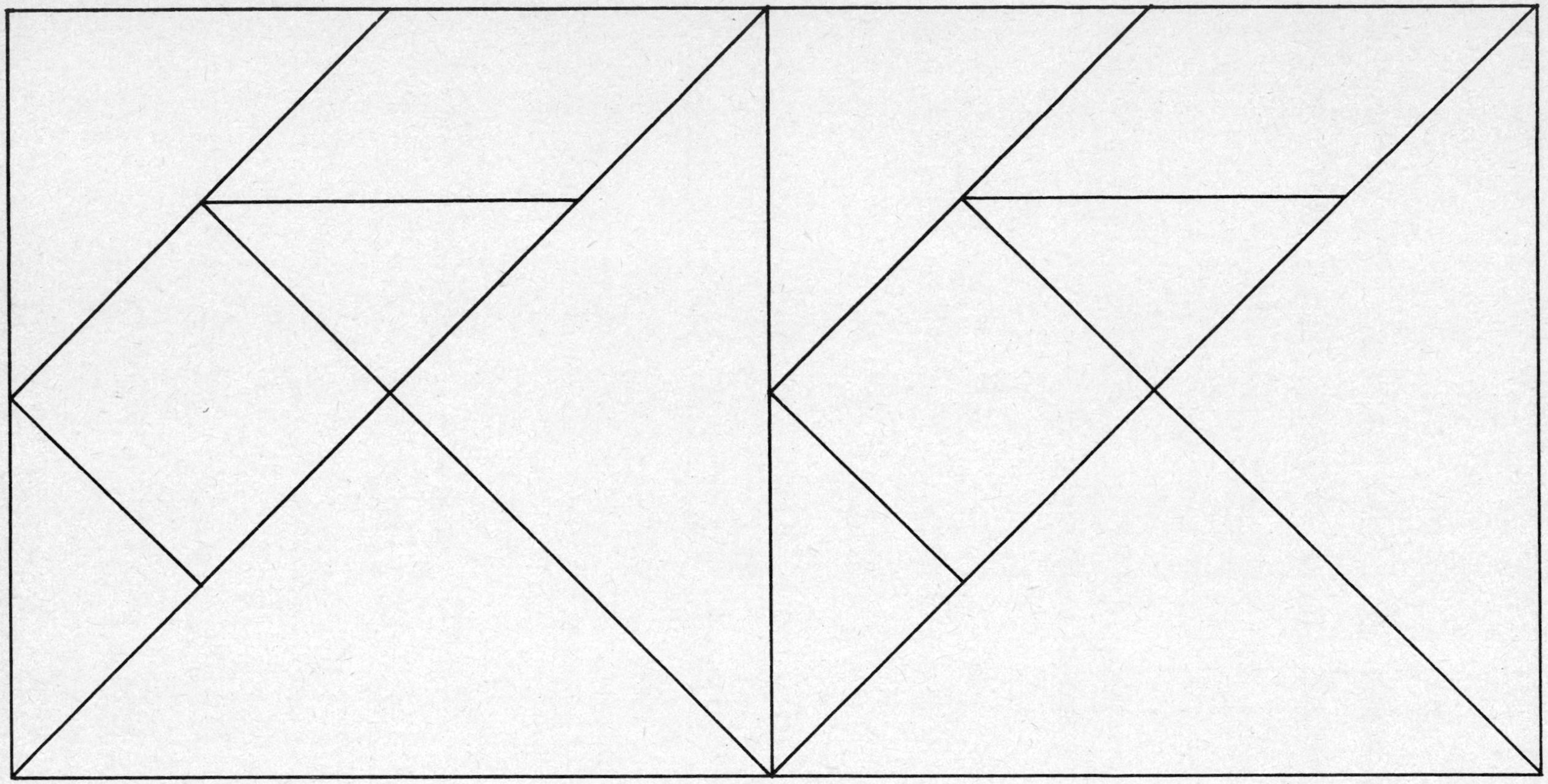

For instructions see page 192

For instructions see page 192

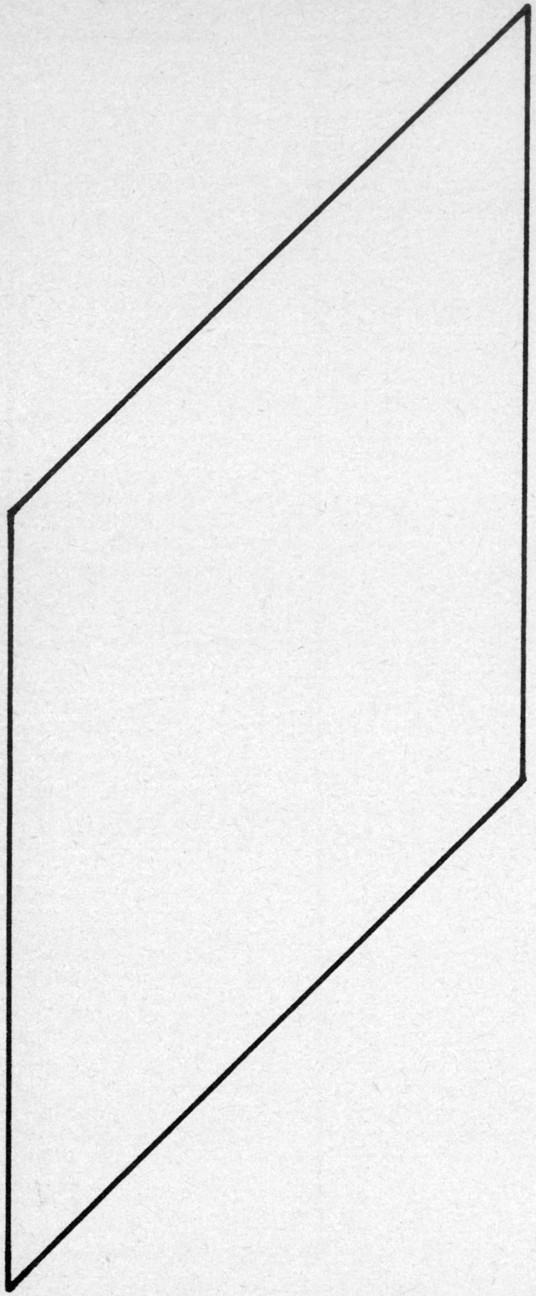

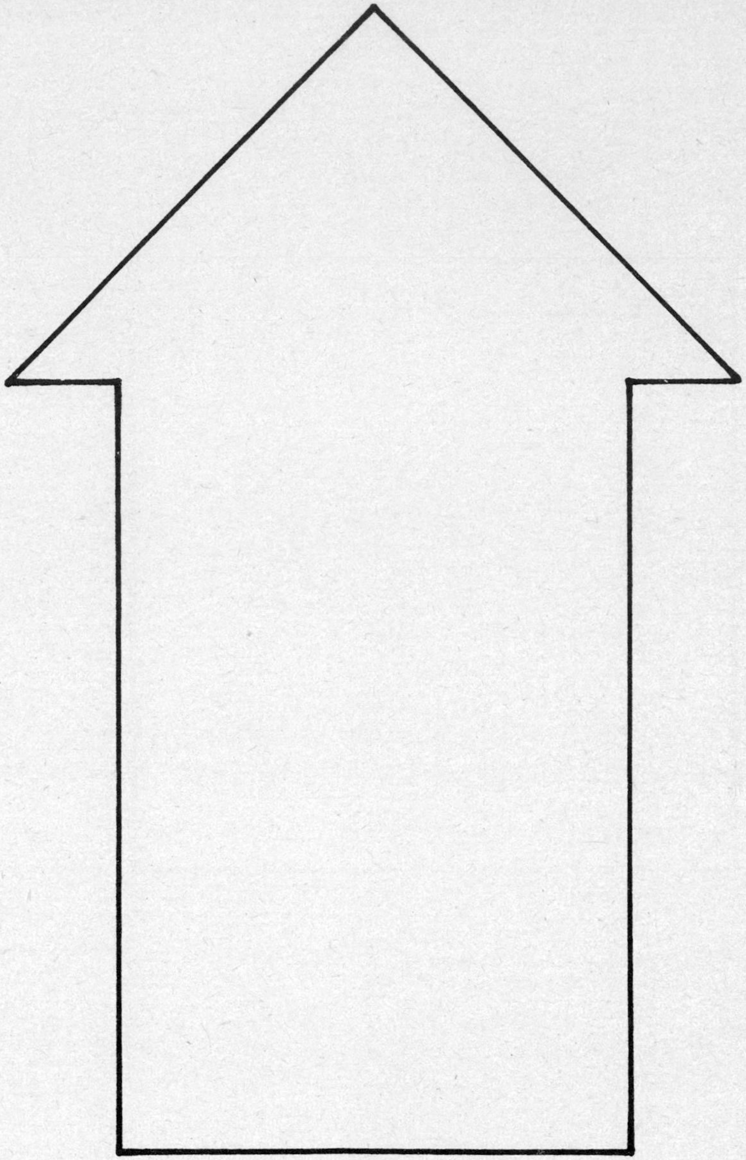

For instructions see page 192

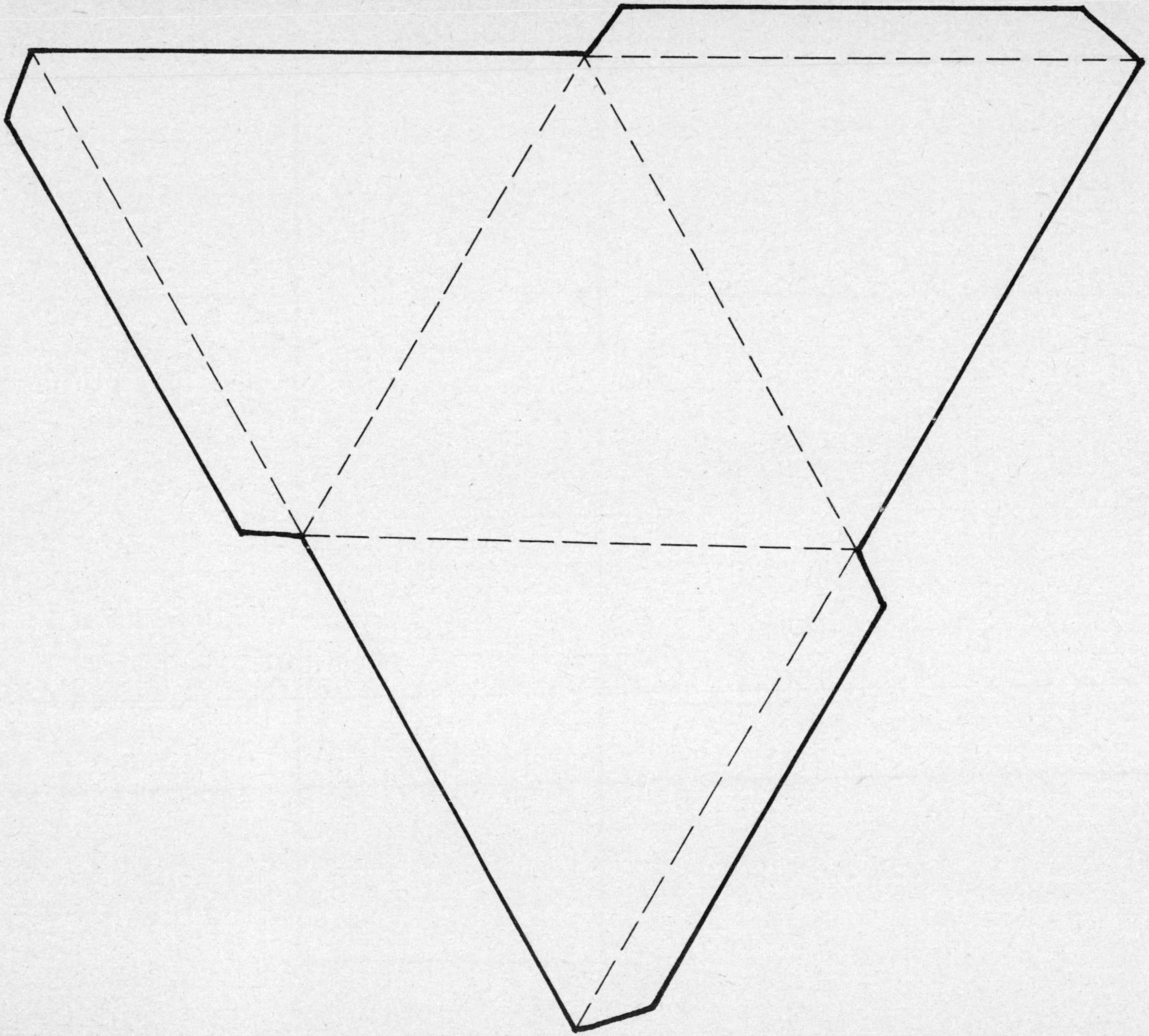

For instructions see page 194

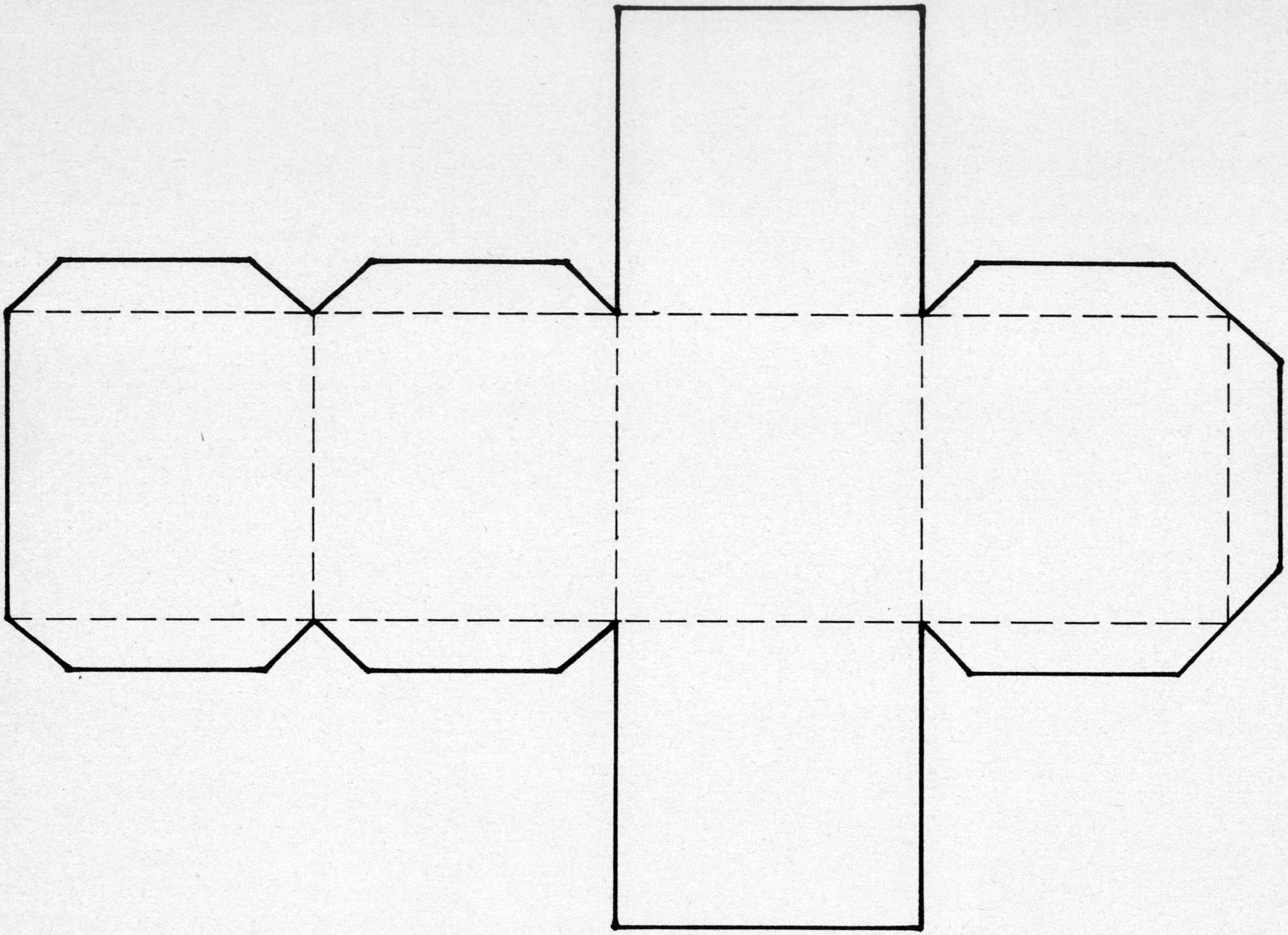

For instructions see page 194

For instructions see page 196

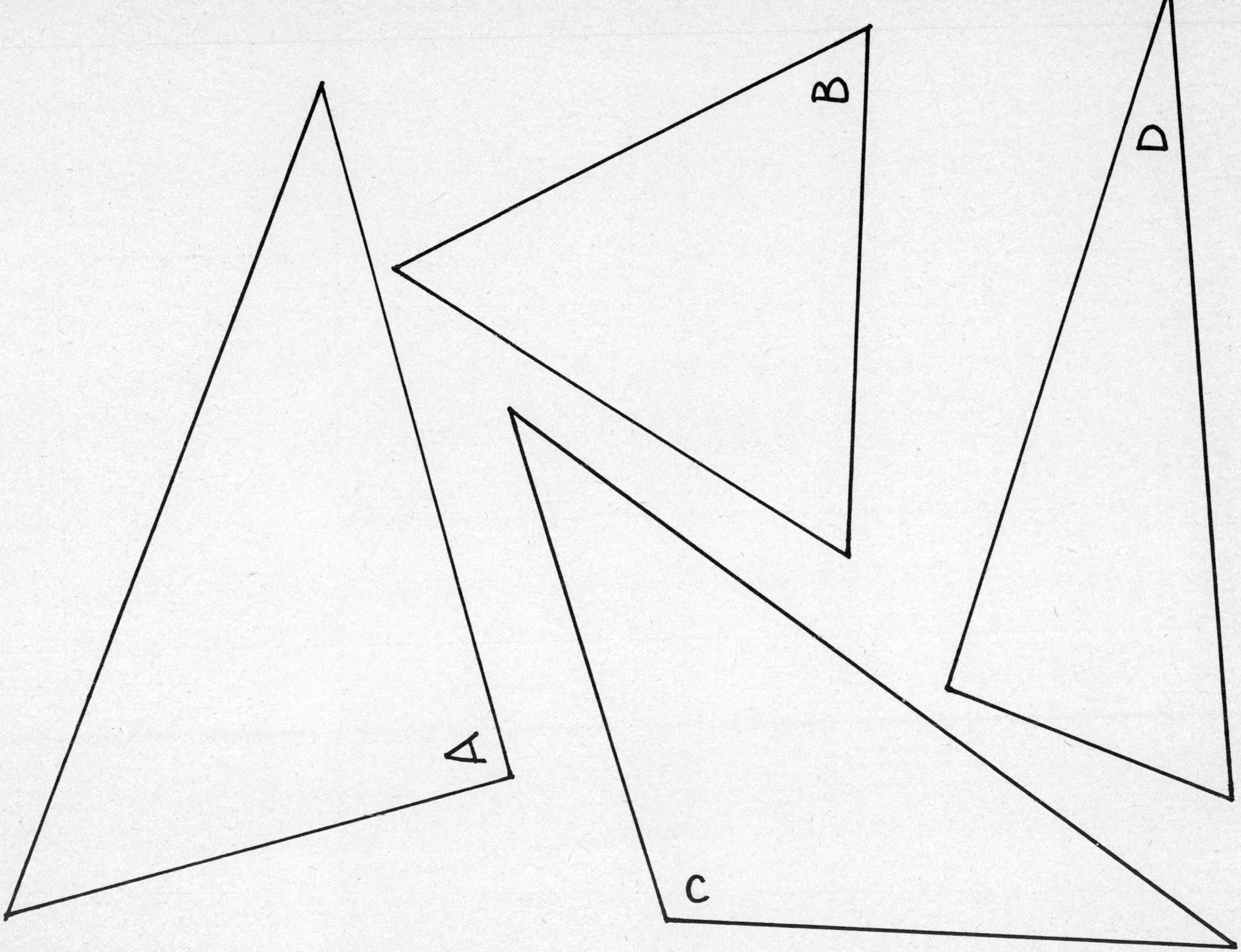

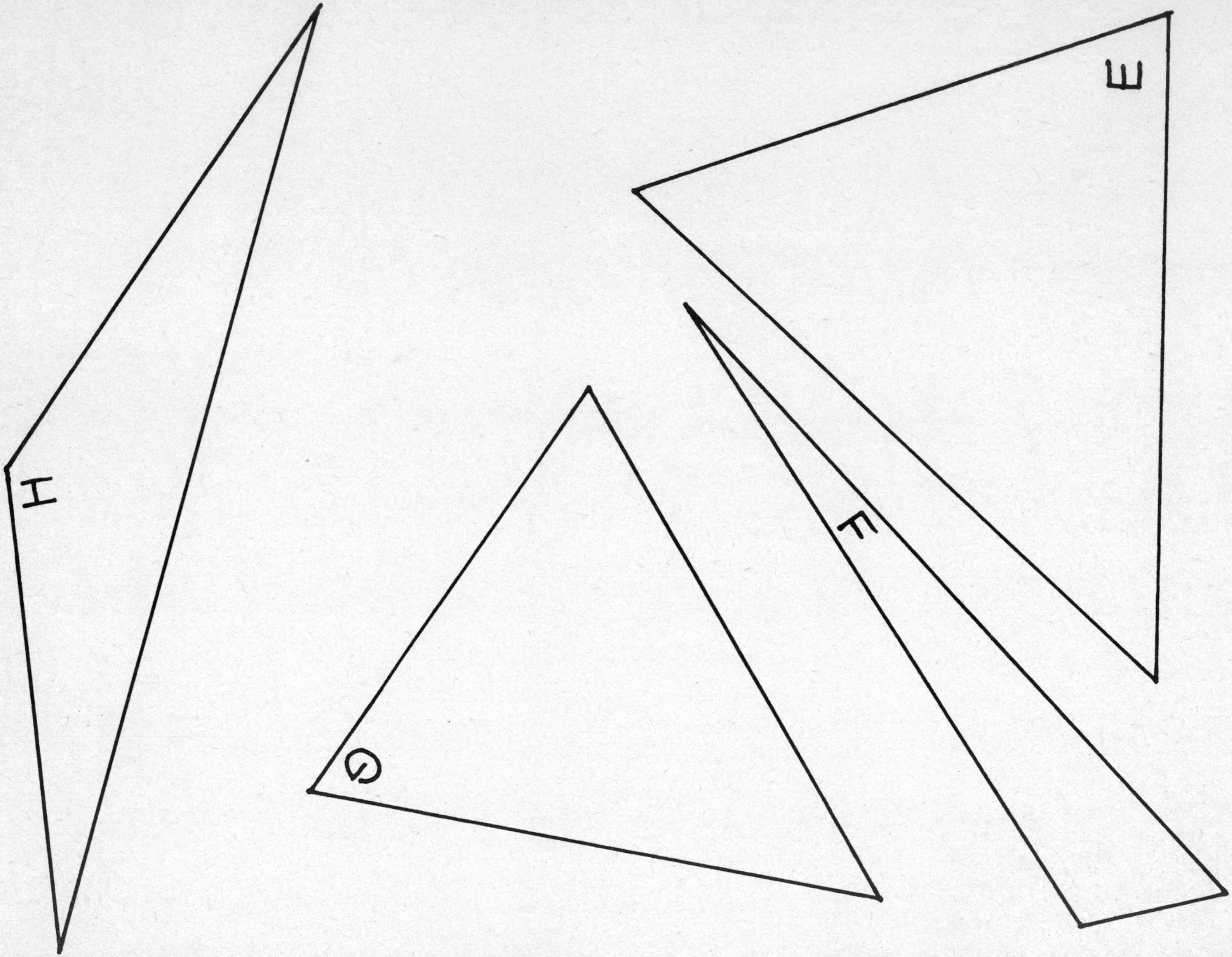

For instructions see page 196

For instructions see page 200

METRIC LINEAR MEASUREMENT #1

Name ____________

thousands	kilometre
hundreds	hectometre
tens	dekametre
ones	metre
tenths	decimetre
hundredths	centimetre
thousandths	millimetre

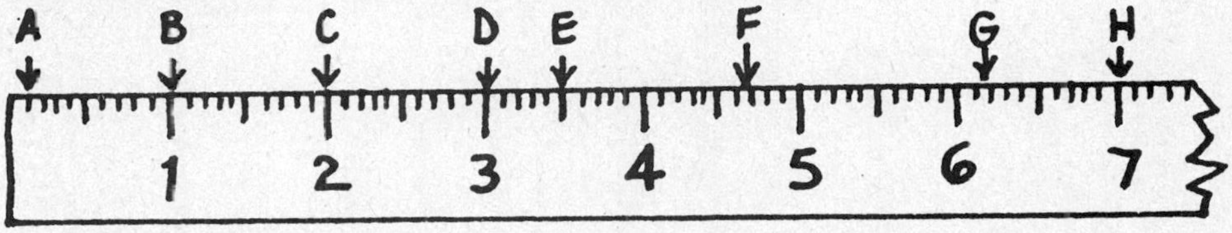

The millimetre (mm) is the smallest distance marked on this metric ruler.

* Start from the left end of the ruler.

Distance to A is 1mm   Distance to B is 10mm

C points to ____ mm   D points to ____ mm
E points to ____ mm   F points to ____ mm

The centimetre (cm) is the distance equal to 10mm

10 mm = 1cm   (1 cm = .10 dm)

D points to ____ mm, or ____ cm
H points to ____ mm, or ____ cm
G points to ____ mm, or ____ cm

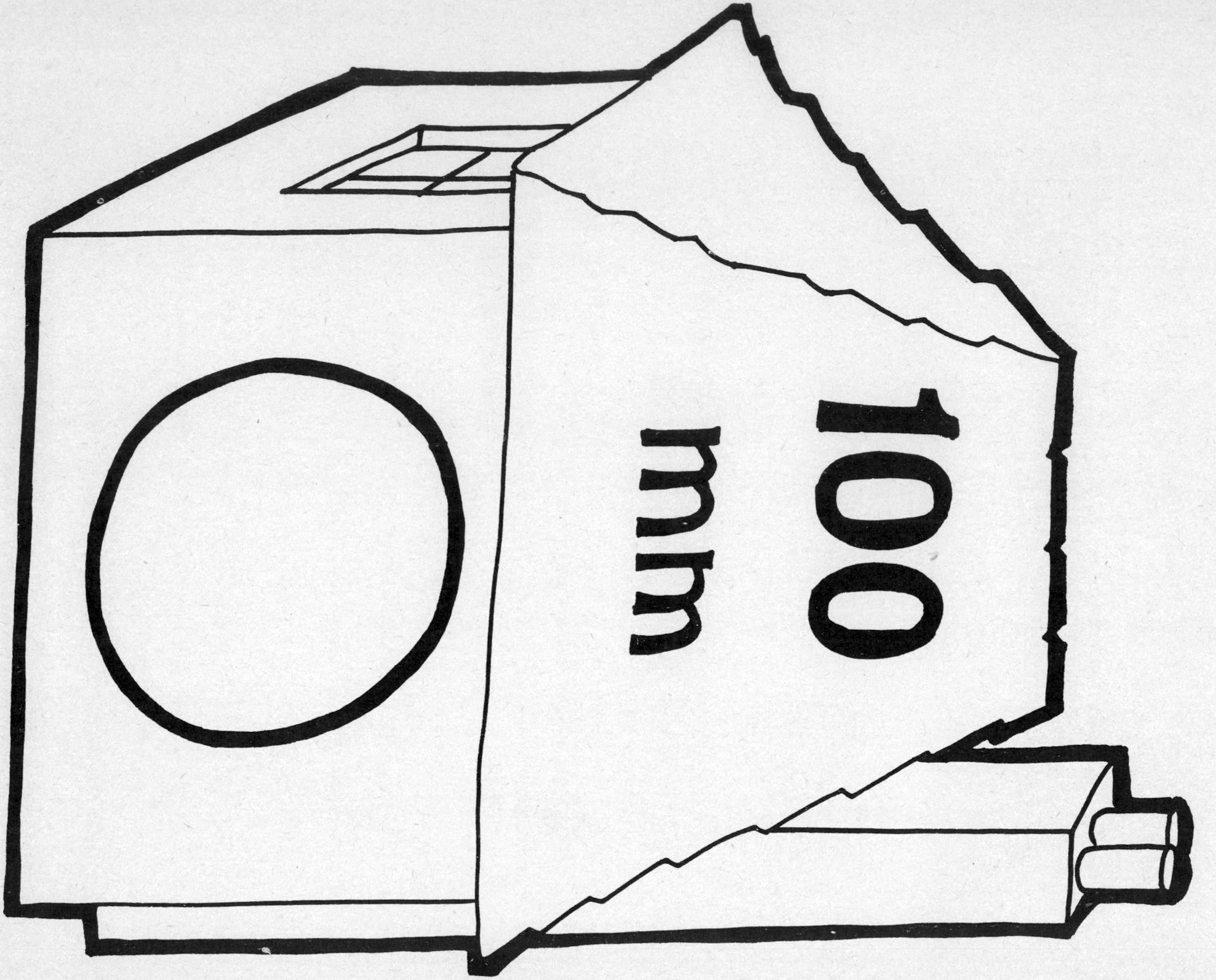

For instructions see page 202

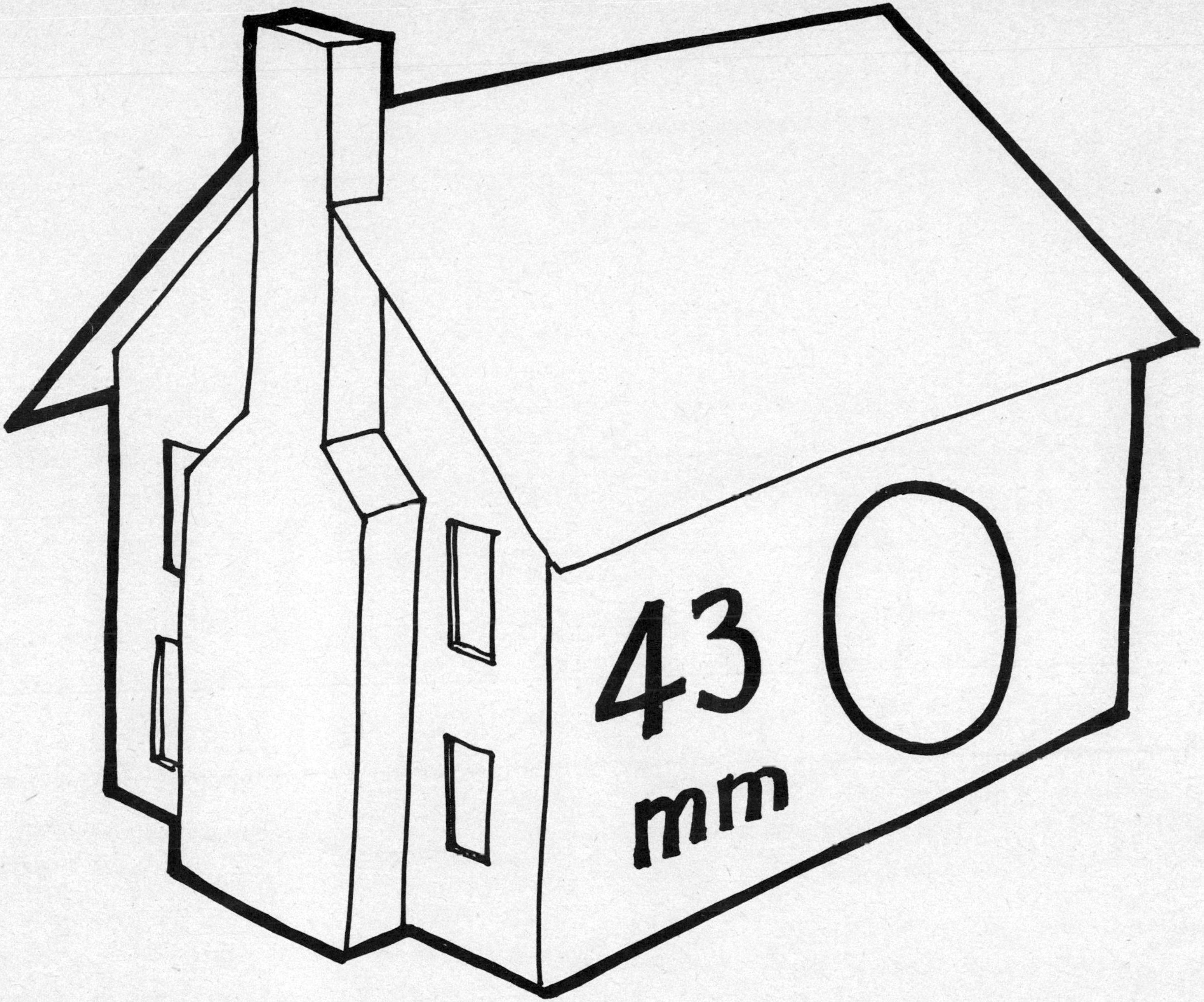

For instructions see page 202

For instructions see page 202

For instructions see page 202

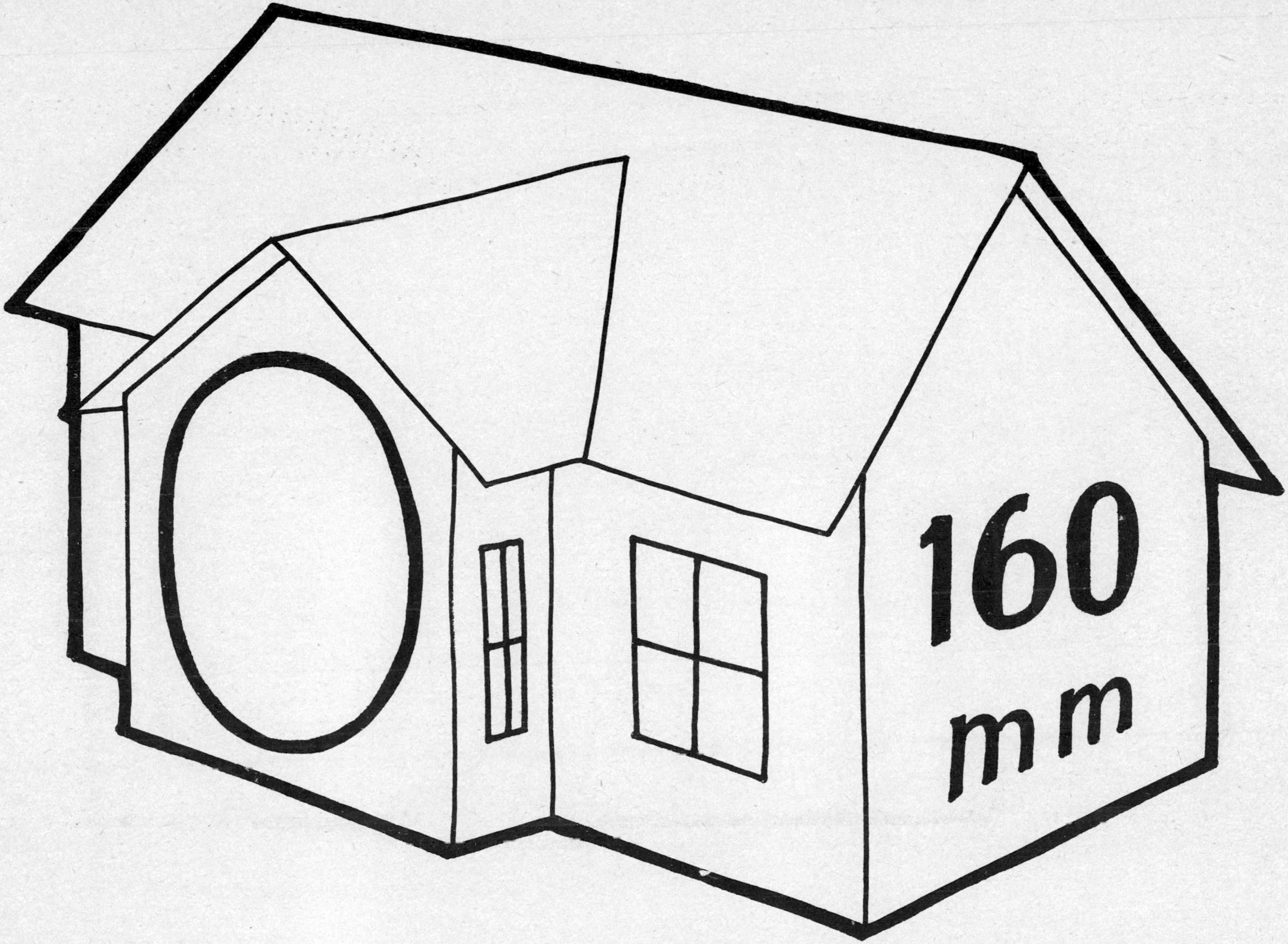

For instructions see page 202

For instructions see page 202

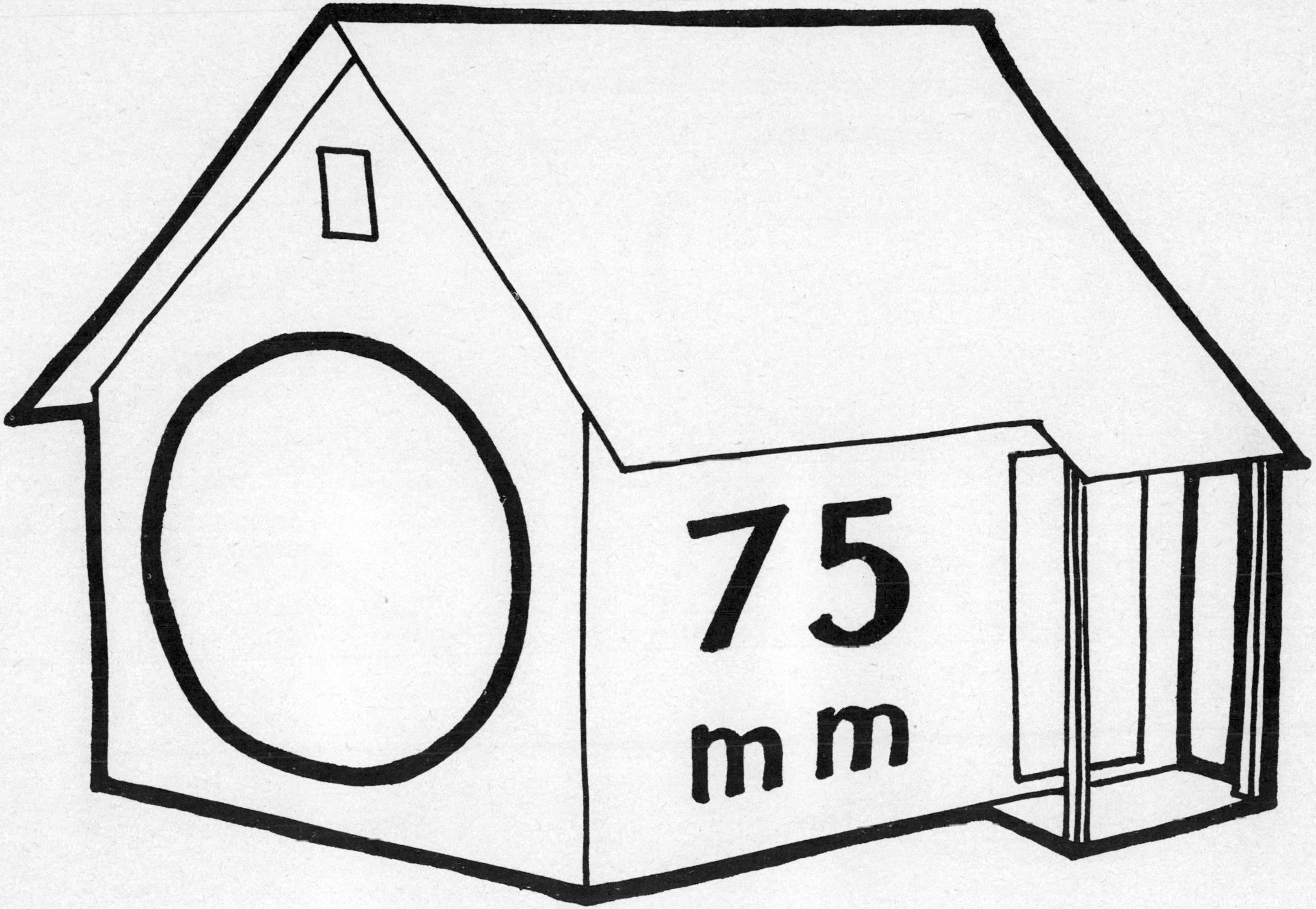

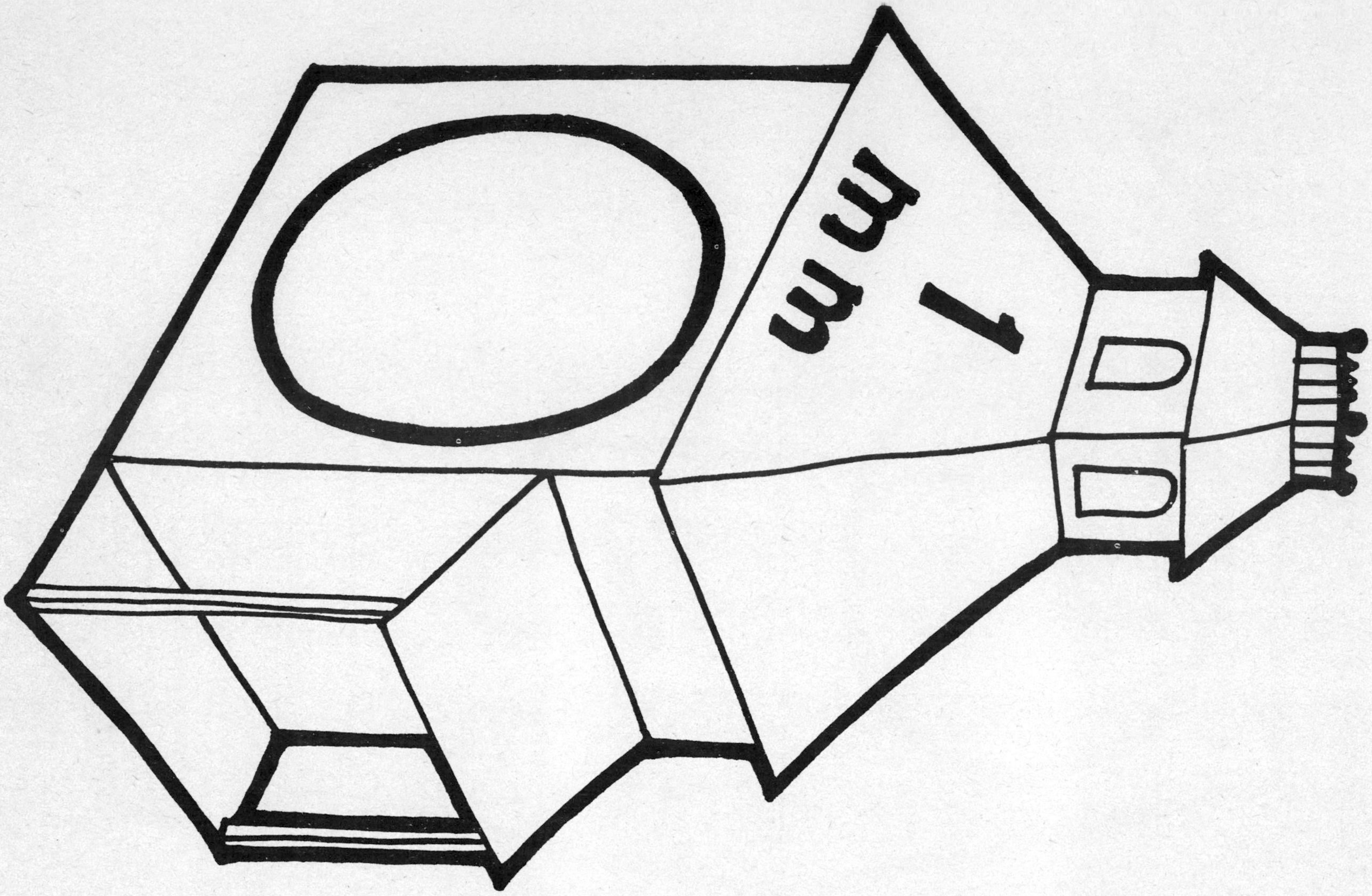

For instructions see page 202

For instructions see page 208

Name________

Hold each of the puzzle packages in your hand. Place them in order from the lightest to the heaviest.

Record your estimate:

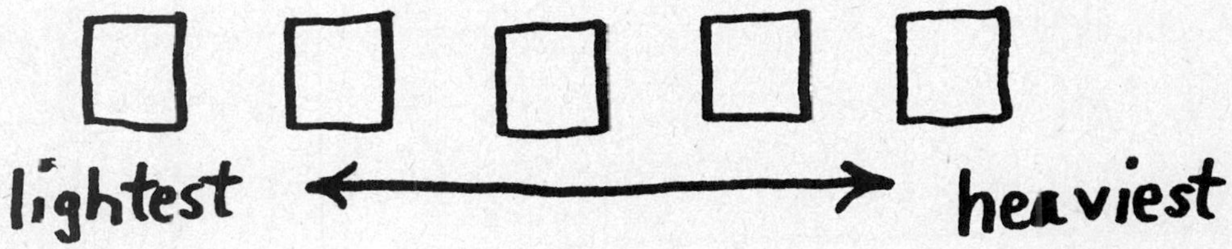

Weigh each puzzle package against one of the standard metric weights.

Record your discovery:

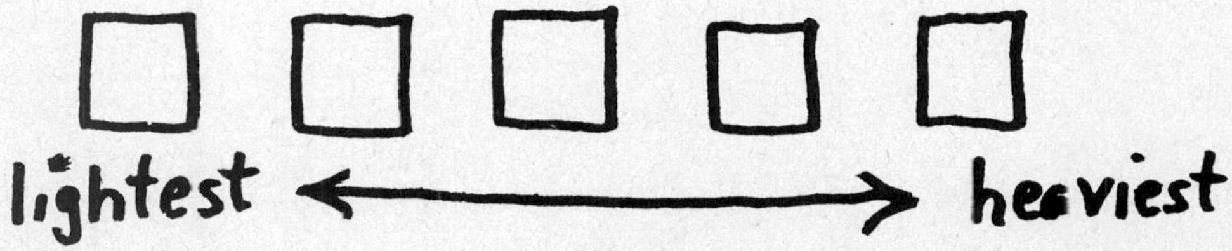

For instructions see page 208

Name ________

thousands	kilogram (or Kilo)
hundreds	hectogram
tens	dekagram
units	gram
tenths	decigram
hundredths	centigram
thousandths	milligram

1. One kilogram is ________ grams.
2. One hundredth of a gram is ______.
3. Ten grams would equal ______.
4. One hundred grams would equal ________.
5. One milligram is ________ of a gram.
6. One tenth of a gram is ______.

Name ________

...ate... Measure... Record...

OBJECT	NON-STANDARD UNIT		STANDARD UNIT	
	ESTIMATE	DISCOVERY	ESTIMATE	DISCOVERY
1. PENCIL				
2. PAPER CLIP				
3. PENNY				
4. WASHER				
5. (CHOOSE AN OBJECT)				